Throwaway Dads

Ross D. Parke & Armin A. Brott

Throwaway Dads

The Myths and Barriers
That Keep Men
from Being the Fathers
They Want to Be

HOUGHTON MIFFLIN COMPANY
BOSTON · NEW YORK   1999

For information about permission to reproduce
selections from this book, write to Permissions,
Houghton Mifflin Company, 215 Park Avenue South,
New York, New York 10003.

Library of Congress Cataloging-in-Publication Data
Parke, Ross D.
    Throwaway dads : the myths and barriers that keep men
from being the fathers they want to be / Ross D. Parke and
Armin A. Brott.
        p.   cm.
    Includes index.
    ISBN 0-395-86041-5
    1. Fatherhood — United States. 2. Fathers — United
States. 3. Men in mass media. 4. Sex roles — United States.
I. Brott, Armin A.   II. Title.
HQ756.P382   1999
306.874'2 — dc21   98-39656 CIP

Printed in the United States of America

Book design by Robert Overholtzer

QUM 10 9 8 7 6 5 4 3 2 1

To my wife, Barbara, to our children, Gillian, Timothy, Megan,
Sarah, Jennifer, and Zachary, and to our grandson, Ben,
all of whom continue to teach me about fathering. — R.D.P.

To my daughters, Tirzah and Talya, for whom any obstacle is
worth overcoming, to my grandfather, Ben Sutz, 1895–1998 (really),
who was in so many ways the most dedicated family man
I ever knew, and to Evie, just for being so incredible. — A.A.B.

Acknowledgments

Like many books, this one spent many years percolating as a set of ideas and concerns.

My part of this book owes a great deal to the students and colleagues who have participated in my research program on fathers and shared their ideas and insights at the University of Wisconsin, the Fels Research Institute, the University of Cincinnati College of Medicine, the University of Illinois, and, most recently, the University of California, Riverside. Grants from several agencies have supported my work on fathers, including the National Science Foundation, the National Institute of Health and Human Development, the National Institute of Mental Health, and the Spencer Foundation. Their support over the last thirty years is gratefully acknowledged. I want to thank my wife, friend, and colleague, Barbara Tinsley, for her advice, feedback, and support during this project and all of my undertakings. She is truly a partner in parenting. Finally, none of the work on this book would have been possible without the cooperation of the hundreds of fathers, mothers, and children who have participated in our projects. Their willingness to share their thoughts and feelings about their roles and relationships is truly appreciated and has been invaluable in moving us from mere speculation about fathers and families to a set of well-grounded scientific principles.

Ross D. Parke,
Riverside, California

The process of writing a book is largely a solitary one, but the process of *making* a book is very much a group effort. And if it hadn't been for a wonderful collection of friends, colleagues, and associates, this book simply wouldn't be the same.

Eve Aldridge read the first draft and never let me lose track of the all-important woman's perspective. She spent countless hours helping me hone my arguments on our runs through the Oakland hills. Lisa Alcalay Klug also read some of the early drafts and made things sharper. Lou Ann Bassan and Anne E. Mitchell were great sources of information and shining examples of how women can welcome fathers into families. Jimmy Boyd, Ron Henry, and Stuart Miller opened their databases and files and flooded me with information, research, sources, and wisdom throughout the entire process. June and Gene Brott, my parents, provided generous financial, emotional, and moral support during the tough — and not so tough — times. Doug Fizel, the public affairs director of the American Psychological Association, and the folks at ProfNet hooked me up with experts in all the right fields. Cathy Young, social critic and writer extraordinaire, selflessly let me read and quote from drafts of her forthcoming book on women and men. And then there were the dozens of men and women who responded to my Internet posts or let me interview them for this book and whose suggestions contributed greatly.

Finally, although he's out of alphabetical order, I'd like to thank Ross Parke, who was (and still is) a bit of a hero of mine, someone whose commitment to fatherhood has inspired me since I began my own research and writing on the subject.

Armin A. Brott
Berkeley, California

In addition, we'd both like to thank the following people for their invaluable contributions: Larry Cooper and Robin Locke Monda, for refining the book, inside and out; Heather Guzman and Jorie Lozano, for preparing the manuscript and spending endless hours researching endnotes; James Levine, our agent, for recognizing that the two of us would yield a better book than either of us alone; John Radziewicz, our editor at Houghton Mifflin, for his insight, wisdom, and humor; and Jenna Terry, for keeping things on track.

Contents

Introduction

Ross Parke: It was in 1968, while still an associate professor of psychology at the University of Wisconsin, that I first realized there was a strong maternal bias in research on children and families. Fathers, in fact, had been all but neglected. As a young father myself, I intuitively knew that fathers play a critical role in their children's lives, a role that is no less important than the one mothers play. Over the ensuing three decades I have made it my mission to educate academics and the public alike about the importance of fathers. I have written two books on the subject (which are used in graduate and undergraduate courses throughout the United States and Canada) and more than one hundred academic papers.

Armin Brott: I didn't think much about fatherhood until my wife was pregnant with our first child in 1989. While searching for information to help me cope with the flood of worries, emotions, and confusion I was experiencing, I came face to face with a maternal bias similar to the one Ross Parke had discovered two decades earlier: bookstores and magazine racks were filled with information and support for new and expectant mothers, yet there was little if anything available for fathers. Not only were written resources for fathers in short supply, but fathers who wanted to be actively involved with their children couldn't expect much support from their employers, the medical community, the media, and, in many cases, even their spouses. Dissatisfied with society's overall disrespect for fathers, I set out to change things. Over the following eight years I've written dozens of magazine articles on the importance of fathers as well as three books on the subject.

The two of us had one simple goal in mind when writing this book: we wanted to increase the public's awareness of the barriers — some subtle, some blatant — that have limited men's involvement with their families. Our hope is that once we all become aware of how pervasive and damaging these barriers are to all of us, we will waste no time in working together to break them down. The evidence, both scientific and anecdotal, is clear: if we support fathers in their quest to become more involved with their families, if we give them the tools to do so, everyone — women, children, and men themselves — will benefit greatly.

So what is it that we feel keeps fathers from being as actively involved as they'd like to be? There are lots of culprits, some of them historical. Under the sway of Freud and others, society came to believe that fathers didn't matter much in the lives of infants and young children — only mothers did. Other causes are more contemporary. As a culture, we have created a series of myths about fathers, which has justified the charge that men are incapable, uninterested, and unresponsive as fathers. One of these myths is the widely held belief that fathers are naturally inept caregivers — biologically unfit and thus unprepared for the caregiving that is a central part of parenting.

Another myth that pervades our thinking about fathers is that of the dangerous father, which portrays men as a threat to women and children and routinely blames them for the thousands of missing children and the high rates of child abuse. These images are hardly compatible with men as competent fathers. They're also misleading and harmful, and inadvertently limit men's opportunities to be the kinds of involved fathers that they strive to be. And consider the stereotype about fathers' limited participation in family life. There is no question that women do more than men in some household tasks, but the impression that men are lazy is simply wrong. Men contribute in myriad ways to domestic chores, but men and women often do so in different ways. What of the deadbeat dad who abandons his family and won't pay child support? Again, a few real deadbeats are assumed to represent the majority of fathers who are doing their best to provide for their children after divorce. The media have helped to both create and sustain these myths about fatherhood in their depictions of fathers in books, films, and on television.

One of the main reasons that these myths about fatherhood have been so pervasive and persuasive is that the father's role is less culturally scripted and less determined than the mother's. The expectations of the good mother are undergoing change but are still clearer and more widely accepted than our expectations of the good father. Mothers are still expected to be the primarily responsible parent, to receive custody following divorce, and to balance work and family responsibilities. For fathers there is a great deal of ambiguity and discretion in how roles are defined. In the absence of clear guidelines, myths and stereotypes are more likely to find fertile ground.

Likewise, the families we grow up in provide us with images and models about how men and women should behave and the kinds of roles they should assume. Boys are taught that baby-sitting is girls' work — a lesson that may limit boys' later involvement as parents.

It's not just the family you were reared in that shapes your behavior and attitudes as a parent — whom you marry matters too. Although not often recognized, women's attitudes may determine how active a role fathers will play in the family. It is true that women have made inroads in the world of work, but there are glass ceilings and lower wages that remind all of us that equity in the workplace has still not arrived. To compensate, some women feel they need to retain control over the homefront — especially parenting — which often means limiting men's involvement in child care.

And men share the blame too. Men are often reluctant to take time off from work for family reasons. Workplace policies that clearly limit men's family time need to be changed to accommodate men's desires to find a better balance between work and family. Beyond the politics of work and family, larger forces have perhaps unintentionally contributed to limiting fathers' involvement. Both the men's movement and feminist groups have led to a hardening of gender lines. Instead of promoting involved fatherhood, each of these important cultural trends has encouraged a self-oriented focus that is often incompatible with active fatherhood.

There are solutions that will help make it easier and more likely that fathers will get involved. Again, *solutions* (plural) are the key, since no single change will do the trick. We are experiencing a cultural evolution in the way that fatherhood is understood and enacted. Men can and do change. There are lots of programs for fathers of children of all ages. And these programs can help men build self-confidence in their abilities to be effective parents. Women can change too, by recognizing that fathers are more capable and by making more opportunities for fathers to become involved. Men need to be positive about their parenting style. By all means celebrate differences between the sexes; men and women parent differently, but both can parent well and make a difference in their children's lives. Women can help in many ways — by letting dads learn, by encouraging their participation, and by being nonjudgmental. Men may do things differently, and maybe not up to their partners' standards, but tolerance leads to involvement.

Society can make it easier for fathers to become involved. Schools that provide parenting classes at an earlier age — for both boys and girls — would help. So would the liberalization of workplace policies to allow men more time with their families.

Men want to be more involved, and a first step in reaching this goal is to increase our awareness of the barriers faced by men who want to be active fathers. This book is an invitation both to explore these issues and to join in the process of getting men more involved.

Part 1
The Stakes

1

Do Fathers Really Matter?

EVERY GENERATION has its scapegoat for contemporary social ills: communism, rock and roll, drugs, feminism, television. Now it seems to be the absence of fathers in the family. It's hard to pick up a newspaper or magazine without encountering a story about the continuing deterioration of the American family and how the absence of a father is at least partly responsible. "For 19 Million There's No Father Home," blasts the *Washington Post*. The *Los Angeles Times* announces "Fatherless Families: A Violent Link," while *Newsweek* talks of "Deadbeat Dads" and "No Father, No Answers."

Our national fixation on fathers — or, more precisely, on their absence — has spawned a new genre in publishing. Since 1990, there have been at least fifty new books about fathers. Some are scholarly, such as Lerman and Ooms's *Young Unwed Fathers* and McLanahan and Sandefur's *Growing Up with a Single Parent*. Others are more political and ideological, such as David Blankenhorn's highly successful *Fatherless America* and David Popenoe's *Life Without Father*, both of which endorse a very conservative agenda that promotes a nearly mythical family structure in which all marriages are stable and fathers are little more than support agents for mothers.

This isn't to say that all coverage of fathers is bad. Newspapers occasionally run feature articles such as "No Longer Missing in Action" (*Los Angeles Times*) and "Does Society Underrate Fathers' Value to Families?" (*Sacramento Bee*). Some new books are trumpeting the importance of fathers and how to be a better one. One of us (Brott) has published a series of guides for fathers: *The Expectant Father, The New Father,* and *A Dad's Guide to the Toddler Years.* Other recent titles, such as *Father Love* and *The Father Factor,* also reflect a slowly increasing interest in fathers' roles in children's lives. At the same time, new conceptions of what fatherhood is and creative visions of what it could be are gradually emerging.

This focus on fatherhood has given rise to a heated debate among academics, politicians, and others about how much fathers actually matter. "Fatherlessness is the most harmful demographic trend of this generation," writes David Blankenhorn. "It is the leading cause of declining child well-being in this society. It is also the engine driving our most urgent social problems, from crime to adolescent pregnancy to child sexual abuse to domestic violence against women." Many others — especially men in the more radical branches of the Fathers' Rights Movement — believe that fathers are so important that their mere presence in a family (or granting them full custody of children after divorce) will do just about everything, from decreasing alcohol and drug abuse and reducing welfare payments to single mothers to improving children's grades. Their implication? Dropping an involved father into every household would readily solve our most urgent social problems.

In the other corner are those who have tried to prove that fathers are not important at all. Children raised without dads are doing just fine, they say, and any problems kids do suffer are the result of economic factors rather than the physical or psychological absence of a father.

Although diametrically opposed, the fathers-aren't-necessary and the father-as-panacea camps share one important feature: they present views that are based more on politics than on actual research. As a result, both views are far too simplistic to shed any real light on the issue of the importance of fathers in their children's — as well as in their partners' and their own — lives.

Nearly silent in this debate has been the academic community, and it is this silence that perhaps hurts fathers the most. For while politicians change their views to suit the prevailing electoral climate, academic researchers over the past two decades have been nearly unanimous in their findings: fathers matter. And they matter a lot.

We all know that babies are better off when they have two parents to love them, cuddle them, and contribute to their college fund. And even though mothers are the ones who breast-feed and undoubtedly change more than their fair share of a newborn's diapers, fathers play a unique and very important role from the start. Children benefit developmentally from the special ways their fathers interact with them, and from the different ways of being that dads bring to their parenting experience.

So what exactly do fathers do? To start with, they tend to allow their infants more freedom to explore, while mothers are usually more cautious. Fathers also encourage their children's independence by promoting exploration. They even speak to their children differently than mothers do. Overall, fathers seem more interested in doing practical, educational things rather than talking about them.

The area in which fathers' parenting style is most obvious and most important is play. Anyone who has ever watched new parents in action can attest that women tend to play more visual games with their babies and are often more verbal with them. Men, on the other hand, are far more physical, right from the time their kids are infants.

These differences are more than just anecdotal. Pediatricians Michael Yogman, T. Berry Brazelton, and their colleagues found clear differences in the ways adults — mothers, fathers, and strangers — played with a group of two week-old to twenty-four-week old infants. Mothers spoke softly, repeating words and phrases frequently and imitating the infants' sounds more than either the fathers or the strangers. A "burst/pause" pattern was common for these mothers: a rapidly spoken series of words and sounds followed by a short period of silence. Fathers were less verbal but more tactile than mothers. They touched their infants with a rhythmic tapping more often than the mothers or the strangers. Father-infant play shifted rapidly from peaks of high infant attention and excitement to valleys of minimal attention; mother-infant play demonstrated more gradual shifts. As Brazelton observed: "Most fathers seem to present a more playful, jazzing-up approach. As one watches this interaction, it seems that a father is expecting more heightened, playful response from the baby. And he gets it! Amazingly enough, an infant by two or three weeks displays an entirely different attitude (more wide-eyed, playful and bright-faced) toward his father than to his mother. The cycles might be characterized as higher, deeper, and even a bit more jagged."

Differences between fathers' and mothers' play styles are not lost on children, who generally respond more positively to play with their fathers than with their mothers. In fact, when given a choice of play partners, more than two-thirds of two-and-a-half-year-olds choose their fathers over their mothers. This preference for the paternal play style is so strong that most children chose it — no matter whom they're playing with. In one study, researchers observed a group of boys as they played with each parent in two different playrooms, one containing books and puzzles conducive to maternal play, the other containing large, soft balls and pillows conducive to paternal play. Boys reacted more positively to both their parents when their play style was more physical and active, resembling the typical paternal style.

Playing with dad is almost always fun for a child, but there are other benefits as well. Children who get along best with other children often have fathers who spend a lot of time playing physically with them. In addition, three-year-olds who had good relationships with their fathers (and at this age a good relationship means lots of play) have better, longer-lasting friendships at age five.

How is this possible? What could children learn from playing that would influence their friendships — or anything else, for that matter? On the most basic level, "while they're roughhousing with their fathers, infants are already learning some valuable lessons in self-control," says John Snarey, a professor of human development at Emory University. Fathers also help children learn how to express and appropriately manage their emotions, recognize others' emotional cues, and understand that biting, kicking, and other forms of physical violence are not acceptable.

Fathers also influence their children's emotional lives in other ways. "The kids who did best in terms of peer relationships . . . were those whose dads validated their feelings and praised their accomplish-ments," writes John Gottman in *The Heart of Parenting*. "These fathers were Emotion Coaches, who neither dismissed nor disapproved of their kids' negative emotions, but showed empathy and provided guidance to help their kids deal with negative feelings." Specifically, Gottman found that fathers' acceptance of and assistance with their children's sadness and anger at five years of age were related to chil-dren's social competence among their peers three years later. Kids with supporting and emotionally accepting fathers were less aggressive, had better relationships with friends, and had less trouble in school. Inter-estingly, the mothers' management of emotions was a less strong pre-dictor of the children's later social success. Fathers, it seems, make an important but often unrecognized contribution to the development of their children's "emotional intelligence" — and it's a contribution that lasts a lifetime.

In the 1950s psychologist Robert Sears and his colleagues examined the child-rearing practices of more than three hundred American par-ents when their children were five years old. Twenty-six years later, an-other group of researchers contacted some of the children from the original study to assess their level of empathy (the tendency to experi-ence emotions or feelings similar to those experienced by others) and compare it to Sears's original findings. The most powerful predictor of empathy in adulthood, the later researchers found, was paternal child-rearing involvement at age five. This factor proved to be a better pre-dictor than several maternal predictors and was equally evident for boys and girls.

In yet another follow-up, when the original children were forty-one, those who had better social relationships in midlife (for example, having a long, happy marriage; having children; engaging in recre-ational activities with others outside the family) were the ones who had experienced more paternal warmth when they were children.

If nothing else, these studies should make us seriously rethink our views about the ways mothers and fathers influence their children. It has long been accepted, for example, that mothers are the emo-tional brokers in the family, while fathers play a mostly instrumental role. Clearly, though, fathers have a much larger and more complex impact on their children's emotional lives than anyone had previously thought.

Besides being "emotionally intelligent," children of involved fathers tend to be intellectually smarter as well. "The evidence is quite robust that kids who have contact with a father have an advantage over kids without that kind of contact," says Norma Radin, a professor emeritus at the University of Michigan who conducted research on fathers for more than twenty years. And these advantages are evident very early in life. In one study, Radin found that children who were raised by actively involved fathers scored higher on verbal ability tests than children whose fathers were less involved. In another study, toddlers whose fathers took a special interest in childcare were consistently rated two to six months ahead of the expected schedule on tests of development, problem-solving skills, and even social skills. In addition, Radin believes that "there's a strong connection between kids' math skills and the amount of contact they have with their fathers."

Radin is far from alone in her findings. In a study of working-class Irish fathers, Kevin Nugent of Harvard University found that a father's level of caregiving during the first year of life was related to his baby's score on an infant IQ test given at twelve months. And the more caregiving the fathers did, the higher and more advanced their babies' cognitive skills.

Interestingly, fathers' skills as playmates are excellent predictors of their children's intellectual development. Fathers who were good at peekaboo, ball toss, and bouncing, for example, had more intellectually advanced children than those who couldn't keep their children interested in their games. Fathers also apparently contribute to their children's intellectual capacity by encouraging them to be independent. In one study, the earlier (within reason) the father expected his child to be able to handle a pair of scissors or take a bath alone, the more advanced the child's intellectual development.

Another way of assessing fathers' impact on their children is to examine what happens to kids who grow up in families without a father around. The evidence is both striking and clear: children growing up in homes without a father tend to have poorer intellectual development. The risk of dropping out of high school, for example, is twice as high in single-parent (father-absent) families than in two-parent families. Adolescents from single-parent families had lower test scores, grade point averages, school attendance, and college expectations than those from two-parent families. And young adults from single-parent families were less likely to enroll in college and less likely to graduate. In their early to mid-twenties young men from these homes were more likely to be out of school and out of work than men from two-parent homes. Women in their twenties, especially those with children, show similar trends.

Even in intact families, fathers can be "absent." In a classic study from the late 1960s, psychologists Robert Blanchard and Henry Biller demonstrated that fathers' availability, as well as their absence, affects their children's academic performance. Blanchard and Biller compared four groups of third-grade boys, all of whom had average IQs, all were from working-class or middle-class backgrounds, and all had the same number and gender of siblings. Only their paternal situation was different. Simply put, the underachievers (kids who were working below their grade level) came from homes where the father had left before the child was five. The superior academic performers were the boys whose fathers were present and available to them. The boys who had lost their fathers after age five and those whose fathers were living at home but generally unavailable were functioning somewhat below grade level.

"Highly available fathers can be models of perseverance and achievement motivation," Biller reported. "The father can be an example of a male successfully functioning outside of the home atmosphere. Frequent opportunity to observe and imitate an adequate father contributes to the development of the boys' overall instrumental and problem-solving ability. Having a competent father will not facilitate a boy's intellectual development if the father is not consistently accessible to the boy or if the father-son relationship is negative in quality."

As all this research suggests, the quality of a father's involvement is crucial. Simply being there is not enough; being available and involved is what really counts. Too many fathers who are still in two-parent families are unavailable to their children because of their work schedule, travel, or lack of interest. Furthermore, kids whose fathers are cold and authoritarian, derogatory, and intrusive have the hardest time with grades and social relationships. They are, says John Gottman, even worse off than kids who live in homes with no father at all. Kids with nonsupportive dads and dads who humiliate them were the ones most likely to be headed for trouble, he says. They were the ones who displayed aggressive behavior toward their friends, they were the ones who had the most trouble in school, and they were the ones with problems often linked to delinquency and youth violence.

Interestingly, fathers don't treat — and thus don't affect — their sons and their daughters in the same way. (Mothers also treat their boys and girls differently, but the difference is not so marked.) To start with, fathers tend to play and interact more physically with their boy infants than with their girls. Later on, fathers give their boys more encouragement to explore and be independent. Boys are allowed to cross the street alone at an earlier age, to stay away from home more, and to explore a wider area of their neighborhood than are girls. There's some speculation that these distinctions may make a difference. Lois Hoffman of the University of Michigan suggests that "boys' greater experience in these independent explorations, which girls lack, very likely has considerable importance in the development of independent coping styles, a sense of competence, and even some specific skills." These skills include such traits as curiosity, assertiveness, and a sense of adventure.

It's important to remember that despite differences in the way fathers treat sons and daughters, girls still have a lot to gain emotionally, socially, intellectually, and psychologically from greater contact with their fathers. Girls whose fathers play with them a lot, for example, tend to be more popular with their peers and more assertive in their interpersonal relationships throughout their lives. Other research has found that extremely competent and successful women frequently recall their fathers as active and encouraging, playful and exciting. As the anthropologist Margaret Mead wrote about her father, "He taught me the importance of thinking clearly and of keeping one's premises clear. . . . It was proper for women to be committed to pure goodness and purely intellectual activities. . . . It was my father even more than my mother . . . who defined for me my place in the world."

It's not completely clear why fathers treat boys and girls differently.

Perhaps fathers are reacting to biological differences in the rates at which boys and girls develop. Girls generally acquire language earlier than boys, while boys are more physically active. Or fathers may treat boys and girls differently because of gender stereotypes concerning the appropriate ways to interact with sons and daughters (girls are more fragile, goes the logic, therefore they shouldn't be played with too much).

Biology may also have a role. Male monkeys, for example, show the same preferences for male infants and tend to respond more positively to bids for rough-and-tumble play in the same way that human fathers do. "Perhaps both monkey and human males are more susceptible to being aroused into states of positive excitement and unpredictability than females," writes child development expert Eleanor Maccoby. In short, fathers and sons may share a biological predisposition that makes them more comfortable with each other's style of play. And there's little doubt that cultural, ethnic, and environmental factors play a role here too. Boys and girls in African-American families are treated more similarly by their fathers than boys and girls in white families.

Children aren't the only ones who benefit from spending more time with their fathers. Wives of active, involved fathers seem to gain as well. The more support mothers get from their husbands (including, of course, taking care of the children), the happier they are in their marriages and the better they perform their own parenting duties. This may be due in part to the fact that women who have involved partners are more likely to work outside the home. And women who are employed are generally more satisfied and less depressed than stay-at-home mothers — especially those who want to work.

This, in turn, benefits fathers. Men whose wives are happy in their marriages tend to be happier themselves. And men who are happy in their marriages are generally more involved in their fathering role.

Conventional wisdom has it that a man's health is affected more by his work than by his family relationships. But according to Rosalind Barnett and Caryl Rivers, the authors of She Works/He Works, the opposite is true. "One of the most surprising findings of our study was that problems in a man's relationship with his child had a significant impact on his physical health, while his problems at his job did not! Being a father who is deeply involved with his children is good for a man's health. The men who had the fewest worries about their relationships with their children also had the fewest health problems. Those who had the most troubled relationships with their children had the most health problems."

These comments echo those made by Maureen Green more than twenty years ago, in her book *Fathering*. "One of the first things a father learns from his children is that his needs can match theirs. They look to him for instruction; he can enjoy giving instruction. The children look to him as a model, and being a model adds an extra dimension to his decisions. His ambitions and achievements look different to him if he can look at them through their eyes as well as his own. Fathering, in short, may be good for men as well as for children."

The benefits of involved fathering on fathers themselves last a lifetime. Using data going back as far as the 1940s and adding much recent research, John Snarey examined the impact of fathers' involvement in child rearing on their own development as adults. Fathers who provided high levels of socioemotional support for their children from birth through age ten and high levels of intellectual, academic, social, and emotional support from age eleven through twenty-one were more likely to be happily married at midlife. Snarey also found that a father's involvement in child rearing during the first two decades of the child's life seemed to predict his occupational mobility at age forty-seven far more than any other factor (including, for example, his parents' occupations, his IQ, and whether or not his wife works outside the home). In sum, it turns out that involved fathers tend to have happier marriages and more successful careers.

Fatherhood also seems to promote men's abilities to understand themselves as adults and to care sympathetically for other adults. According to Snarey, men who take an active role at home are, by the time their children are grown, better managers, community leaders, and mentors. Overall, they're more concerned with the next generation than with themselves.

*   *   *

Although no one completely understands the processes involved, active fathering clearly benefits children, mothers, and fathers themselves. Encouraging fathers to be involved — and supporting them in their efforts to do so — is an investment that could yield important social dividends for all. Sadly, though, our society has both wittingly and unwittingly erected a series of nearly insurmountable barriers that effectively reduce men's involvement with their children and families. As a result, women, children, and men have suffered greatly. And until we stop tacitly supporting these barriers, we are unlikely ever to experience fully the positive benefits of involved fathering.

Part 2
The Myths

2

The Biologically Unfit Father

MARGARET MEAD once said that fathers are a biological necessity but a social accident. Throughout much of the nineteenth and twentieth centuries our culture has been trying very hard to make this statement a reality. Socialized into being the family breadwinner, "traditional" fathers provided strong moral and material support for their families, meted out discipline to their children, but did little else. They paced the waiting room during childbirth, rarely if ever changed a diaper or warmed a bottle, and generally steered clear of the nursery, leaving the responsibility for child rearing almost entirely to their wives.

The notion of fathers as "accidental" was shared by those who studied parenthood and child development. Sigmund Freud, for example, who had a major influence in shaping the twentieth century's cultural views of parenting, believed that since mothers usually fed and cared for babies, they were biologically better suited to be parents, and they would exert more influence over their children than fathers would.

But there were some challenges. One of the fiercest critics of Freud's focus on feeding as the centerpiece of early development was John Bowlby, a British psychiatrist. "The conventional wisdom was that infants were only interested in mothers because mothers fed them," he said in a 1977 interview. "I was profoundly unimpressed by that."

Rather than consider the importance of fathers, Bowlby continued to promote the idea that mothers were superior, but for slightly different reasons. For Bowlby, any emotional and social problems suffered by children resulted from the lack of an "attachment bond," the process by which the infant comes to prefer a certain adult — specifically his mother — over others. Bowlby suggested that attachment is a result of instinctive responses important for the protection and survival of the species. Crying, smiling, sucking, clinging, and following all elicit necessary maternal care and protection for the infant and promote contact between mother and infant. He stressed that the mother is the first and most important object of infant attachment, relegating fathers to the role of mother's little helper.

That notion got a big boost from the primate researcher Harry Harlow. In his now famous experiments, Harlow showed that rhesus monkeys would develop an attachment to a surrogate caregiver. Or, to use Harlow's non-neutral term, surrogate "mother." To prove this, he constructed two stand-ins, a wire-mesh mother and a cloth-covered mother. Although the wire-mesh mother provided the food, Harlow found that the monkeys spent most of their time — sixteen to eighteen hours a day — clinging to the cloth mother.

What this experiment proved was that attachment (in monkeys, at least) was based more on the "contact comfort" provided by the terrycloth covering than on the chance to feed. Fathers could have easily provided this kind of warmth and comfort, even if they couldn't nurse their offspring. Nevertheless, Harlow persisted in labeling these experimental caregivers as mothers — a label that perpetuated the myth of the biological primacy of mothers.

There's no question that throughout history, fathers have taken on less of the care and feeding of infants and young children than mothers. It would be a mistake, however, to conclude that this is true because mothers have some sort of biologically based nurturing or caretaking superiority. If so, one might expect fathers in all cultures to play a relatively minor role in childcare. But this is not the case.

Fathers in a number of other cultures share infant and childcare more or less equally with their wives. In our own culture, many, many men are actively involved in nurturing their children, and there are thousands more who, as stay-at-home fathers, do nearly all of the childcare. And, as Kyle Pruett, a Yale psychiatrist and the author of *The Nurturing Father*, has documented, these primary-caretaker fathers do an excellent job. Clearly, the family roles played by mothers and fathers are not biologically fixed. Instead, they vary with prevailing social, ideological, and other conditions.

Some proponents of the biologically-unfit-father theory have attempted to prove their point by looking at the differences between males and females of other species. One study by Harry Harlow found that female rhesus monkeys, for example, are four times as likely as males to express nurturing behavior toward infants, and most males are ten times as hostile to infants as females.

But the evidence is hardly conclusive. The males of dozens of species of fish, frogs, birds, and monkeys either share the parenting or assume the dominant nurturing role — even with their infants. As with humans, it appears that the level of male participation in caretaking varies, in part, with the amount of involvement that females will allow. And, as with humans, a male animal's presence often has great impact on his children. The male California mouse is responsible for bringing food into the nest and for huddling with the young to keep them warm (the pups aren't born with the ability to regulate their own body temperature). As a result, his pups weigh more, their ears and eyes open earlier, and they have a better survival rate than pups who are separated from their fathers.

Animal researchers (and the theorists who attempt to apply their findings to humans) have also suggested that the hormonal changes females experience during pregnancy and childbirth are further proof that they are biologically superior parents. But as Rutgers University psychobiologist Daniel Lehrman observed, "Such arguments involved using what look like scientific considerations to justify our social prejudices."

Most of the evidence that males are biologically unequipped for parenting is based on studies with laboratory rats. But as Michael Lamb says, "The variability among rodent species and the stereotypic nature of rodent parenting compared with the complexity of socialization and parenting in humans . . . combine to make the rodent model totally inappropriate."

As it turns out, the role that hormones play in determining sexual behaviors decreases as one ascends the phylogenetic scale, whereas the impact of learned behavior increases. "There is every reason to believe that among humans societal prescriptions are at least as important in the regulation of parental as well as sexual behavior," Lamb comments.

Recent evidence on humans suggests that women aren't the only ones who experience hormonal changes with the birth of a baby. Fathers experience a drop in testosterone when their babies are born, which some researchers believe may be associated with nurturing feelings. This suggests that men may be more prepared — even biologically — for parenting than we previously thought.

Researchers generally agree that environmental conditions can override the effects of hormones and, in the long run, be more important than short-lived hormonal shifts in determining the reactions of both males and females to infants. Even in animal species in which the male typically does not demonstrate active fathering, nurturing paternal behavior can be elicited under the right conditions. Virgin female and male rats, for example, who have sufficient exposure to newborn infants show parenting behavior.

In humans, perhaps the most compelling evidence that biology has little if anything to do with successful parenting comes from studies of adoption. In one recent study, adoptive mothers and fathers reported feeling just as attached to their babies as biological parents — both before and after the adoption. Adoptive fathers and mothers were better able to cope with the physical demands of parenthood and reported being more satisfied in their parental roles than biological parents. And there were no differences between mothers and fathers; regardless of gender, males and females reacted in similar ways to the adoption experience. As David Brodzinsky, co-editor of *The Psychology of Adoption,* recently concluded, "Pregnancy may set the stage for parenthood, but parental behavior — maternal as well as paternal — can develop quite nicely without it." Once again, biology is not destiny!

Women, of course, bear the physical burdens of pregnancy and childbirth. Psychologically, however, the process affects men just as powerfully as it does women — perhaps even more. Yet until fairly recently,

there has been little research on the man's emotional and psychological experiences during pregnancy.

The very title of one of the first articles to appear on the subject
should give you some idea of the medical and psychiatric communities' attitudes toward the impact of pregnancy on men. Written by
William H. Wainwright, M.D., and published in the July 1966 issue of
The American Journal of Psychiatry, it was called "Fatherhood as a Pre-
cipitant of Mental Illness." But an expectant father's experience during
the transition to fatherhood is not confined simply to excitement —
or mental illness. Expectant fathers feel everything from relief to denial, fear to frustration, anger to joy, the same emotions felt by expectant mothers.

One of the factors that makes it easy to ignore men's reactions to
pregnancy is that men and women aren't having the same experiences
at the same time: men are generally about a trimester behind their female partners. Women's emotional ups and downs are considered
"normal" at any given stage of pregnancy, but since men aren't in the
same place at the same time, their experiences are seen as abnormal,
funny, or not even worth mentioning.

Although most of what expectant fathers go through during their
spouse's pregnancy is psychological, various studies estimate that anywhere from 22 to 79 percent experience "sympathetic pregnancy" or
"couvade syndrome" (from the French word meaning "to hatch").
Most couvade symptoms are the same as those traditionally associated
with pregnant women: weight gain, nausea, mood swings, food crav-
ings. And there are often other symptoms that women don't get:
headaches, toothaches, itching, and cysts. These physical symptoms
are often accompanied by psychological problems such as depression,
tension, insomnia, irritability, and stuttering.

Physical symptoms are only a small portion of the changes that
expectant fathers undergo. In anticipation of approaching fatherhood, men show increased interest in babies. Some start reading
books about children and parenting. Many men react to the antici-
pated financial burden of parenthood by working longer hours or taking second jobs, especially during the last few months of pregnancy.
Whatever husbands are worrying about during that time, they sure
worry about it a lot.

One recent study found that men were more anxious than their wives during this period. They even worried more about their wives' aches and pains than their wives did! Fathers also experience the more typical anxieties about getting to the hospital on time when labor begins and whether the baby will be healthy. Their chief worry is money — to pay the hospital bills, to raise the baby — not an unreasonable concern, considering that as of the mid-1990s the average cost of having a baby in the United States was about $7,000, more if there were any complications, such as a cesarean section or a premature birth.

For some expectant fathers these worries may result in more severe psychological symptoms. A small percentage experience severe depression and nearly half suffer from low self-esteem. Fathers with low incomes are more likely to report depressive symptoms than fathers with higher incomes. Certain men, especially those with a history of violence, are more likely to assault their wives during pregnancy. And the assaults are mainly directed toward the belly. Whether the cause is jealousy or some other factor remains unknown.

Men — like women — vary greatly in terms of their readiness for parenthood, and this sense of readiness may affect how they react during pregnancy. Katharyn May identified several factors that are important in men's emotional preparedness for fathering, the most basic of which is whether a man has ever wanted to become a father. Some men — like some women — never wanted to have children and thus come to parenthood reluctantly; others see being a father as an important part of their life's plan. Most men, though, no matter how prepared or ready they are, experience at least some ambivalence during their partners' pregnancy.

The concept of parent-infant bonding didn't really emerge until the 1970s when two pediatricians, Marshall Klaus and John Kennell, argued that opportunities for extended mother-infant contact during the first weeks and months after birth would enhance the attachment bond. It wasn't until the mid-1980s that other researchers thought to test the bonding notion with fathers as well. Some evidence suggests that fathers who have more extended contact with their newborn infants in the hospital (even as little as four hours), as opposed to a traditional schedule of only briefly visiting the wife and baby together, become more involved with the baby later on at home.

Today, though, most scholars view the early bonding notion with considerable skepticism — not just for fathers but for mothers too. The process of developing a close relationship between parent and infant is a gradual one that emerges over the course of the first year of life. Fathers who are not present at the birth of their baby, mothers who deliver by cesarean section, and, of course, adoptive parents all manage to develop healthy relationships with their infants and children. "This bonding business is nonsense. We've sold parents a bill of goods," says Katharyn May. "They believe that if they don't have skin-to-skin contact within the first fifteen minutes, they won't bond. Science just doesn't show that."

Still, parents and infants do bond, and men's early attachments to their babies are just as powerful as women's. In the early 1970s, Martin Greenberg and Norman Morris were among the first researchers to notice how delighted and pleased fathers were with their newborns. They interviewed new fathers and discovered that "fathers begin developing a bond to their newborn by the first three days after birth and often earlier. Furthermore, there are certain characteristics of this bond which we call 'engrossment' . . . a feeling of preoccupation, absorption and interest in their newborn."

While almost no researchers have questioned that mothers develop a close attachment to their infants, many can't seem to accept that fathers develop the same kind of ties to their offspring. The assumption is that fathers may exaggerate and distort their feelings in the excitement of a new baby's arrival. To find out whether men walk the walk as well as talk the talk, Ross Parke and his colleagues decided to observe fathers with their newborns instead of only asking them how they felt about their babies. The results were fascinating.

Contrary to the view of the biologically unfit father, dads were just as interested as moms in their babies. Fathers held their infants and rocked them in their arms more than mothers did and equaled mothers in how much they talked, kissed, explored (examined skin, counted toes), and imitated their newborns.

This study may have been flawed, however. First, since both mother and father were in the same room, the high degree of father-infant interaction may have been due to the supporting presence of the mother, who may have encouraged the father and provided physical assistance and verbal instructions. Second, most of the fathers in this study had attended childbirth classes and had been present during the delivery. They therefore may have been better prepared for their parental role and more likely to involve themselves with their infants than other fathers.

To control for these flaws, Parke observed men who had not taken classes and not been present when their children were born. Again, the fathers were interested and active participants in the first few days after delivery. Whether alone with their newborn or together with their wife and baby, the fathers were just as warm and stimulating as the mothers. In fact, the only nurturing behavior in which mothers surpassed fathers was smiling. It has been well established, however, that women generally smile more than men, not just at babies but at all kinds of people.

If they are going to be competent caregivers, fathers (and mothers) need to be able to recognize and properly interpret their babies' signals. According to the biologically-unfit-father theory, men should be less capable of unscrambling their babies' messages than women. The truth is that fathers and mothers react nearly identically to one of the earliest and most persistent signals that a baby uses to express her wants and needs: crying. More surprising — and more damaging to the biologically based argument — is that the blood pressure of both mothers and fathers rises in response to the crying infant, but not to a smiling baby.

Fathers, like mothers, are also capable of discriminating among different types of crying patterns. The cry of a premature infant, for instance, differs from the cry of a full-term baby; it is shrill and high-pitched. When listening to tapes of premature and full-term babies crying, both mothers and fathers found the wail of the premature infant more unpleasant than that of a full-term baby. Even more impressive is the fact that men and women are equally able to discriminate among different crying patterns. Babies, of course, cry for various reasons: because they are hungry, because a pin is pricking them, or for some other reason. Mothers can differentiate between types of cries, such as pain and anger, particularly when listening to their own infants. Fathers can accurately identify the cries of their infants, but they aren't as capable as mothers in distinguishing among different kinds of cries. (They are, however, better than childless men at interpreting the cause of an infant's cry.)

Fathers are not only able to recognize infant signals but are just as competent as mothers in knowing what to do to help the baby. Different signals mean different needs: sometimes babies are hungry, other times bored, or something hurts. After an infant vocalizes, both mothers and fathers immediately talk to her more, touch her more, and look at her more closely. But they don't do these things in the same way. Fathers are more likely than mothers to respond to infant vocalization by talking to the baby; mothers react more by touching. The baby's mouth movements, like vocalizations, also elicit responses from his parents: fathers and mothers increase their talking, touching, and stimulation in response to mouth movements. Again, we see that fathers, rather than being biologically unfit, are very capable and sensitive caregivers, and they react quickly and appropriately to the often subtle signals of their newborn infants.

Fathers are often excluded from one of the most important parenting activities, feeding, because it is assumed they just aren't good at it. As one mother said, "I'd let him feed the baby but he just doesn't know how." Another mother commented, "Men just aren't trained to feed babies." As with so many of the myths about fathers, this one turns out to be groundless.

When Parke and his co-workers watched mothers and fathers feeding their babies and measured the amount of milk consumed, they found that the babies took almost the same amount from fathers as from mothers. Of course there is more to being a competent caregiver than merely getting food into a baby. By sucking, pausing, coughing, or spitting up, babies indicate whether the feeding is going smoothly or they are experiencing some discomfort. And one way to measure how capable parents are as feeders is to examine how quickly they modify their behavior in response to an infant's distress signals.

Fathers, like mothers, respond to these infant cues by momentarily stopping the feeding, looking more closely, and speaking to the baby.

Although they tend to spend less time feeding their babies, fathers are as sensitive and responsive as mothers to infant signals during feeding. The only difference between mothers and fathers is that fathers are less likely than mothers to stimulate the baby by touching him when he signals discomfort.

A father's presumed biological limits clearly do not prevent him from showing a great deal of skill and competence in his interaction with an infant. "Current data do not prove that there are no biological sex differences," one researcher concluded. "But they do speak against the notion that 'maternal' responsiveness reflects predominantly biological influences."

Unfortunately, many medical institutions do not recognize the importance of fathers during pregnancy and childbirth. As a result, despite the critical role they could play in preparing men for the challenges of fatherhood and encouraging their involvement, most medical professionals actually inhibit fathering. This process starts months before men become fathers.

Fathers who are involved during their partners' pregnancies have been shown to be more involved after the birth. And one of the simplest ways to start on the right course is for the father to accompany his partner on her regular prenatal medical checkups. Sadly, most men don't feel particularly welcome there. Pamela Jordan, a nurse and pregnancy expert, found that most men feel that their presence at the prenatal visits was perceived as "cute" or "novel." And many men, especially if they are feeling emotionally left out of the pregnancy by their partners, complain that obstetricians treat them as mere onlookers or even intruders. Men are generally ignored, and if they are talked to at all, it is only to discuss how they can support their partners. Rarely does an obstetrician recognize that expectant dads have fears, worries, and concerns too.

There are, of course, other ways for expectant fathers to get involved. Childbirth preparation classes are now a standard part of the prenatal services offered at most hospitals, and between 50 and 80 percent of all pregnant women, and often their male partners, attend them. Although these classes ostensibly welcome men and teach them lots of valuable information, many inadvertently reinforce the idea that fathers are peripheral players. Some of this has to do with the word "coach."

At first glance, this seems like a perfectly appropriate term for the father. But researcher Katharyn May has found that the use of the word "coach," and the concept behind it, has negative side effects. In part, it focuses attention on the father's role only during the brief period of labor and delivery and minimizes his importance during the entire pregnancy and beyond. It also reinforces the sexist stereotype of the father as a sort of fifth wheel in the delivery room instead of recognizing that he is a unique individual who is sharing a challenging life experience with his partner. Finally, the whole concept puts far too much pressure on the father by implying he should be capable of handling any and all contingencies — like a professional sports coach — after completing just twelve to fifteen hours of classes. What if he can't handle something? Should he be fired — both as coach and as father too?

One recent innovation in childbirth preparation may go a long way toward alleviating the "coach" problem. A team of New Jersey obstetricians, Myron Levine and Robert Block, encourage fathers to "play doctor" for the day and deliver their babies themselves (only in normal, uncomplicated births) under the supervision of the obstetrician. Their intent is "to bring the home aspect into the safety of the hospital setting and to make giving birth more family-centered." Fathers who deliver their babies are enthusiastic and also become more involved in the daily care of their infants at home. Three months after the birth, more than twice as many of the fathers who had performed the delivery were spending an hour or more with their babies daily, compared with fathers who had not delivered their babies.

Childbirth preparation classes are a fairly recent innovation, and until the 1980s fathers were routinely excluded from participating in childbirth. This exclusion was in part an effort to reduce infection in the delivery room; fathers, and any other unscrubbed person, were viewed as a possible source of contamination. Unable to be with their wives during labor and delivery, fathers were relegated to the waiting room, where they could fret, pace, and sleep. Even as late as 1972, one survey reported, fathers were permitted in the delivery room in only 27 percent of American hospitals. Not until 1974 did the American

College of Obstetricians and Gynecologists endorse the father's presence during labor and delivery.

Although the occasional father can still be seen pacing in a hospital corridor, hospital practices have greatly changed, and since the early 1990s fathers have been allowed into delivery rooms in nearly all U.S. hospitals. As a result, about 90 percent of all American males, married or not, now witness the birth of their infants.

Being permitted into the delivery room has made a big difference to fathers, allowing them to take an active role in the birth. It has also affected the quality of fathers' labor and delivery experience. Sharing the delivery was more important to men than just being with their wives during labor. Of those who were present, 95 percent reported a positive experience. "I felt tremendous," one man recalled. "I felt like I was part of it too." Of the husbands in one study who were not in the delivery room, however, 88 percent had negative feelings about missing the delivery. One said, "I felt anxious. Very anxious. Boy, it's taking a long time. And disappointed, like I'd let her down. Because I heard her — a nurse came out, and I heard my wife saying, 'I want my husband!' and I thought, Oh, God, what's happening? I felt like — possibly — I hadn't done my job. I don't know why he [the doctor] made me leave."

Being present at the child's birth has other advantages for fathers: in one study, more fathers (51 percent) than mothers (25 percent) held their babies while still in the delivery room. As this study's investigators noted, however, "The father, of course, is not lying down with an intravenous tube inserted in one arm and perhaps a blood pressure cuff on the other."

While there's still some debate about whether early contact with a baby strengthens a man's feelings of fatherhood, there's little question that being present at the delivery encourages his later involvement with his infant. Moreover, the husband's experience is closely tied to that of his wife. Women who have a positive birth experience contribute to their husbands' enjoyment of the birth. Preparation for childbirth leads to more active participation by fathers in labor and delivery, which in turn makes the whole birth event better for both mother and father — and gets the father's relationship with his infant off to a better start.

Obstetricians aren't the only medical professionals who have excluded fathers. When the children are sick or need their teeth cleaned, mothers are usually the ones who make the appointments and get the kids where they have to go. While some critics claim that this is because fathers aren't as interested in their children's health as mothers are, a more plausible explanation is that the medical community has erected barriers that exclude fathers. Most doctors' offices are open from nine to five, which doesn't accommodate working parents of either sex very well. But this schedule has a more profound effect on fathers, whose employers make it nearly impossible for them to take time off to care for a sick child. A recent study in London demonstrated the impact of doctors' office hours on fathers' participation in health care. Fathers were more than twice as likely to bring their children to a health clinic when it offered services in the evening as when it was open only during the day.

Since medical professionals are often the first people outside the family who help shape a father's role, their policies and practices could play a large part in preparing and encouraging a father's involvement. As pediatrician and fatherhood expert Michael Yogman recently noted, "Fathers are more often coming to office visits and pediatricians need to use any opportunity to engage the father and reinforce his participation. Invitations to fathers to attend office visits where the pediatrician meets them either prenatally or in the hospital can be an effective outreach. Appropriate magazines and waiting room materials for fathers can make them feel more welcome."

Sadly, though, most medical professionals don't seem to agree. Although the theories of women's biological primacy in parenting have been shown to be false, their legacy lives on. Welcoming men as equal partners in the pregnancy, including male-specific topics in birth preparation classes, and creating a father-friendly atmosphere in hospitals and obstetricians' offices have yet to be considered priorities by medical and mental health professionals.

The evidence that men are biologically fit for fatherhood is overwhelming. But until we all recognize this fact, the alienation of men from their families, which begins even before they become fathers, will continue.

3

The Dangerous Father

A S HARMFUL AS the image of the biologically unfit father is, it is nowhere near as damaging as another of the common and equally incorrect stereotypes about men: that they're dangerous. For decades, feminist writers such as Marilyn French (*The War Against Women*), Susan Brownmiller (*Femininity*), Andrea Dworkin (*Intercourse*), and, more recently, Susan Faludi (*Backlash*) and Naomi Wolf (*The Beauty Myth*) have told us that men by their very nature pose a significant and constant threat to women and children.

In one form or another, this attitude has permeated the public's consciousness. It's rare for a day to go by without hearing, often in graphic detail, about rapes, kidnappings, murders, and molestations, all committed by men, often against their wives and girlfriends.

While the public is certainly outraged by the way it thinks men treat women, that outrage is far greater when the perceived victims are children. Few people command more respect on that subject than John Walsh, the host of television's *America's Most Wanted*. So when Walsh testified before Congress that 1.5 million children go missing every year, the entire country snapped to attention. "We don't have a clue what happens to over 50,000 of them," said Walsh, whose six-year-old son, Adam, had been abducted and murdered several years earlier. "This country is littered with mutilated, decapitated, raped, and strangled children."

The response to Walsh's claims was startling and immediate: pictures of missing children suddenly appeared on milk cartons, Congress passed the Missing Children Act and created the National Center for Missing and Exploited Children, and parents across the country had their children fingerprinted. Thousands of parents had radio transponders implanted and ID numbers etched in their children's teeth. Millions of children were instructed by their parents to run away from any adult they didn't know, and millions of parents began living in fear that one of their own children would become "another Adam."

Fortunately, these fears were overblown. The actual number of children abducted by strangers each year is smaller than the number of preschoolers who die as a result of choking on food. But thanks to the images put out by a variety of advocacy groups and disseminated by the media, the inflated figures have been seared into the public's consciousness, alongside the media-created image we have of those potential kidnappers and murderers: men. Mustachioed pedophiles lurking in the dark, waiting to offer a piece of candy to their unsuspecting victims.

One might reasonably wonder where Walsh and others get the figures they cite. The National Incidence Studies of Missing, Abducted, Runaway, and Thrownaway Children (NISMART) — a report mandated by the 1984 Missing Children Act — identifies five categories of "missing" children. According to their most recent figures, there were

> 354,100 children abducted by family members
> 114,600 child abductions by non–family members
> 450,700 runaways
> 127,000 children who were "thrown away"
> 438,200 children who were lost, injured, or otherwise missing

That does add up to about 1.5 million, but a closer look reveals some problems. First, it's nearly impossible to come up with a definition for each of the five kinds of missing children. In some states, for example, the law defines "abduction" as the coerced movement of a person as little as a few feet. But when people hear the word "abduction," they often think of Adam Walsh, Polly Klass, or some other high-profile case where a kidnapper snatches a child away and then kills him.

To account for the significant differences in definitions, NISMART breaks down the incidents in each of the five categories into two distinct subcategories: "broad scope" and "policy focal." "Broad scope" defines a particular event the way an affected family might define it, and includes "both serious and minor episodes that may nonetheless be alarming to the participants." (The numbers given above are broad-scope incidents.) "Policy focal," defines an incident the way the police or other social agency might, and includes only episodes "of a more serious nature, where without intervention, the child may be further endangered or at risk of harm." The broad-scope numbers in every category are far higher than the more important policy-focal numbers. But even the lower figures greatly exaggerate the problem they're attempting to describe, and contribute to an artificially manufactured "missing children epidemic."

Let's take a look at a few examples, starting with children who may be missing but certainly weren't kidnapped (but who nevertheless constitute 60 percent of all "missing children"): runaways.

If we eliminate the kids over fifteen who leave home without permission to stay with a friend, the 450,700 broad-scope figure for runaways drops to just over 133,000. That's still a big group, but two-thirds of those children were sixteen or older (many running away with boyfriends or girlfriends) and nearly half of them returned home within two days. Only a quarter of the parents or guardians didn't know where the child was.

In a similar fashion, eliminating children who were missing for as little as a few minutes lowers the number of "lost, injured, missing" children from 438,200 to 139,100. Even the lower figure warrants a closer look. Nearly 20 percent of these children were recovered within two hours; 73 percent within twenty-four hours. Seventy-nine percent suffered no physical harm. In 12 percent of the policy-focal cases the child went out and lost track of the time, and in 19 percent either the parent or the child had simply misunderstood expectations.

What about the kids that NISMART classifies as actually having been "abducted" (a term that brings up powerful images of children kidnapped, raped, and murdered by strangers)? Using the policy-focal definition cuts this figure by more than half, to 163,200. But that still exaggerates the problem. To start with, 75 percent (354,100) of all "kidnap" victims were taken by family members and were never in any danger. The vast majority of these "family abductions" were child-custody-related delays, such as one parent returning a child a few minutes late after a court-ordered visitation, while only 2 percent of the cases involved what we might think of as a "child snatching" from a school or daycare center.

A slight majority of the perpetrators of "family abductions" are, in fact, noncustodial fathers or other father figures. Given the inequities in awarding custody, this is hardly surprising. And most of the family abductions are reported in January and August, when school vacations and visitations are ending. More than half of these abductions occur in the South, while the Midwest is underrepresented. "It is possible that the more traditional legal system in the South makes noncustodial fathers pessimistic about getting a favorable outcome, so that they take matters into their own hands," the NISMART report speculates.

Despite the popular image of divorced fathers who snatch their children, change their identities, and take off for another city or country, most of these "kidnappings" lasted from only a few days to a week, and only 10 percent went on for a month or more. And in only 17 percent of the cases did the parent or guardian from whom the child was allegedly taken not know where the "abducted" child was. So how many children are really snatched and hidden away in ugly custody battles? Around three thousand per year, says Tom Riley, president of STATS, a nonpartisan statistical analysis firm — less than 1 percent of the original broad-scope number.

Within the category of family abductions there are two large groups that NISMART doesn't report on and which get almost no media attention. First, there are the approximately six million incidents each year when mothers actively prevent their children from spending time with their fathers. While this is not strictly kidnapping, it feels that way to many noncustodial fathers and could justifiably have been included under at least the broad-scope definition. Second, thousands of children are moved by their custodial mothers far enough away from the children's father that the father is unable to visit them.

Except in a very few cases, these men (and their children) have no recourse. The police won't pursue an abducted child without writing a report, and they won't write one if the child has been abducted by a custodial parent. And the National Center for Missing and Exploited Children, which helps custodial parents (about 85 percent of whom are women) track down their "kidnapped" children, refuses to help noncustodial parents (85 percent of whom are men).

As troubling as family abductions are, it's the threat of an abduction by a stranger that every parent fears the most. But of the 114,600 incidents that NISMART puts in this category, only 3 percent (3,200 to 4,600) involved actual abductions. The rest — more than 110,000 — were only *attempts*. (Remember, the definition of "abduction" doesn't always match up with the public's image of what a kidnapping is. According to NISMART, "abduction" means detaining a child for more than an hour; the unauthorized taking of a child into a building or a vehicle; carrying a child more than twenty feet; or luring a child for the purpose of committing another crime.) Fewer than 300 incidents in this category were actual abductions by strangers, or what the U.S. Department of Justice calls "stereotypical kidnappings." Of these, about 100 end in murder — a horrifying number, but less than one-tenth of one percent of NISMART's original 114,600 figure.

So where are the 1.5 million children who go "missing" each year and the 50,000 "mutilated, decapitated, raped, and strangled children" John Walsh refers to? For the most part, they're right where they're supposed to be: at home.

This isn't meant to minimize or discount the horror and pain suffered by real victims and their families. And of course children should learn caution around strangers, and parents shouldn't let their kids go out alone for long walks in the middle of the night. Caution is reasonable and prudent, but as Tom Riley asks, "Are we really helping combat this problem by overstating it by a factor of hundreds and whipping parents around the country into a frenzy of suspicion and paranoia?"

Most certainly not. Here's how Mark Warr, a criminologist who specializes in people's fear of becoming crime victims, puts it: "A few years ago the police came to my kids' school and wanted each of the children to participate in a national program where they'd put an ID number on the children's teeth. They came right out and told the kids that if they were ever abducted and murdered, the police would use the ID numbers to identify them. Why on earth are we teaching our children something like that? The probability of being abducted and murdered is less than a million to one, but we're scaring the hell out of thousands and thousands of our kids and their parents. What happens is we end up with a society in which nobody trusts each other."

And leading the list of people not to be trusted are men — especially men you don't know. When it comes to abductions and murders committed by strangers, men do in fact comprise the majority of perpetrators. But of all murders of children under twelve, more than 60 percent are committed by family members, 55 percent of whom are women. Overall, then, a child has a greater chance of getting killed by a female relative than by a strange man hiding in the shadows.

This kind of information doesn't make good copy or bring in federal funding to advocacy groups. But fear does — especially when it has a face. Take the case of Polly Klass, a beautiful twelve-year-old girl who was kidnapped from her Petaluma, California, home and killed. The search for Polly, and later for her killer, captured the nation's heart, and for months the media ran pictures of her next to those of the prime suspect, Richard Alan Davis, who fit the public's image of a sociopathic kidnapper-murderer: male, somewhat swarthy, with plenty of facial hair. Davis was ultimately convicted of the murder.

Obviously, it doesn't make sense to take an isolated and extreme case like that of Polly Klass or Adam Walsh and apply it to the rest of the country. But by neatly combining the images of Polly and Davis with frequent reference to the "1.5 million missing children," the media created the unmistakable impression that many of those children were going to suffer the same fate and that a veritable army of men like Richard Alan Davis were roaming the land, searching for more victims.

The image of man as the sole perpetrator is compounded in the printed materials provided by advocacy groups in their well-meaning attempts to educate parents and protect children. Take, for example, Kenneth Wooden's book, *Child Lures: What Every Parent and Child Should Know about Preventing Sexual Abuse and Abduction.* On the one hand, Wooden acknowledges that "while the proverbial stranger can still pose a threat to the safety of children, we owe it to our kids to teach them much more than the 'don't talk to strangers' mantra." On the other hand, of the illustrations that accompany the descriptions of each of the fifteen "lures" that Wooden describes, fourteen show only males as the people to fear. Nearly half of them are sporting a beard, mustache, or sideburns. (In the fifteenth illustration, the perpetrator isn't actually shown. Instead, a message, "Meet me at the park," appears on a child's computer screen. But in the text, Wooden describes the on-line perpetrator only as "he.")

Treating all men as though they are potential threats to our children can have damaging consequences. Lawrence Wright, a writer who lives in Texas, came face to face with this artificially constructed anti-male bias one day when he went to pick up his daughter, Caroline, at her after-school daycare center:

> She had a new teacher, a man, in fact. I made a point of going over to introduce myself and make him feel welcome. The new man was out on the playground with a walkie-talkie. "I'm Caroline's dad," I said, but before I could get around to my welcoming speech, he said, "I'm sorry, but I'm going to have to ask you for a picture I.D." As Caroline's father, I appreciated the security, but as a man, I took offense at having to prove that I was not a pervert. True, women are also asked to show identification, but I suspect that is done in the spirit of fairness. Everybody assumes it is men that are the problem.

Like coverage of missing and murdered children, media reports on child abuse are everywhere. The coverage follows much the same pattern as it does for the "epidemic" of missing and murdered children, starting with a wild exaggeration of the scope of the problem. No matter how or where the crime took place, the news story nearly always includes a sentence along the lines of, "Every year there are three million cases of child abuse reported in the United States." When people read such a statement, what image pops into their heads? asks Richard Wexler, the author of *Wounded Innocents*. Three million battered and bruised children? Probably. And an army of violent sexual predators, most of whom are men.

Both of these images are false. To start with, remember that there's a distinction between reports of abuse and actual cases of abuse. This is especially important because two-thirds of those three million reports turn out to be false. That leaves about a million substantiated cases of abuse, which is still a horrifyingly huge number. But as we saw when we looked at "missing" children, the public has an impression of what "abuse" means that is very different from the definition used by various government agencies that compile the statistics.

Of the million substantiated cases, more than half involve "neglect": physical (inadequate supervision, inadequate attention to the need for food, clothing, or personal hygiene), emotional (inadequate nurturance or affection, inattention to the child's developmental or emotional needs), or educational (permitting chronic truancy, keeping the child home for illegitimate reasons, or failure to enroll a school-age child in school). A quarter of all substantiated cases involve "physical abuse," meaning the child suffered a "moderate injury" (defined as a physical, mental, or emotional injury or condition resulting from physical abuse that was serious enough to persist in observable form for at least forty-eight hours). Twelve-and-a-half percent of substantiated cases (a relatively small percentage, but still well over 100,000) involve sexual abuse. In this category, men are the predominant abusers, accounting for more than 85 percent of the perpetrators. But remember that although the sheer number of sexually abused children is large, in percentage terms about three-tenths of one percent of children are sexually abused — that's 3 per 1,000.

Still, the impression persists that millions of children are being sexually abused every year. One widely heard claim is that one girl in three or four will be sexually molested before leaving high school. "The figure is constantly recited by authorities in the field of child sexual abuse prevention, and there is some evidence that it has made an impact on how the public perceives the magnitude of the problem," says Neil Gilbert, a professor of social welfare at the University of California, Berkeley. "According to surveys, a huge majority of parents . . . believe that 25% or more of all children are victims of sexual abuse."

Despite the alarming difference between 0.3 percent and 25 percent, the truth about the real prevalence of sexual abuse goes unreported. "Contrary to popular belief," writes Richard Wexler, "the six worst words a reporter can say to an editor are not, 'it won't be ready by deadline.' The six words most guaranteed to get a reporter in trouble are, 'actually, it's more complex than that.' "

There is no shortage of accurate, reliable data on child abuse, but the media still tend to base their coverage on the findings of advocacy groups in the child sexual abuse prevention movement. The problem with relying on advocacy research is that while such groups undoubtedly have their hearts in the right place, they also have an ideological imperative. They seem to think the results of their research are more important than the quality of that research. In other words, distorting the facts and statistics is justifiable in the name of a good cause.

That's exactly what happens with research produced by advocates for missing and sexually abused children. One of the best and most widely cited examples of this flawed research comes from Diana Russell, who in 1984 asked 930 women a number of questions about sexual abuse. The questions included, "Did anyone ever try or succeed in touching your breasts or genitals against your wishes before you turned 14?" and "Did anyone ever feel you, grab you, or kiss you in a way you felt was threatening?"

Russell compiled her answers and came up with an unusual definition of sexual abuse that included unwanted hugs and kisses and even being confronted by an exhibitionist. Her conclusion: 54 percent of women had been the victims of incest (by a father or brother) or sexual abuse by a non–family member (usually a male).

Later, perhaps surprised by her own conclusion, Russell lowered her 54-percent figure to 38 percent by counting only those incidents that involved physical contact. This supposedly narrower focus included not only forced vaginal intercourse or other penetration but also attempted petting, threatening kisses, and unwanted touches on the leg.

While all these things are far from pleasant, they are not what most people have in mind when they think of sexual abuse, nor are they considered sexual abuse under any federal or state law. But "by designing research that lumps together possibly harmless behavior with the trauma of child rape, advocates have inflated the estimates of child sexual abuse to critical proportions," writes Gilbert. And by continuing to cite Russell's (and others') inaccurate statistics, the media compound the problem, contributing to a climate in which women are unnecessarily afraid.

Who are they afraid of? As usual, one need look no further than the nearest male. As Gilbert puts it, if one accepts as fact the claim that somewhere between 38 and 54 percent of women were sexually abused or raped as children, the nearly inescapable conclusion is that at least the same percentage of men are pedophiles or rapists.

All these suspicions, perceptions, and "inescapable conclusions" have a decidedly negative impact on men. But when our fears give way to actual allegations, the results are far worse.

Charges of abuse are sometimes made against men in intact families, but they are much more common in cases of divorce. So common, in fact, that there's a clinically recognized syndrome: SAID, or Sexual Allegations In Divorce. A variety of studies have concluded, however, that 75 to 80 percent of these divorce-related allegations of child abuse are completely false.

Still, helped along by the widely disseminated view that fathers — especially divorced or divorcing ones — are abusive, a veritable child abuse industry has sprouted up, populated by people whose livelihoods depend on bringing more and more allegations into the system.

In divorce cases, allegations of abuse can arise in a variety of ways. Thanks to the media, child abuse is on everyone's mind, and under the stress of a divorce, people frequently overreact to ordinary symptoms, such as diaper rash and bruises, and jump to the wrong conclusions. In this type of situation, the concerned mother — and studies have shown that nearly 95 percent of the accusers are women — will usually try to get some advice from a therapist, physician, or child protective services worker.

But far too many women falsely accuse their estranged or former husbands of child abuse who say they are doing it by mistake or out of an attempt to protect their children. Richard Gardner, Lee Coleman, Melvin Guyer, and other researchers have independently concluded that women who deliberately make false allegations are obsessed with hurting their husbands as much as possible. "They'll frequently coach their children into making statements against the father, and will shop around until they find a therapist, a doctor, or some other professional who will support their claims," says Gardner, a clinical professor of child psychiatry at Columbia University. "A parent who is genuinely concerned that a child has been abused typically hopes that the child was not sexually abused and tends to be relieved when an investigator concludes that abuse is unlikely."

"It's a way of getting even, a way of gaining control over your child at a time when you feel very out of control," writes Arthur Green. "It's a way of getting this guy you hate out of your life forever." Attorney Anne Mitchell puts it more succinctly, calling an allegation of abuse the perfect weapon. "It's simple, fast, and guaranteed to achieve the desired result." There's also some evidence that women are being encouraged to make false charges. "With child abuse and spouse abuse, you don't have to prove anything, you just have to accuse," says Jan Ross, one of the leaders of a for-women-only seminar on divorce.

Whether a false allegation of abuse is made maliciously or out of genuine concern for the welfare of a child, the result is the same for the accused. Unlike alleged perpetrators of other crimes, a father accused of child abuse is guilty until he proves himself innocent. "And that's not easy," says attorney Peter Firpo. "By the time a man hears he's been accused, his children have probably been seen by therapists or child protective services officers, who see their role as validating the accusation." Things move pretty quickly from there. The instant the allegation is made, the father's contact with his children is cut off and an investigation begins.

In most states, child abuse investigations are supposed to be handled jointly by law enforcement officials and local child protective services workers (they're called different things in different states, but for consistency "CPS" will be used here). In general, police officers have received extensive training in investigative techniques and are, at least ostensibly, impartial. Most CPS workers, however, don't even make a pretense of neutrality. "They're advocates who seek to promote the welfare of their clients," says Dr. Lee Coleman, a child psychiatrist and frequent expert witness in child abuse cases. "They're taught to believe and support their clients, no matter what those clients say."

Dr. Gardner, who has more than thirty years of experience evaluating allegations of child abuse, notes that many CPS workers refer to themselves as "validators," a term that at best raises questions about their objectivity. "They of course hold that 'children never lie about sexual abuse,' and they accept as valid every statement a child makes that might verify sex abuse," he says.

The "believe the children" idea was first popularized by Dr. Roland Summit in an influential article in the journal *Child Abuse and Neglect* in 1983. He wrote that "children never fabricate the kinds of explicit sexual manipulations they divulge in complaints or interrogations." Summit, who developed his theories without the benefit of any scientific evidence, also claimed that denial of abuse is itself frequently a sign of abuse. "If a child suspected of being abused is unable to volunteer information, it must be elicited with warm reassurance and specific, potentially leading questions."

The problem with this approach is that it veers dangerously close to, and is often inseparable from, coercion. According to Stephen Ceci and Maggie Bruck, two of the country's leading experts in this field, children, and especially preschoolers six years of age and younger, are extremely suggestible. They're also very concerned with pleasing adults and will say just about anything in order to do so. So if an interviewer creates an atmosphere of accusation ("Are you afraid to talk? You'll feel better once you've told"), the likelihood that a child will give a false answer goes up significantly.

Ceci and Bruck identified a variety of other factors that can lead to false accusations on the part of children. Children are more likely to make untrue statements when interviewers are of high status (people the children have been trained or socialized to respect). In the infamous Kelly Michaels daycare case, in New Jersey in 1985, children were interviewed by police or social workers who made explicit reference to their connection to law enforcement agencies — such comments as, "I'm a policeman and if you were a bad girl, I would punish you wouldn't I? Police punish bad people." In this case, the alleged perpetrator was convicted of 115 counts of sexual abuse against 20 three- to five-year-old children and sentenced to 47 years in jail. Based on the fact that suggestive and coercive interviewing techniques were used, the verdict was later overturned and all charges were dropped.

Interview bias — as is often the case when social workers interview potential victims — also contributes to increased false reports. "When children's responses contained discrepant, inconsistent, incomprehensible or no information, the investigators only considered these responses to be consistent with the fact that abuse had taken place or else they chose to ignore these students," says Lee Coleman.

But child abuse victims are worthless without perpetrators, especially if one is trying to raise the public's consciousness on a particular issue — or, to be cynical, trying to raise money. And it didn't take Roland Summit long to find a convenient perpetrator: "Unless there is a special support for the child and immediate intervention to force responsibility on the father, the girl will follow the 'normal' course and retract her complaint."

This approach to child abuse allegations is based on the assumption that the abuse took place and that the father is the most likely perpetrator — an assumption incompatible with the role of an investigator, who is supposed to be neutral and determine whether a crime was committed at all. Nevertheless, despite their biased orientation, CPS workers have taken on the task of determining the guilt or innocence of an accused father. This unfortunate scenario is further complicated by the fact that the police — the other presumably neutral voice in an investigation — often rely heavily on CPS's conclusions. In San Diego, California, for example, a grand jury probe found that detectives "will integrate elements of the social workers' investigation into their own reports, instead of performing an independent investigation."

In 97 percent of the cases where the police conduct an actual investigation, they are not able to substantiate the allegations, so no criminal charges are filed. But to the dismay of the thousands of men who are falsely accused each year, this doesn't mean that the investigation will end, or that they'll be able to see their children again anytime soon. Even after the police drop the criminal investigation, CPS agencies can still conduct their own. And to help them do so, the courts have given them incredibly broad powers.

For example, CPS workers — armed with nothing more than an allegation, and without a court order or a hearing — can force parents and children into therapy for an unlimited amount of time, can compel an accused man to take lie detector or other "diagnostic" tests, and can deny a father access to his children — even if he has a court order allowing such access. "These are people who, at least for a limited amount of time, are given an enormous amount of power over somebody else. And they routinely abuse that power," says Dr. Melvin Guyer, a psychiatry professor at the University of Michigan and a practicing attorney.

As part of an "investigation," CPS will frequently send a child for evaluation to an outside mental health professional selected from a court-approved list. Although a skilled therapist should be able to weed out obviously false charges, by and large the therapists to whom CPS refers children are all too willing to confirm what may be false reports against an innocent father.

In some cases, therapists are simply afraid to rule out abuse. To be eligible for federal funding under the Mondale Act — the Child Abuse Prevention and Treatment Act — every state has passed laws requiring certain people (doctors, therapists, teachers, etc.) to report suspected abuse to the proper authority. To back up this requirement, these "mandated reporters" are subject to fines or imprisonment for not reporting. "As a result, everyone's on the defensive — they're afraid that if they don't make a report, they'll be deemed criminals if they inadvertently put a child back in the hands of a real abuser," says Dr. Gardner.

This fear often leads child abuse evaluators to outlandish, and tragic, conclusions. In a series of studies, Dr. Guyer and other researchers presented to a panel of mental health professionals the synopsis of an actual case — one in which the researchers knew the allegation had been false. The following facts were presented: the mother had alleged abuse based on her discovery of a bruise on her two-year-old daughter's leg and of a single pubic hair (that she thought looked like the father's) in the girl's diaper.

Four medical exams of the girl had shown no evidence of abuse. In addition, two lie detector tests, a police investigation, and a CPS investigation had cleared the father. Based on this evidence alone, 76 percent of the professionals recommended that the father's contact with the daughter be either highly supervised or terminated altogether. Several of these "child abuse experts" even managed to conclude that the girl had been sodomized as well as subjected to cunnilingus.

In other cases, a false report of abuse is quickly confirmed because the therapist, like the referring CPS worker, has already made a decision before hearing what all the parties, including the father, have to say. When Dr. Gardner, who has reviewed hundreds of cases of alleged child abuse, asked various "validators" why they did not interview the father as part of their evaluation, he was frequently told, "[The father] would deny it anyway so there's no point in my seeing him," or "My job is not to do an investigation; my job is only to interview the child to find out whether the child was sexually abused."

Validators also tend to rely heavily on "behavioral and emotional indicators of abuse," which include acting out, bed-wetting, changed eating habits, nightmares, whining, temper tantrums, thumb-sucking, or behavior that is overly compliant or overly fearful. But these supposed indicators of abuse are so common they could apply to just about anyone. "Any normal child might at some point in childhood exhibit one or more of these behaviors and thereby risk being perceived as an abuse victim," one researcher, Ross Legrand, writes. Furthermore, many of the indicators of abuse can also be attributed to stress and anxiety — exactly what would be experienced by a child whose parents are undergoing a bitter divorce.

By far the most powerful incentive to rubber-stamp an abuse charge is financial. Therapists appearing before the San Diego grand jury, for example, testified that they feared removal from the approved list (and, of course, a corresponding drop in income) if they opposed the recommendations of the CPS department. Therapists who do dare to disagree openly with a CPS worker's opinion risk "never getting to see their patient again."

Private validators have additional ways to profit from abuse charges against fathers. In Alameda County, California, for example, the Victim/Witness program will pay directly to a licensed therapist up to $10,000 per child for counseling, as long as the child was alleged to have been abused. An additional $10,000 is available to counsel the child's mother. To get their therapy paid for, the child victim and her mother must see a therapist from an approved list. And who directs the mother to a therapist who would be best for her and her child? CPS, of course.

All it takes to start the funding process is a police report or a child abuse report containing an allegation of abuse. No proof that the allegation actually took place is required. "Just because there wasn't a conviction, doesn't mean a crime wasn't committed," said an official of the California state agency that manages the Victim/Witness program. "If someone believes she's been a victim, we don't have the right to question that."

From the therapist's perspective, all he or she has to do to collect a regular government paycheck is provide an occasional progress report claiming that additional counseling is necessary because the patient still suffers from the trauma of having been abused. A therapist who might otherwise be honest enough to say that a child hasn't been abused might not want to risk killing the goose that lays the golden eggs.

Some therapists have found other sources of long-term income: the alleged victims' fathers. Not long ago, one such father, Nick O., called the therapist who was treating his daughter to get a status report. "She told me that her work with my daughter was done, but that she was going to keep her in therapy 'in anticipation of an unpleasant custody battle.' " Nick's daughter, who was three when Nick was accused of abuse, has been in therapy for more than two years. "There's no question in my mind," Nick says, "that if I were some poor shmuck on the street who didn't have a dime to my name, this would have been over a long time ago."

A typical CPS investigation may also involve referring the alleged child victim for a medical exam. Some doctors, too, seem inclined to support the "findings" of the CPS workers. Like therapists, doctors may confirm abuse because they're afraid not to. And like therapists, they have financial incentives: if they don't back up CPS, they will no longer be called upon to perform evaluations.

But unlike therapists and CPS workers, who may substantiate an abuse claim based on their opinions alone, doctors are usually required to document their reasons. However, "in medicine, statements made by patients or family are generally taken at face value," says Dr. Coleman. "So when a mother or a CPS worker sends a child to the doctor and says, 'I think she's been abused by her father,' the doctor will frequently make a diagnosis of abuse based on this 'history.' "

Because sexual abuse rarely leaves any physical signs, a physical exam is not likely to give a doctor much to go on. A doctor's report might say that although no indication of abuse was found, the examination's findings were "consistent with abuse." "Technically, there's a kernel of truth there," says Dr. Coleman. "But what gets ignored is that a normal physical exam is also consistent with no abuse. Saying 'consistent with abuse' is simply a fraud — it's language designed to help the prosecution without adding anything to the investigation." It also means that although there's no evidence that the father committed any abuse, the door is always open.

Other times, doctors may file misleading or ambiguous reports, with disastrous results. In one disturbing case, an Ohio physician conducted an examination of a girl alleged to have been abused. In his report, the doctor claimed to have found a "suspicious looking scar" in the little girl's anus. In a later review of the slides that he himself had taken during the exam, the doctor admitted that "there is nothing that looks suspicious." But the damage had already been done: the girl testified that the reason she believed her father had abused her was because she believed she had this scar.

The doctor testified in court that other factors he relied on to determine that the girl had been abused — her recurring urinary tract infections and an asymmetrically shaped hymen — are quite common in nonabused children. "Nevertheless, there are doctors still basing their opinions on this type of medical misinformation," says attorney Peter Firpo. "And men are in prison because of it."

When CPS workers have finally assembled the conclusions of the outside therapists and medical professionals, they prepare a report for the court that will usually touch on such items as whether the child should be allowed contact with her father and whether continued therapy is required. Not surprisingly, these reports are frequently filled with incorrect, misinterpreted, or even fabricated evidence against accused men. "CPS workers very selectively look through an enormous amount of data, pick out just those things that are consistent with their opinions, and ignore anything that might show that the guy is innocent," says Guyer. Therapists told the San Diego grand jury that CPS workers "frequently distort reports they have been given about patients," and if the therapists disagree with the CPS worker, their recommendations "may not even appear in the report to the court."

As part of his attempt to prove his innocence, one accused father, Rob W., subjected himself to a lie detector test, extensive psychological evaluations, and a penile plethysmograph, an exam that purports to determine whether a man is a pedophile by wiring his penis to a machine and measuring his responses while he's looking at pictures or listening to recordings of various sexual scenarios — some involving children, some not. All these exams concluded that Rob had done nothing wrong. In fact, one examiner reported that based on the evidence, Rob "may have been falsely accused." He recommended that CPS "look for possible motives for falsely accusing Rob, such as protecting some other perpetrator . . . or an attempt on the part of his ex-wife to secure total control over their children and preclude Robert from any contact with them."

In a report to the court, however, the CPS worker involved in the case apparently ignored the examiner's recommendation, the "no deception" reading of the lie detector test, and the reports of the two outside therapists who believed Rob was innocent. She also ignored the daughter's own statements that nothing really happened, that she was sad about not being able to be with her father, and that her mommy had told her to tell things to other examiners. Instead, this CPS worker recommended to the court that no paternal visitation be allowed at all.

The case of Alicia W., a girl who was allegedly raped by her father, provides an even more disturbing example of the lengths to which CPS will go to prove an abuse charge against an innocent father. During one videotaped interview, Alicia was asked by a CPS worker, "With whom do you feel safe?" She clearly answers, "My mom, dad, and brother." But in the official transcript of the tape, her response appears as, "My mom and brother." Later, the altered transcript was used by several other people — including the CPS worker and the head of the medical clinic where the girl was examined — to "prove" that she didn't feel safe with her father. "The best that can be said is that these people heard what they wanted to hear," say independent investigators who recently reviewed this case. "The worst is that they committed perjury."

CPS's influence also extends to the courts. Because of the huge backlog of court cases, many counties allow "referees" — temporarily appointed officials, usually attorneys — to listen to the facts and present their findings to a judge for signature. But many referees owe their jobs, and their two- or three-hundred-dollar-an-hour fees, to the continued support of CPS workers. The San Diego grand jury found, for example, "there is a strong perception that referees are hesitant to go against the recommendations" of CPS and that evidence contrary to CPS's position "is either excluded or ignored."

Clearly, the fear of making a mistake, combined with the financial incentives and total immunity provided by the Mondale Act, help explain the high number of false charges of abuse and the child abuse industry's willingness to go along with them. Some people feel that perhaps the most compelling explanation is our society's deep-rooted anti-male and anti-father bias.

"There's this feeling out there that men are inherently violent and abusive, and that women and children need to be protected from them," says Guyer. "There's also an expectation that if a man hasn't already abused his children, it's only a matter of time until he does, and therefore he shouldn't have access to them. To people who think that way, making a false allegation of abuse doesn't seem so outlandish."

Given the obvious bias and even malicious nature of some CPS investigations, one might expect that the agencies would be sued quite often. But this isn't the case. To be eligible for federal funding under the Mondale Act, states must pass laws protecting their mandated reporters from prosecution. "This was a pretty well-meaning provision, and it gave many people the confidence to come forward," says Dr. Gardner. "But the same immunity protects people who are making frivolous and even completely fabricated accusations."

A recent court case demonstrates what a powerful protection this immunity can be. One physician examined a one-year-old boy and failed to recognize that the child was exhibiting symptoms of a congenital brain defect. Instead, the doctor insisted that the child was "suffering from injuries of a non-accidental nature which could only have resulted from a violent shaking or a fall." When the boy died a few days later, the doctor noted that the death had been "caused by a blunt injury to the side of the head."

A few weeks later, the physician sent a letter to his district attorney's office expressing his opinion about the infant's death and urging that the parents' other child be removed from the home. The D.A. agreed. Outraged, the parents hired a lawyer and an independent medical expert to review the autopsy. As a result, the parents were cleared of all charges.

When the parents sued the doctor, however, the judges threw the case out, finding that even if the doctor had committed "malicious acts" in filing his reports, he could not be held liable for doing so. The court concluded that the absolute immunity from civil or criminal liability enjoyed by mandated reporters applies not only to mistaken or negligent reports but also to "reckless, or intentionally false reports."

Unlike mandated reporters, ordinary people who make false allegations, such as vindictive ex-spouses, can be fined or imprisoned. But as a practical matter, this rarely happens. "You have to prove malice, and that's almost impossible," says Kim Hart, director of the National Child Abuse Defense and Resource Center in Holland, Ohio.

While anyone wrongly accused of a crime may suffer (legal fees, incarceration, etc.), those wrongly accused of abusing their children suffer far more. Nick O., for example, has spent more than $150,000 so far in defending himself. Bankruptcy, unemployment, stress, health problems, alcoholism, and suicide are not uncommon. Once accused, many fathers are afraid to be alone with their, or anyone else's, children. Even some who haven't been accused, but have heard about the devastation an abuse charge brings, have become afraid of being affectionate with their own children out of fear that somehow, someone will misinterpret what they're doing and they'll be dragged into the criminal justice system.

Most falsely accused fathers find themselves in a kind of catch-22. Despite never having been charged with any crime, they're kept away from their children because CPS continues to believe that they're guilty. The only possible way to get to see their kids would be to be exonerated in court. But because they've never been charged . . .

Not being able to clear one's name in court has other effects. Whenever a child abuse report is made, the alleged offender's name is entered into the Child Abuse Central Index, a national database of sex offenders. Anyone applying for a license (real estate, childcare, etc.) or undergoing a background check will show up on the CACI as a suspected sex offender. "And when it comes to child abuse, suspected is as good as guilty," Kim Hart says. "Unless a man is found not guilty in a criminal trial, or unless CPS reports that the allegation was false, the accused's name will stay on the list for life."

One might argue here that when it comes to child abuse, it's better to err on the side of caution. In other words, it's better to prosecute a few innocent men as long as we get all the guilty ones. However, this shotgun approach has not been successful: researchers have found that there are twenty times more "false positives" (innocent people inaccurately identified as abusers) than "false negatives" (true abusers who slip through the cracks).

Even if one agrees that a twenty-to-one error ratio is acceptable, what's not acceptable is the impact all these false positives have on the children. Obviously, if a child has really been abused, he or she has suffered horribly. But the child put in therapy to deal with the trauma of an abuse that never happened may suffer at least as painful a fate. "Often the therapist actively fosters expressions of hostility and vengeance against the innocent parent, which may result in permanent alienation," writes Dr. Gardner. And even those rare men who are able to prevail against a false allegation may never be able to reestablish a loving relationship with their children.

Of the more than half million substantiated cases of child neglect of all kinds reported each year, 87 percent are of children neglected by a female, almost always the child's mother. When it comes to physical abuse, women are just as likely as men to hurt a child, and of the people who physically abuse their own children, 60 percent are mothers. Recent analyses of confirmed cases of child abuse provided by CPS agencies across the country reveal that overall, mothers abuse their children twice as often as fathers do. And in 1994, the U.S. Department of Justice released a study showing that 55 percent of people who kill their own children are mothers. Even when it comes to sexual abuse, a significant minority of incidents are committed by women. These figures are far from secret. They're available from a variety of government sources. Yet hardly any of them ever get reported.

There's also quite a bit of data that indicate that the problem of female abusers — especially sexual abusers — is vastly underreported. Researcher Craig Allen suggests three reasons for this. First, female abuse might be easier to hide and/or mask as role-appropriate behavior. After all, women have been the primary caretakers and have ample opportunity for sexual contact with children as they perform such daily tasks as bathing and diapering. Second, women might be more likely to abuse boys, but boys are less likely to report the abuse. And third, female sexual abuse of children might occur more often as incest and thus be less likely reported than extrafamilial abuse.

What it all comes down to is that we just don't see female sex abuse. "Society tends to be more concerned with fathers sleeping with or genitally manipulating daughters or sons than mothers doing the same things . . . ," wrote C. K. Kempe and R. E. Helfer in *The Battered Child*. "Intervention is very difficult because mothers are given an enormous leeway in their actions, while fathers and brothers are not."

One of the markers of advocacy research is its willingness (perhaps eagerness) to overlook or condemn any data that challenge either its hypotheses or conclusions. As a result, it's almost understandable that data on male child abusers — especially sexual abusers — have been emphasized while female offenders have been largely invisible. What's not understandable is how the psychological community, which prides itself on its unbiased investigations, has essentially ignored the issue and all but refused to study it more. "That she might seduce a helpless child into sexplay is unthinkable . . . ," wrote J. L. Mathis in 1972, "and even if she did so, what harm can be done without a penis?"

Others, such as Diana Russell, have gone a step further and attacked the idea that there might be more female abusers out there than previously thought. "The explanation of male preponderance is significant to virtually every theory of child sexual abuse. . . . Every theory of child molestation must explain not just why adults become sexually interested in children, but why that explanation applies primarily to males and not females." In other words, acknowledging female sexual aggression — and, presumably, doing something about it — appears to be politically incorrect.

While Russell and other feminist advocates view child abuse as a male-only crime, they also seem to believe that the victims are almost exclusively female. But it is now widely accepted — by everyone, that is, but advocacy groups — that between 25 and 40 percent of sexual abuse victims are boys. It's also widely accepted that the percentage may be higher. Boys almost never report being the victims of abuse, largely because of the social stigma that haunts "weak" boys — what could be a bigger sign of weakness in the mind of a young boy than being taken advantage of by a woman? Although far from every female abuse victim reports her abuse, girls are, by and large, significantly more likely to report it. Interestingly, when boys do acknowledge their own abuse, they report having been sexually abused as children as often by females as by males.

One can argue back and forth about why women abuse (one common argument is that mothers spend more time with children than fathers do and therefore have more opportunity), but the one thing that you can't argue about is that the prevailing stereotype that men are the only abusers is flat-out wrong. The writer and commentator Linda Ellerbee summed it up this way: "The truth is that women, like it or not, can be brutal too. Brutality's not sexist."

Our continued tendency to view all men as potential child molesters and kidnappers has contributed significantly to the marginalizing of America's fathers. Several years ago, one of the authors (Brott) had an experience that has become commonplace among men who have tried to be involved with their children:

> I was pushing my daughter on the swing at our favorite park when I heard the screams. Just a few feet away, a panicked little girl was teetering on the small platform at the top of a long, steep slide. As I watched, she lost her grip on the handrail and began to fall. Without thinking, I leapt over to the slide, plucked the girl out of the air, and set her down on the sand. I knelt down and was about to ask her if she was all right, when a woman picked the girl up, gave me one of the most wilting

looks I've ever seen, and hustled the child away. "Didn't I tell you not to talk to strange men in the park?" the woman asked her daughter, glaring over her shoulder at me. "Did he hurt you?"

African Americans often describe the pain, anger, and frustration they feel, even in their own neighborhoods, when white people cross the street to avoid facing them. And they're rightfully outraged that white people who know nothing about them make all sorts of assumptions based simply on race. Many of us have probably done the same thing. Many more have treated fathers in a similar way, responding not to who the man is but to his gender. That's clearly what happened with the woman in the park. Her reaction was based less on what had actually happened than on her ingrained and automatic fear of men in parks, whom she saw as menacing and solitary.

Ironically, women are not the only ones who are suspicious of men. Many men report that they, too, fall victim to society's anti-male sexism and view unfamiliar men with suspicion. When hiring babysitters, for example, some men don't even bother to interview the (admittedly few) male applicants. And there's little doubt that if a father had turned around to find a strange man kneeling by his daughter in the park, he would have jumped to a very negative conclusion.

Parents are faced with the daunting task of trying to teach their children to strike a balance between a healthy wariness of strangers and an equally healthy politeness toward new neighbors. But as a society, we should understand how unfair and how painful it is to automatically label men as abusers. We should have more compassion for how the victims of our prejudices feel.

We need to encourage men to get more involved at home, and we need to make them feel safe and welcome there. By viewing men with suspicion and fear, we are driving them farther away from their families. "The misconception that child abuse is solely or even primarily a male phenomenon skews public policy on the issue," writes Andrew Kimbrell. "Moreover, by focusing solely on male abuse of children, our society gives young men an image of fatherhood as abusive and motherhood as benign that does not comport with reality and that destroys a boy's sense of respect for his own gender."

It's easier on the ego (and there's a lot more social support) to be less involved than to have to be treated like a potential rapist. Most important, we need to look at a man holding hands with a child and see a father, not a molester. When we can do that, we'll know we've made some progress.

4

The Lazy Dad
and the Deadbeat Dad

IT SEEMS THAT every few months there's a new report announcing that mothers are not only working more outside the home, they're doing just about everything inside the home as well. Fathers' contributions to the domestic labor load, say these studies, consist of little more than lifting their feet so their wives can vacuum the rug in front of the television.

This stereotype of the lazy dad has been around for a while and was popularized by Arlie Hochschild in her 1989 book, *The Second Shift: Working Parents and the Revolution at Home*. Hochschild, a sociologist at the University of California, Berkeley, made the startling claims that men do only seventeen minutes of household-related work a day compared to their wives' three hours a day, and that fathers interact with their children only twelve minutes a day compared to mothers' fifty minutes.

Given this outrageous difference between men's and women's domestic work hours, the media, the government, and nearly every feminist group has turned Hochschild's phrase "second shift" into a kind of slogan demonstrating that fathers are basically slugs. But there's one problem: neither the seventeen-minute figure nor the twelve-minute figure — nor, for that matter, much of the entire "second shift" concept — is anywhere near accurate.

Working in the late 1980s, Hochschild relied heavily on a study conducted two decades before by Alexander Szalai, even though there were far newer and far more accurate data available. Using stale, inaccurate source material is usually enough to invalidate anyone's conclusions, but besides that, Hochschild excluded some of Szalai's data that apparently didn't support her thesis. Put another way, "In navigating through the territory of men's and women's experiences," write James Levine and Todd Pittinsky, "Hochschild was not only using an already outdated map, but looking at only part of it."

When counting men's hours, Hochschild included only workdays, conveniently omitting weekends, when men — and women — spend more time on housework and childcare. But when tallying women's hours, she counted the whole week. She also didn't include the hours men spend playing with their kids. Granted, playing is arguably more fun than cooking, yet it seems unfair to include mom's meal preparation hours while not counting at all the time dad spends taking care of his children.

Researcher Joseph Pleck analyzed Szalai's 1965 numbers (and Hochschild's misinterpretation of those numbers) and, when he included non-workdays (but still not play time), found that "employed fathers actually spent an average of 91 minutes per day in housework and child care combined." Remember, this was in 1965; men's involvement at home has grown steadily since then, especially the time they spend on childcare-related activities.

In the 1970s and early 1980s, compared to their partners, fathers spent about one-third as much time engaged with their children (doing something directly with them) and half as much time being accessible (being on hand and available to the child). These numbers went up in the late 1980s to 40 percent as much time engaged and two-thirds as much time being accessible. (While "being accessible" sounds like little more than an excuse for a father to just sit and watch football, the fact is that most kids don't need or want to be entertained every second of the day, but an adult still needs to be around just in case.) Over this same period, women's average time spent on housework decreased.

In 1993, University of Illinois researchers Brent McBride and Gail Mills found that fathers were engaged with their children an average of 1.9 hours on weekdays and 6.5 hours per day on weekends — in all,

83 percent of mothers' time. Fathers were accessible an average of 4.9 hours per day on weekdays and 9.8 hours per day on Saturday and Sunday — 82 percent of mothers' time.

One of the flaws in studies of paternal involvement or domestic division of labor is that they include only such tasks as cooking, cleaning, planning meals, carpooling, shopping, changing diapers, and arranging play dates for the kids. Hardly ever mentioned are such things as mowing lawns, taking out the trash, changing the oil or performing other minor car repairs, cleaning gutters, and, of course, earning the bulk of the money that pays for the meals, the cars, the mortgage, the private school tuition, and the televisions. In other words, the things researchers count toward "involvement" are nearly all performed by mothers. Many of the things they don't count are done by fathers.

Fortunately, a small number of studies have taken a look at men's and women's participation in and out of the home. When employed parents' paid and unpaid work hours are totaled, women end up doing 11 more hours per week of work inside the home and men do about 9 more hours of work outside the home. Including commuting time, women put in a total of 60 hours a week of paid and unpaid work. Men do 59.

Clearly, the question of mothers' second shift and fathers' laziness is more complex than it's been made out to be. Still, when reporting on the issue, the media continue to use only the traditional female definition of involvement.

One recent article, entitled "Men's Role About the House Still Minor," reported the findings of a study that looked at how men and women spend their time. The study found that men spend 10.5 percent of their time on household work and 30 percent on paid work; women spend 25.9 percent of their time on household work and 12.6 percent on paid work. The fact that men's and women's total hours are roughly the same wasn't mentioned. A graph accompanying the article showed the relative amount of time men and women spend on a series of household tasks but didn't show work for pay. "Women continue to bear a larger part of the burden of household work," said the report, and a man "who shares housework and childcare with his partner . . . seems to be largely a figment of the imagination."

"Had the reporter not been so interested in presenting men as

villains," wrote Peter Vogel in a critique of media coverage of men's issues, "he might have also mentioned that men continue to bear the
burden of the breadwinner and that women who share the family financing are also 'largely a figment of the imagination.' "

As likely as Vogel's comments are to anger many women, they're
accurate: despite all the talk about how women are entering the
workplace in droves, working mothers are still a significant minority,
especially when compared with their working husbands. In 1997,
94.6 percent of all fathers — and only 71.9 percent of all mothers —
with children under eighteen were working in some capacity. And
96.8 percent of those employed fathers were working full-time jobs,
compared to 73.2 percent of working mothers.

These numbers need some clarification. Women and men have different definitions of what "full time" means. According to a study conducted by the nonpartisan, nonprofit Families and Work Institute, fathers who work full time put in six hours a week more at their paid
jobs than mothers who work full time. And don't forget to add that
extra hour a week more than women that men spend commuting.
Overall, "the average working father is still putting in an extra day of
paid work a week compared to his full-time working spouse," write
James Levine and Todd Pittinsky.

So are fathers really watching TV while their wives work a "second
shift"? Hardly. "The good news," wrote researcher Rosalind Barnett,
"is that in dual-earner couples, women are no longer alone in working a second shift. The bad news is that everyone is working long
hours . . . nobody is doing much time in the easy chair." And as John
Robinson, a demographer, has observed, the "time crunch" may be the
newest problem for families throughout America. Neither fathers nor
mothers in today's hectic society have enough time for the kids, themselves, their relationships, or to just "do nothing."

Using a gender-neutral definition of involvement, men and women
devote an equal amount of time to their families. But certain groups,
particularly radical feminist ones, still insist that women bear an unfair burden. Despite the relative equality in hours worked, they argue,
the things that women do more of — traditional housework and

childcare — are more important than the things men do more of, such as earning a paycheck or fixing the car. Using this kind of "weighted average" to devalue fathers' financial contributions makes it possible to continue to praise women for putting in a (nonexistent) "second shift" while criticizing men for being uninvolved at home.

This approach to measuring involvement yields one other rather bizarre (and completely political) conclusion: earning money, rather than being seen as a demonstration of men's love, concern, and commitment to their families, is instead regarded as nothing more than an attempt to control and dominate women.

"The linkage between fatherhood and breadwinning," writes social historian Robert Griswold, has "justified men's limited commitment to child care," and consequently, has been "part and parcel of male dominance." No one seems to have wondered who, in light of women's smaller contribution to their families' income, is going to pay the bills if men quit doing it.

And it only gets worse. In *The Battered Woman,* psychologist Lenore Walker exonerates a violent woman who started a fight with her husband, hit him with a chair, and tried to bean him with a glass. Why? Because he "had been battering her by ignoring her and by working late."

The idea of measuring men by the size of their wallets is nothing new, especially for women. One recent study in *Behavior and Brain Sciences* found that while men in all cultures see beauty as the most important quality in a prospective mate, for women the determining quality is the man's earning power and ambition. According to psychologist David Buss, "The evolution of the female preference for males who offer resources may be the most ancient and pervasive basis for female choice in the animal kingdom."

If a man's earning capacity is important to his being able to attract a mate, it is even more important once he becomes a father. In the minds of a large majority of men and women, being a "good provider" is synonymous with being a "good father." Nearly 60 percent of men, for example, regularly rate "good provider" as one of the essential traits of an ideal father. And most women, "no matter how much they themselves may contribute to the family's resources, still expect the male to be a resource provider," writes researcher David Popenoe.

For men much more than for women, providing for their families is inextricably tied to their self-image and even to masculinity itself. For twenty years Yankelovich, the research and polling firm, has asked men to define masculinity. And for twenty years men have consistently rated "being a good provider for his family" as number one — higher than being a leader, an athlete, a lover, a decision-maker, or even being born male.

There are two serious problems that have arisen as a result of our having encouraged the good provider–equals–good father equation, and both have damaged the institution of fatherhood. First, in our willingness to consider only fathers' economic contributions to their families, we've forgotten about their psychological, emotional, and social impact on children. "Emphasizing fatherhood in largely economic terms has helped contribute to its demise," writes Wade Horn, director of the National Fatherhood Initiative. "If we want fathers to be more than just money machines, we need a culture that supports their work as teachers, coaches, nurturers, disciplinarians, and moral instructors." With the focus on the man-as-breadwinner model, however, men are effectively kept from any other kind of involvement with their children. Second, by so closely linking employment and masculinity, men and women alike are drawn to the nearly inescapable conclusion that a man who can't provide for his family is somehow not a man at all.

Nowhere is this more obvious than in inner-city communities. "African Americans are still living in the shadows of slavery, which demolished the male protector/provider role and the dignity and strength that came with it," write Sylvia Ann Hewlett and Cornel West. "Black males are thus especially susceptible to the belief that they are disposable and dispensable. Many black boys growing up are used to hearing that 'black men ain't shit, they ain't never going to be shit, and you are just like your daddy.' "

This has some devastating effects. For inner-city teenage fathers (who are the prime targets of current public attacks on absent fathers), for example, there is a direct correlation between a father's experience as a breadwinner and his level of involvement with his children. Young fathers who felt they weren't earning enough money to support their families experienced such shame and embarrassment that their level of involvement went down.

Of course, poor fathers aren't the only ones who suffer from the if-you-aren't-making-money-you-aren't-a-man syndrome. Men from all walks of life who lose their jobs and remain unemployed for a long period of time usually experience feelings of despair, self-loathing, and worthlessness. They see themselves as a burden to their families, as social failures with no hope.

Unemployed women suffer too, but it's not the same. "Women know the same confusion and shame as unemployed men who felt themselves pushed out in the cold," Gloria Emerson wrote in *Some American Men*. "The difference was they did not see themselves as ruined women, suspect as females, people now exposed as profoundly defective." Unemployed men commit suicide twice as often as employed men. For women, there's no difference in the suicide rates of the employed and the unemployed.

Susan Faludi, in *Backlash*, says that the link between masculinity and being the breadwinner is a major cause of the threats men feel from women's increased presence in the workplace. And she's got a point. For generations, most men were employed in heavy industry: steel, mining, construction. These very industries have experienced huge recessions and corresponding layoffs — mostly of men. Meanwhile, high-tech jobs — jobs that a typical miner or steelworker hasn't got the training or education to do — are increasingly being filled by women. "Men are being doubly emasculated both by unemployment and by their replacement in the work force by women," writes David Thomas.

Jane Young, a professor at the City University of New York, puts it a different way: "I think men increasingly feel that women don't need them for the things they used to — as providers, protectors, and heads of households — and, therefore, their status in relationships is limited. Media and government are telling women: 'Get rid of this guy. You don't need him. You're probably better off on your own. We'll help you out so you can raise your children by yourself.' So there is a tremendous sense of being rejected, scorned, vilified, and ultimately of not being important, except as a distant provider of money — and that creates a lot of rage."

That rage can produce tragic, yet widely reported, consequences. In Boston, a struggling salesman named Charles Stuart killed his better-educated and more successful pregnant wife because she was gaining the "upper hand." In New York, an unemployed man, Yusef Salaam, who felt "like a midget, a mouse, something less than a man," raped and bashed in the head of a female jogger. In Canada, Marc Lepine, an unemployed engineer, shot and killed fifteen women because they were "all a bunch of fucking feminists." These are rare and egregious crimes, and we can — and should — never forgive such behavior. At the same time, we can't — and shouldn't — lose track of the impact that equating masculinity with earning power has had on men.

Nowhere is the inappropriate emphasis on fathers' economic contributions more salient than when the talk turns to "deadbeat dads." They've been on the cover of *Newsweek* and featured in newspapers and television news programs. In political campaigns around the nation, from small-town mayor to president of the United States, one of the only issues candidates will agree on is that deadbeat dads should be hunted down and jailed. Fathers who don't pay child support are being blamed for everything from poverty and crime to the breakdown in family values. But while the image of uncaring, selfish, abandoning men dominate the media, one question remains unexplored: Have these men really run away from their families or are they being chased away?

When they hear about deadbeat dads, most people think of men like Michael Kojima, who, although delinquent by more than $100,000 in child support, managed to come up with $500,000 for a seat at George Bush's table at a 1992 Republican Party fund-raising dinner. Or of Jeffrey Nichols, who lived in luxury as he owed $580,000 in court-ordered payments to his three children. Men like Kojima and Nichols make great anecdotes in newspaper articles and political stump speeches, but they are the exception rather than the rule. Sixty-six percent of mothers who receive less child support than they are entitled to say the fathers are simply financially unable to pay, for a number of legitimate reasons. In fact, the unemployment rate during the previous year is one of the most accurate predictors of whether child support will be paid. One large study found that 81 percent of men who were consistently employed over a given year made all their support payments, and only 45 percent of men who experienced employment problems did.

Here is a typical example. A few years ago, Lloyd R., a divorced father of two who lives in a sparsely furnished apartment in San Rafael, California, broke his leg and was unable to work. With workers' compensation as his sole income, he found he could no longer make his support payments. So, during the year he was out of work, Lloyd fell further and further behind. His debts continued to mount. When he finally found a new job, his wages were garnished and the IRS seized his tax refund.

Lloyd certainly wasn't alone in not being able to pay his child-support obligation because of a serious injury. Brian G., a former logger who lives with his new wife and child in Oregon, went to prison several times for his failure to pay support. In January 1990, Brian underwent back surgery and was told by his doctor that because he could no longer do strenuous physical labor, he would have to find another line of work or be retrained. Unable to find other employment, Brian enrolled in a local community college and began taking classes in — ironically — criminal justice. His new wife, Linda, was trying to support her husband, herself, and their newborn baby on her minimum-wage salary as a grocery store checker. Things were so bad that the family needed food stamps to survive.

Brian's former wife, who, according to Brian, had inherited several hundred thousand dollars not long after the divorce, complained to the district attorney that Brian was delinquent on his child support. Without bothering to ask for Brian's side of the story, two sheriffs arrested him at the college, leaving Linda to work and to care for their six-week-old baby alone.

Of course not all men who are having employment problems were injured; some just aren't in particularly lucrative professions. A recent list of the top ten child-support evaders in the state of Virginia revealed such occupations as construction worker, mechanic, health care assistant, laborer, truck driver, painter, and roofer — not lawyer, doctor, commodities trader, or software developer. A recent study conducted by the Institute for Research on Poverty revealed that 52 percent of nonpaying fathers had incomes of less than $6,155 per year, and only 12 percent made more than $18,464.

Things are particularly tough for teenage men who become fathers. This group is especially likely to be unemployed or in low-paying and unstable jobs. Even though he has the time to spend with his child, a young man without a job, who can't lend financial support, may avoid contact with the child — as if he hasn't earned the right to be part of the child's daily life. As one young man puts it, "Sometimes a guy got a nice job, you know, he don't mind trying, but if he ain't got no job, maybe he's afraid to try."

"Men can be brought back into the family only when they have more resources — material and emotional — to invest in their children," observes Frank Furstenberg, a sociologist and an expert on adolescent parenthood. "Only then will they be admitted into the family by women and their kin and only then will they have confidence that they have a rightful claim."

As unfeeling as the legal system may at times appear, it does (theoretically, at least) allow men who are legitimately unable to pay child support to have their payments reduced or waived altogether. Unfortunately, very few men ever find out — until it's too late — that such options exist. Still, hiring a lawyer to present the case in court often proves too expensive for most men. "Even if I would have known," says Lloyd, the divorced father of two, "how could I have paid for a lawyer when I was on workers' comp?" When he fell behind on his child support and his ex-wife tried to collect, the district attorney represented her for free, although her financial position was far better than Lloyd's.

Getting legal help in dealing with their child-support problems is even harder for fathers who are on welfare. In most cases, the amount these men were ordered to pay exceeds their ability to pay. And applying for a reduction takes time and, more important, money — which of course they don't have. There's also "a reluctance to reduce child support orders on the assumption that incomes will eventually im-

prove, but in the meantime arrears accumulate," wrote Elaine Sorensen, a senior researcher with the Urban Institute, a Washington, D.C.,
think tank. Only 4 percent of noncustodial fathers who were paying
court-ordered child support received a downward adjustment when
their earnings fell by more than 15 percent from one year to the next.

Not all men who don't pay their support are on welfare, on disability,
or unemployed. Some really are driving fancy cars and living in man-
sions while their ex-wives and kids live in squalor. There's no question
that for men who don't pay their child support when they are financially able, every reasonable effort should be made to enforce payment.

In recent years Congress has passed a number of laws that make
it easier to crack down on deadbeats using a variety of methods, such
as mandatory wage garnishment, nonrenewal of business licenses,
restrictions on interstate travel, and jail. And in 1998 President Bill
Clinton signed the Deadbeat Parents Punishment Act into law. Yet according to many experts, such drastic enforcement methods present
serious problems. First, automatic wage garnishment is humiliating
for the majority of men who have every intention of paying what they
owe, and it reinforces the incorrect presumption that all men are going to default. Second, putting men in jail for being behind on child
support seems too much like a modern debtors' prison which, along
with travel restrictions, is constitutionally prohibited.

One federal law, for example, makes it illegal for a father who is behind on his child support, regardless of the reason, to leave his state.
Thus an unemployed father who moves to another state to find work
is presumed to be guilty of avoiding his obligations. The intent of this
law has been so twisted that it has been used to prosecute a man
whose ex-wife had moved to another state with the couple's children.
The rationale? Since he was no longer living in the same state as his
child, the court decided that he was trying to avoid paying support.

Other enforcement efforts are just as bizarre, and just as short-
sighted. In April 1998, child-support collection officials in Rock
County, Wisconsin, arrested Marc Ames because he was delinquent in
the amount of forty cents (interest and fees brought the total to a
whopping $173.53). The first time Ames heard of his debt was when his

1997 tax returns were intercepted. County officials indicated that as small as the amount in question was, they planned to prosecute and perhaps jail Ames for up to 180 days — at a cost to taxpayers of thousands of dollars.

Ample evidence exists that sending men to prison is counterproductive. The second time Brian G. was arrested, he had just started a new job and resumed making his payments as scheduled. But because he had been unable to reduce his child-support obligation while he was disabled, he found himself more than $6,000 in arrears. "It seemed pretty idiotic that they would take me away from a job where I was finally earning enough to make my payments just to punish me for being behind," he says. "How the hell can I come up with the payment when I'm in jail?" Many other men have asked the same question. Clarence Lee Brandley spent nearly a decade in Texas prisons, mostly on death row, for a murder he was ultimately cleared of. But Texas's attorney general still insisted that Brandley come up with $22,000 in support arrearages that accrued while he was wrongfully behind bars.

These punitive child-support collection efforts are especially hard on low-income fathers. One proposed piece of legislation, part of the 1998 Welfare Reform Act, would deny welfare benefits, food stamps, and Medicaid to noncustodial fathers who are more than two months behind on child support. More than three million men would be affected by this bill. In a sense, coercing men to pay their obligations in this way seems like a good idea, but consider this: in 1990 the median income of these men was $430 a month, 30 percent less than that year's poverty line. Not surprisingly, two-thirds of these fathers weren't working. Forty percent were receiving Supplemental Security Income or Medicaid (meaning they were disabled or otherwise unable to work), and half were receiving food stamps or lived in public housing.

However well meaning this legislation is, the costs would far exceed the benefits. "The perverse effect would be not to increase child-support collections significantly but to plunge more children further into poverty and alienate noncustodial fathers from the child-support system," wrote Elaine Sorensen.

* * *

Some of the most extensive child-support collection efforts have been created with the stated intention of reducing the $200 billion our government pays out each year in welfare benefits — an admirable goal. The sponsors of the Deadbeat Parents Punishment Act, for example, claim it will result in removing 800,000 women and children from the welfare rolls if only half of delinquent dads pay their child support in full. Other politicians, most notably President Bill Clinton and his secretary of health and human services, Donna Shalala, have made more specific promises. They say that collecting $48 billion in delinquent child support would reduce welfare expenditures by nearly 25 percent. Unfortunately, this $48 billion solution, which has been quoted by just about every politician in the country, is a fantasy.

In 1993 the Urban Institute released a report in which it speculated that if every custodial mother was awarded child support of $5,000 per child a year, and if every penny was collected, the total would be $48 billion. The report further stated that $14 billion had already been paid, leaving a "balance due" of $34 billion. That's still a pretty big number, and the ifs it is based on are even bigger.

First, more than 42 percent of the ten million divorced, single, or remarried women theoretically eligible for a child-support award were not awarded one. (It's not that these women were being mistreated by family court judges: around 40 percent didn't want or pursue an award, and 23 percent of the time, the father either was still living with the family or was unable to pay.) Second, the average court-ordered child-support award was really $2,800, not $5,000. That means the total amount that could conceivably have been collected was not $48 billion but only $16 billion. Subtracting the $14 billion that Shalala and Clinton acknowledge has been paid, the actual amount owed by delinquent parents is $2 billion — still a lot of money, but at only 1 percent of the welfare budget, not enough to make much of a dent, either.

Even this $2 billion doesn't accurately reflect how much child support is truly owed. The assumption is that the $2 billion is all collectible, that every penny is out there in some father's pocket, waiting to be found. In fact, a 1992 General Accounting Office report found that as many as 14 percent of "deadbeat" fathers were dead. Many, as we've discussed, are unemployed and a small number are in prison.

By far the most guarded secret in the child-support numbers game is what it costs us to collect what's supposedly owed. The Office of Child Support Enforcement has a budget of about $4 billion, more than twice what it could, under the most optimistic scenario, ever hope to bring in.

After seeing how much money federal and state governments are willing to burn in their relentless pursuit of phantom child-support money, private companies have begun offering child-support collection services. Lockheed-Martin and another company have cooperated on a $17.5 million contract to build a new computer system to track parents who haven't paid support. Lockheed-Martin has already won 32 contracts in 24 states and counties, including a $50 million contract to collect child-support payments in Baltimore.

On a smaller scale, an organization called Find Dad America uses federal funds to finance its operations, including its catchy toll-free phone number: 1-800-PAY-MOMS. Find Dad America also uses these funds to sprinkle national and local newspapers with catchy ads like this:

> Her first day at school.
> Her first bicycle.
> Her child support payments.
> Her father missed them all.

Another claim frequently made by politicians is that by abandoning their children and then refusing to support them, fathers are contributing to the increase in the number of single mothers and to the rise in poverty in this country. From 1980 to 1990, the proportion of children under eighteen living with only one parent doubled, from 12 to 25 percent. Among African Americans the number rose from 29 to 52 percent. One-third of single mothers have incomes below the poverty level and collect government assistance (such as AFDC, Aid to Families with Dependent Children, now called TANF, Temporary Assistance for Needy Families).

Most experts agree that the failed social policies of previous Republican and Democratic administrations, not divorced fathers, are responsible for the increase in poverty and in the breakdown of the family structure in the inner city. Robert Rector, an analyst with the conservative Heritage Foundation, has said that the government offers a single mother assistance of more than $13,000 a year. The only conditions are that she can't work and she can't live with the father of the children. Rector calls this kind of assistance "the incentive program from hell" and credits it with destroying America's poor families.

Even the government has admitted that more stringent child-support enforcement would not significantly reduce child poverty. In fact, perfect compliance would reduce the poverty level of custodial parents by only 3 percent (from 24 to 21 percent). Still, the assault against poor fathers continues. "Since the mid-1960s government policy has moved against fathers. For example, Aid to Families with Dependent Children was set up in a way that deliberately excluded fathers," write Hewlett and West. "For 20 years, welfare agencies staged unannounced midnight raids to make sure that there was no man in the house. If a man was found, the mother lost her AFDC benefits. The effect of these raids was to cause men to be literally pushed out of the nest. Not only did these regulations create a huge disincentive to marry; they made it extremely difficult for poor men to become fathers to their children."

Oppressed by insensitive welfare regulations and denied a higher education by recent budget cuts, many poor fathers find themselves in a peculiar bind. If they want their wives or girlfriends to be able to collect government aid, their only remaining option, and the only responsible one, is to leave home and their children. Are these guys really deadbeats, or are they just some of the thousand points of light that were systematically extinguished by previous "family values" administrations? These aren't divided families, these are families that are forced apart.

There is one approach that is virtually guaranteed to improve child-support compliance, regardless of the income level of either the father or the mother: allow divorced and never-married fathers more time with their children. The U.S. Census Bureau found that more than 90 percent of men with joint custody pay their entire child-support obligation on time, and 79 percent of men with visitation rights pay on time and in full. In both cases, compliance is above 90 percent when adjusted for unemployment, underemployment, disability, or other legitimate inability to pay. It is only when custody and visitation are completely denied and fathers are severed from their children's lives that child-support payments drop below 50 percent.

These statistics, like the ones used to calculate the $34 billion "shortfall," may be too conservative because they are derived from interviews exclusively with women. One of the few national studies that has interviewed men and women (and then matched their answers) found that men claim they pay about 20 percent more in child support than women claim they receive.

While there's little doubt that some men are probably overreporting their payments, it is just as probable that some women — particularly AFDC or other government aid recipients — are underreporting what they receive. Several government reports show that many aid recipients routinely underreport their outside income in order not to jeopardize their benefits.

Census figures — and the women whose responses contribute to them — also neglect to include the money and other services that noncustodial fathers contribute to their families. As University of Maryland sociologist Jay Teachman argues, "Simply making child-support payments only partially fulfills the more general role of fathering. By making economic contributions other than child-support payments, fathers not only increase the material well-being of their children, but they can remain more involved in their children's lives."

Eighty-seven percent of women on AFDC and 68 percent of non-AFDC mothers report occasionally receiving assistance above and beyond the court-ordered child support, including cash gifts, payment of bills, and clothing or in-kind gifts from their children's fathers. And nearly 60 percent of AFDC and 70 percent of non-AFDC mothers say that the fathers' relatives also helped the mother, providing childcare, cash gifts, baby-sitting time, and clothing. To take things a step further, a more recent Census Bureau report states that "increased father custody and joint custody should be evaluated as a means of reducing child poverty."

Money, if you can get it, is certainly important, but it takes more than payments to raise a healthy child, and there are plenty of nonmaterial ways poor or unemployed dads can contribute to their children's social, cognitive, and emotional well-being. One of the best is simply to share in their children's daily lives. This means investing time taking an interest in school, getting to know their children's friends, or taking them to the doctor. Surprisingly, these nonmonetary contributions are all but ignored by researchers. As Jay Teachman points out, "Almost nothing is known about the nature of other forms of social and economic transfers across households from absent fathers to their children."

When child support is defined broadly enough to include time investments, such as helping with homework, going to school events, as well as giving clothing and gifts, four out of five absent fathers have provided some form of assistance to their children — a clear demonstration that the majority of fathers are attempting to make their children's lives better any way they can.

Fathers who contribute in one way are likely to contribute in other ways too. Dads who make child-support payments, for example, are more likely to show up at school events. As in the case of monetary payments, one of the best predictors of whether other forms of assistance will be provided is the quality of the relationship between the parents. According to Teachman, "Assistance is more likely to be transferred across households when both parents are motivated to have fathers continue to fulfill the parental role following divorce."

Interestingly, the correlation between access to the children and payment of child support is not gender specific. In other words, noncustodial mothers who are ordered to pay child support default in at least the same proportions as noncustodial fathers. Recent Census Bureau data revealed that 46.9 percent of noncustodial mothers totally default on support, compared to 26.9 percent of noncustodial fathers. Twenty percent of noncustodial mothers with child-support orders pay at least some part of their obligation, compared to 61 percent of noncustodial fathers.

At first blush, it doesn't seem too surprising that mothers would sometimes default on child-support orders. After all, if it is being suggested that we should have some sympathy for men who lose their jobs, we should have the same sympathy for women who, overall, make less money than men and probably can't afford to pay child support anyway. The legal system, however, already takes women's economic situation into account when it considers ordering them to pay child support. Consequently, while 58 percent of custodial mothers are awarded child support from their former spouses, about 40 percent of custodial fathers are. Custodial mothers' support awards are also a third higher than those given to custodial fathers.

Unfortunately, the critical relationship between custody, access to the children, and child support seems to be lost on most legislators and family law judges. Although almost every state now has some kind of legislation specifically barring judges from granting custodial preference based solely on gender, the legal system continues to favor women by a huge margin. The mother is the sole custodian an overwhelming 82 percent of the time, and only 7 percent have joint custody.

The term "joint custody" is a misnomer, however. In California, for example, joint custody is awarded in about 70 percent of cases. But this figure is deceptive because it refers to joint *legal* and not joint *physical* custody. Fathers with joint legal custody get to sign report cards, but when it comes to seeing their children, they are usually limited to almost the same visitation schedule as noncustodial fathers. Even fathers with joint physical custody aren't getting a 50-50 split. Because most states define joint physical custody as "frequent and continuing contact," the term covers everything from equally splitting expenses, decision-making, and time with the kids to arrangements that are indistinguishable from sole mother custody with occasional visits by the father. Women, it seems, are presumed to be fit parents; men, as in so many other parenting-related areas, have to prove it.

Nearly 40 percent of noncustodial fathers have no access (visitation) or custody rights at all. And the men who do have court-ordered access to their children are traditionally limited to visits every other weekend, on alternate holidays, and for a couple of weeks in the summer.

The courts are not alone in making it difficult for single fathers to be with their kids. Mothers themselves often see no value to the father's relationship with his children and often try to interfere with it. In their book *Surviving the Breakup,* Judith Wallerstein and Joan Kelly found that between 20 and 50 percent of custodial mothers "actively tried to sabotage the meetings by sending the children away just before the father's arrival, by insisting that the child was ill," and so on. Other studies, such as those conducted by psychologist Joyce Arditti, found that 47 percent of divorced fathers felt that their ex-wives' interference with their visitation was a problem; 27 percent said it was a serious problem. Translated, this means that each year more than six million children are denied access to their fathers.

"Many times, mothers will disrupt visitation by getting the kids involved in something really fun just before the father gets there," says Dr. Richard Warshak, author of *The Custody Revolution.* "That way, if the father tries to enforce his visitation, the kids will see him as the bad guy — the guy who made them stop having fun."

In most cases, however, the interference is less subtle. On at least forty occasions, when Larry K. has gone to pick up his children, his former wife has refused to let them out of the house, claiming they were ill. "My daughter was supposedly sick for the whole month of December, 1991," Larry says. He has also documented an additional fifty visitation refusals for other reasons. "The visits I miss are lost forever — my ex never lets me make them up."

For most fathers, going to court to enforce their visitation rights is prohibitively expensive: attorneys' fees to cover one challenge run an average of $4,000. And even if they win, visitation still isn't guaranteed. While family court judges are quite willing to lock up men who fall behind on their child support, they are extremely reluctant to jail mothers who refuse to comply with visitation orders. A recent survey in Indiana turned up 272 fathers who had gone to court to try to enforce their court-ordered visitation. Only 62 percent of them were granted a hearing, and not one mother was jailed for having violated a court order. And 77 percent of the men who had hearings reported that the visitation problem got worse after going to court.

For these men and thousands of others, the message is clear: there are basically no consequences — for women, anyway — for violating court orders. In 1998 Lisa Barbosa, a divorced mother from Mississauga, Canada, became perhaps the first woman ever to be sentenced to jail for failing to allow the father of her child his court-ordered access. Far more typical is the case of Cyndy Garvey, the ex-wife of former Dodgers star Steve Garvey, who was found guilty in 1989 of forty-two counts of willfully violating a court order that permitted her ex-husband to visit his daughters. She received a suspended sentence.

Many fathers who are being denied their court-ordered visitation have — theoretically, at least — other recourse as well. As part of the Personal Responsibility and Work Opportunity Reconciliation Act of 1996, Congress gave the Federal Parent Locator Service some new functions. In addition to "establishing parentage, setting, modifying or enforcing support orders," parents can use the FPLS for "enforcing custody and visitation orders." But that's easier said than done. In 1997 Virgil Chase's former wife, Gloria Ann Chase, kidnapped their children and has hidden them from their father ever since — a clear violation of the couple's court order. Judges in Prince George's County, Virginia, where Virgil still lives, admit that they know exactly where Gloria Ann is. And so does the Office of Child Support Enforcement, which dutifully passes Virgil's $660 child-support checks on to his ex-wife each month. Yet despite their obligations under the FPLS, neither the judges nor the OCSE will tell Virgil where his children are or help enforce his visitation order.

As you might expect, denying a noncustodial parent his or her court-ordered access to the children often has a direct impact on compliance with support orders. A 1988 study of more than two thousand noncustodial parents found that willful nonpayment occurred in only 1.9 percent of cases where the noncustodial parents were allowed to visit the children. But in cases where a custodial parent denied access to the other parent, the compliance rate for support orders was only 36 percent. The whole thing is terribly immature on both sides. Without excusing the behavior, it's important to understand how difficult it is for a noncustodial parent to write a check every month to support a child he or she is kept from seeing.

Some experts have speculated that the real reason parents who don't get to see their kids pay less child support has to do with feeling deprived of the opportunity to have an impact on the child's life, to teach, and to pass on core values. According to researcher Sanford

Points Required	Reward Code	Reward Options
1,500	1RT	1 Six Flags Weekday Admission Ticket
2,000	2AT	1 Six Flags Full Use Admission Ticket, OR
	2GC	1 $25 Six Flags Food & Merchandise Voucher, OR
	2PP	1 Six Flags Season Parking Pass*
4,000	4SP	1 Six Flags Individual Season Pass, OR
	4AT	2 Six Flags Full Use Admission Tickets, OR
	4GC	1 $50 Six Flags Food & Merchandise Voucher
6,000	6AT	3 Six Flags Full Use Admission Tickets, OR
	6GC	1 $75 Six Flags Food & Merchandise Voucher
8,000	8AT	4 Six Flags Full Use Admission Tickets, OR
	8GC	1 $100 Six Flags Food & Merchandise Voucher
10,000	10SP	1 Six Flags Family Season Pass**

*Not valid at Six Flags Magic Mountain, CA; Six Flags Hurricane Harbor, CA; Six Flags AstroWorld, Houston, TX; Six Flags Kentucky Kingdom, Louisville, KY; Six Flags Elitch Gardens, Denver, CO or Six Flags America, Washington, DC. Six Flags Darien Lake offers a parking voucher valid for 5 visits for the 1999 season

**For 3 or 4 people contingent upon park guidelines.

Don't forget to keep saving your **Reward Points** for these valuable **Six Flags Entertainment Rewards!**

When you're ready to redeem your points, just mail in your redemption form that is attached to your statement! It's that easy!

SixFlags

TM & ©1999 Warner Bros.

Six Flags®

Entertainment Card Reward Option Restrictions

Weekday Admission Ticket: Valid Monday - Friday only; Award certificates issued are valid through December 31, 1999; The following blackout dates apply – 5/31/99 & 9/6/99; Present at any Six Flags Theme Park (SFTP) main gate ticket booth; Reward option redeemable only once per calendar year; Normal age/height restrictions apply; Subject to normal park operating hours. **Full Use Admission Ticket:** Award certificates issued are valid through December 31, 1999. Blackout dates apply – 5/31/99, 7/4/99, 9/6/99. Present at any SFTP front gate ticket booth; Normal safety and age/height restrictions apply; Use subject to normal park operating hours. **Food and Merchandise Voucher:** For $25, $50, $75 and $100 amounts; certificates are provided in $10 & $5 increments (may be combined); Valid for use at restaurant and retail store locations throughout the parks. Not valid for games, concerts, skycoaster, or other attractions, on-site hotel or campground accommodations, campground general store, or hotel gift shop, restaurant/bar. Award certificates are valid through December 31, 2000. **Season Parking Pass:** Not available at Six Flags Magic Mountain, CA; Six Flags Hurricane Harbor, CA; Six Flags AstroWorld, Houston, TX; Six Flags Kentucky Kingdom, Louisville, KY; Six Flags Elitch Gardens, Denver, CO; or Six Flags America, Washington, DC. Six Flags Darien Lake offers cardholders a parking voucher valid for complimentary parking 5 times during the 1999 season and is only available to season pass holders. The season parking pass entitles cardholder to complimentary parking at the park where the voucher is redeemed for the 1999 season only. **Individual Season Admission Pass:** Cardholder will receive a letter which must be presented and processed at the park of individual's choice. Each letter entitles cardholder to one single season admission pass, good only for the 1999 season. Each letter is good for either a child or adult pass. Normal safety and age/height restrictions apply. Use subject to normal park operating hours. Usage conditions and benefits on season pass will reflect those in effect at the time pass is processed at specific park. **Family Season Admission Pass:** Cardholder will receive a letter which must be presented and processed at the park of individual's choice. Good only for the 1999 operating season. Each letter entitles cardholder to a single season family pass for 3 or 4 people, as defined at park where processed. Usage conditions and benefits on family season pass will reflect those in effect at the time pass is processed at specific park. Letters issued in 1999 are valid in 1999 only. Normal safety and age/height restrictions apply. Use subject to normal park operating hours.

2/99

Braver, noncustodial parents who feel they have some influence on their children have good child-support payment records. But when they're reduced to infrequent visitors, some end up withdrawing "from the obligations of parenthood, financial support, and an impaired emotional relationship with the child appears likely to follow."

Despite the lack of guidance from the federal government, some states have tried to level the playing field. In Michigan, for example, the Friend of the Court, the state agency that oversees the welfare of children with respect to court-ordered support, custody, and visitation, is now required to enforce orders for visitation as well. What this means is that a custodial parent who repeatedly denies access to the noncustodial parent can be jailed, just like a parent who refuses to make child-support payments. The results? The Friend of the Court's emphasis on visitation enforcement has improved children's relationship with both parents and made Michigan number one in child-support collections for many years. "More parents are willing to pay when they are seeing their children and feel they are being treated equitably by the system," wrote Michigan state senator Debbie Stabenow.

The whole "deadbeat dad" campaign is, in a sense, a microcosm of the way our society willfully disregards the importance of fathers in children's lives and the importance of children in fathers' lives. Once there's a divorce, we act as if the family no longer exists — we amputate one parent or the other and expect the child to grow up healthy. It's painfully obvious to those who aren't blinded by politics that if we preserve the child's relationship with both parents, children will be better off and we'll have far fewer problems with child-support collection. Enforcing fathers' visitation rights is the first step in preserving that relationship.

In the mid-1990s, Don Chavez was a member of the first Commission on Interstate Child Support and tried to do exactly that. Just after the commission was formed, Dr. Chavez made an attempt on the national level to link child-support enforcement with enforcement of visitation rights. He drafted a resolution that defined child support — which had no legal definition — as having both an emotional and a financial component. "I felt that if we were going to make it a crime not to provide for a child's financial needs, it should also be a crime to interfere with noncustodial parents' rights to be with their children." The commission defeated Chavez's resolution by a 14–1 vote.

No matter where people stand on the "deadbeat dad" issue, just about everyone agrees that children are the ones who suffer most when families are torn apart by divorce. Children who grow up in fatherless families have more emotional problems, do worse in school, and have higher rates of criminal involvement. Yet under the guise of protecting children, we've systematically deprived millions of them of one of the most fundamental rights imaginable: the love, guidance, and support of their fathers.

Kids are not the only ones whose suffering is overlooked in the midst of a divorce. The role a father plays in his children's lives is just as important as the role they play in his. Treating men like nothing more than walking wallets bolsters traditional stereotypes of men as uncaring and ignores the deep feeling of loss they experience when their children are taken from them. Unfortunately, our society doesn't acknowledge men's strong feelings for their children. When we hear that a woman has lost custody of her child, our reaction is one of shock, pity, outrage. But when we hear that a man has lost his children, we have no such feelings.

Single fathers, whether they're divorced or unmarried, on the whole love and care for their children as much as any other parents. The day society starts treating them as real parents, we might find that the "deadbeat dad" problem has largely gone away.

5

The Bumbling Father
and the Useless Father

THE MESSAGE that dads are lazy, dangerous, biologically unfit, or deadbeats powerfully shapes our impressions about fathers. There are other negative messages as well. They're sometimes subtle and often amusing, but because they're aimed mostly at children and young people, they can further distort our views of fatherhood and fathers.

What's the first book you remember from when you were a child? *Babar? Goodnight, Moon? Where the Wild Things Are?* Whatever it was, chances are that someone read it to you countless times and that it affected the way you look at the world. And that's just what it was supposed to have done.

Each year, American children have more than five thousand new kids' books to choose from. And recently there's been a push to use these books to portray the important roles that various minority groups have played in shaping our country's history and culture. *Little Black Sambo* and other classics that some felt were perpetuating negative racial stereotypes have all but disappeared from library and bookstore shelves, replaced by books that more accurately reflect the African-American experience. Others are aimed at the contributions of Hispanic Americans to our culture. And dozens of other books tell our children about almost every ethnic group, from the Chinese who helped build America's early rail system, to the Japanese Americans herded into internment camps during World War II, to the European Jews fleeing Nazi persecution.

But by far the biggest effort to modernize children's literature has been focused on women and girls. Today most local libraries have a large selection of children's books with positive female characters — heroines and mothers — books that make every effort to take women characters out of the kitchen and the nursery and give them professional jobs and responsibilities. In many homes, especially those in which girls live, feminist fairy tales by such authors as Jack Zipes have replaced or supplemented the more traditional (and arguably more sexist) fairy tales of past generations. Richard Scarry, one of the most prolific and popular children's writers and illustrators, has reissued some of his old classics. In the new versions, women — female animals, really — are pictured doing the same jobs as male animals. Even the terminology has changed: both males and females are now referred to, in gender-neutral fashion, as "mail carriers" or "firefighters."

There is, however, one large group whose portrayal continues along the same stereotypical lines as always: fathers. Parents who are looking for books with positive father role models are pretty much out of luck. They barely exist. Mothers are, by and large, still shown as the primary caregivers and, more important, as the primary nurturers of their children. Fathers, if they're shown at all, are generally portrayed as indifferent, uncaring, buffoonish characters who do little more than come home late after work and bounce baby around for five minutes before putting her to bed.

Take, for example, a recent retelling of *Mother Goose and the Sly Fox*. The plot line is simple: a single mother (Mother Goose) of seven tiny goslings is pitted against, and naturally outwits, the Sly Fox. Fox, a neglectful and presumably unemployed single father, lives with his filthy, hungry pups in a grimy hovel littered with the bones of their previous meals. Mother Goose, a successful entrepreneur with a thriving lace business, still finds time to serve her goslings homemade soup in pretty porcelain cups. The story is funny and the illustrations are marvelous, but the unwritten message is that women take better care of their kids and men have nothing else to do but hunt down and kill innocent, law-abiding geese.

And what about *Babar?* Once in a while adults complain about the book's colonialist slant (you know, little jungle-dwelling elephant finds happiness in the big city and brings civilization — and fine clothing — to his backward elephant village), but does anyone find it strange that Babar, as well as Arthur and Celeste, seems to be the product of parthenogenesis? Why is it that after Babar's mother is killed by the evil hunter, Babar becomes an orphan? Why can he only find comfort in the arms — and the pocketbook — of another woman, the Old Lady? Why do Arthur's and Celeste's mothers come alone to the city to fetch their children? Don't the fathers care? Do they even have fathers?

In a more recent classic, *Little Gorilla,* by Peggy Rathman, we are told that the little gorilla's "mother loves him," and we see the mama gorilla giving her little one a warm hug. On the next page we're also told that his "father loves him," but in the illustration father and son aren't even touching. In *Toes Are to Tickle* we're told that Mommy is for "one more cuddle . . . one more story . . . and kissing good night." As for Dad, well, just about all he's good for is "one last ride." And in the Berenstain Bears series, which are among the most successful kids' books in history, Papa Bear is routinely portrayed as bumbling, childish, and generally stupid. Mama Bear, on the other hand, is the wise and level-headed one whom the cubs listen to and who always shows Papa Bear up.

A lot of statistical evidence confirms our impression that fathers in children's literature are depicted in largely negative terms. A recent exhaustive review of several hundred popular kids' books of the 1990s revealed that more than half that include references to a parent or parents mention or portray mothers as the only one. If a dad is there at all, he's usually shown as uncaring, unloving, absent, and ultimately irrelevant.

In an even larger study, "The Role of the American Father as Revealed in Selected Fiction Books for Children in the Elementary Grades," researcher Michele Otstott found that 64 percent of fathers were depicted primarily as economic providers. And in books for older kids (grades 4 to 6), the father was primarily an authority figure.

Even those fathers whose roles were not limited to the traditional were surprisingly uninterested in their children. Fathers in the study were involved with their children in 254 distinct activities. But according to Otstott, the number of times each type of activity occurred was "tragically low." (In the few cases where stepfathers were shown, they were also often portrayed as being uninvolved and ineffectual.)

Unlike the overwhelming number of children's books that feature single mothers (or at least women whose husbands are never at home), the majority of fathers in Otstott's study "were shown as being married with a family where the mother was present. While the father is beginning to be portrayed in other types of marital situations, the portrayal is not as frequent as it is in actual life."

Negative portrayals of fathers are not limited to books for young children. In a recent study, English researcher Lesley Boyd examined a large number of young adult novels to determine the ways in which the depiction of fatherhood may have changed. She found that "the position of fathers in society, and their portrayal in adolescent fiction, have changed little over the last 20 years. . . . The majority of fathers in the novels are still portrayed stereotypically in that their roles as breadwinner and authority figure are heavily emphasized and there is only a minimal involvement in domestic or childcare activities. Fathers are also depicted as being more emotionally remote and less involved with their children than mothers are."

One can reasonably argue that the images of men and women in children's literature are simply reflections of reality. It's still true that for a variety of reasons (many of which we'll discuss in later chapters) women in this country do the bulk of the childcare. But if children's literature only reflects reality, why aren't 50 percent of the families in books divorced? Why aren't 15 to 20 percent of the single parents in these books fathers? Why, for that matter, aren't smokers, alcoholics, and drug abusers adequately represented?

The answer is that literature doesn't always reflect reality. In fact, it could be said that it sometimes does quite the opposite, reflecting some kind of reality that doesn't exist — the world the way we imagine it rather than the way it is.

Remember all those gender-neutral firefighters from Richard Scarry and other authors? The truth is that in the real world only 2 percent of the 1.2 million people who risk their lives to fight fires in this country are women. But that hasn't prevented us from all but banishing the word "fireman" from the English language. Far more than 2 percent of all the nurturing parents are men, and in raw numbers there are far more actively involved, nurturing, loving fathers than there are female firefighters. Still, images of nurturing fathers are practically nowhere to be found.

There's little question that reading about female firefighters (and police officers and construction workers and just about any other occupation where women are a small minority) boosts girls' self-esteem and reinforces in their minds — and everyone else's, for that matter — the idea that women have lives beyond the home and that there's nothing girls and women can't do. Little boys, in contrast, are given a far more restricted list of life options: they can do anything they want as long as they financially support their families and leave the nurturing to the nearest female.

The effect of filling our children's heads with negative images of fathers, of ignoring men who share equally in raising their children, and of showing nothing but part-time or no-time fathers is, quite simply, devastating. Left unchecked, these images will remain the self-fulfilling prophecies that they already are, not only influencing the way fathers view themselves but reinforcing in the next generation the belief that mothers are the truer parents and fathers don't care about, and therefore don't belong with, children. After being raised with images of absent, uninvolved, disrespected fathers, why would any little boy ever want to be one? After being raised with the same images, where would a little girl get the idea that fathers are important and worthy of respect? Indeed, why would she want to have either a father or a husband around?

All we're doing is trading one double standard for another. It would be nearly unthinkable to tell a child today that women can't be doctors. But how many parents would spend the time to tell their children that a man can be a nurse? That men can and do nurture and care for others is usually ignored, laughed at, or dismissed as an anomaly.

This isn't to say that there aren't any kids' books that show loving, nurturing fathers who are involved with their children. There are, but they're pretty hard to find.

Can't You Sleep, Little Bear?, by Martin Waddell (illustrated by Barbara Firth), and the sequel, Let's Go Home, Little Bear, do a great job of capturing the warmth of an ursine father-son relationship. Daddy Makes the Best Spaghetti, by Anna Grossnicke Hines, was one of the first of not very many books to depict, without making fun of, a family in which dad is the primary caregiver and mom works outside the home. And before you decide that fathers' involvement is a new phenomenon, read Russell Hoban's 1960 classic Bedtime for Frances.

Unfortunately, though, even books that have outwardly positive father-child interactions often unwittingly perpetuate other damaging stereotypes about fathers.

Take, for example, the relationship between Little Nutbrown Hare, who is going to bed, and his father, Big Nutbrown Hare, as depicted in Sam McBratney's Guess How Much I Love You. "Guess how much I love you," the bunny gleefully says, throwing his arms out "as wide as they could go." But the daddy has even longer arms and easily tops his son. Little's disappointment is evident. "Hmm," he says. "That is a lot." A few pages later, Little declares that he loves Big "as high as I can reach." But Big once again trumps his son: "I love you as high as I can reach." Little's disappointment grows. "I wish I had arms like that," he thinks. The duel continues until Little falls asleep, after which Big gets in the last word.

Admittedly, this book shows a father and son in a warm, affectionate relationship. But the problem with the way this is presented is that Little Nutbrown Hare, like so many real-life little boys, will develop a sense of tremendous inadequacy: he'll never be able to do anything right, he'll never be able to do anything as well as his father does, and he'll never be able to live up to his father's expectations.

One of the primary functions of children's literature is to educate children and help them make sense of their lives. To that end, "Nothing is more important than the impact of parents and others who take care of the child," writes the renowned child psychologist Bruno Bettelheim. "Second in importance is our cultural heritage, when transmitted to the child in the right manner. When children are young, it is literature that carries such information best."

When we want children to understand how important it is to listen to adults, we might tell them about Little Red Riding Hood. When we want them to understand the negative consequences of lying, we read about the little boy who cried wolf. To help them deal with separation anxiety, Hansel and Gretel might help. To fill them with optimism that goodness triumphs over adversity, there's the Cinderella story. And dozens of books can help kids cope with such diverse problems as an alcoholic parent, divorce, moving to a new neighborhood, potty training, and the death of a sibling, a grandparent, a parent, even a pet.

In most cases, as times have changed, children's literature has adapted, reflecting the new cultural heritage and new messages parents want their children to hear. But what do we read our children when we want them to prepare themselves for a more equitable distribution of labor in the home? Well, not much. And why? The unavoidable conclusion is that as a culture, we're pretty satisfied with the way things are and we want to keep them that way.

This is not to suggest that children's literature must be censored or somehow sanitized. Instead, we need to better understand the various roles that literature plays in our children's lives. If we do, we'll be better able to use books — and children's love of them — to effect the kind of social change we've already begun in our quest to eradicate racism and sexism. Young children believe what they hear, especially if it comes from a parent. And since adults are the ones selecting the reading material, at least for the first few years of a child's life, children's books should be held to a high standard. Just as we use literature to empower girls and people of color, we can and must use literature as a way to mold the images children have of fathers.

Boys must come to understand that to be an active, involved, loving, nurturing father is a viable and important life choice, one that a man should be able to make without having to sacrifice his career or his self-respect. And girls must come to understand that a father's role in the family is as valuable as a mother's, and that it is one they, as future wives and mothers, can benefit from enormously.

No matter how much time any parent or caregiver spends reading to a child, sooner or later all kids find themselves in front of a movie or television screen. And from there on out, the time they spend interacting with (or vegetating in front of) one kind of electronic medium or another will dwarf their reading time. While the average American reads just one book a year, ninety-eight percent of Americans have at least one television at home. What's more, the average American watches a hefty thirty hours of television a week, compared with only fifteen minutes a day spent reading for pleasure.

Television viewing starts very early in life. The average six-month-old is in front of a television for almost one and a half hours a day. By age two or three, children are constant viewers, and by adolescence they're on par with adults, logging four to five hours every day. If only because of the sheer number of hours that children spend in front of the TV set, the images of fathers that they get there have the potential to do much more damage than those in books.

Traditionally, both men and women on TV shows and in commercials were portrayed in stereotypical ways. Male characters tended to be independent, knowledgeable, active, and competitive. Female characters were generally more passive, dependent, and emotional. But over the past few decades, the women's roles have greatly expanded. In the 1950s, female characters were twice as likely to be parents as workers. But by the 1980s, this situation had reversed, and they were twice as likely to be workers as parents. Today, while female characters still exhibit some of the same traditional characteristics, they are two to eight times more likely to be independent, aggressive, and respected than before. They also appear far less often in subservient career roles (fewer secretaries, more doctors and lawyers).

But the limits that defined — and confined — men have remained fairly rigid. "Images of autonomous and controlling men were, and still are, the norm in television commercials, and emotionally expressive or vulnerable men are still a rarity," writes Scott Coltrane, a sociologist at the University of California, Riverside. In the fifties only about 15 percent of male characters exhibited forceful, antagonistic, or possessive behavior — qualities traditionally associated with jerks — but by the 1980s half of them behaved that way.

Despite the great shifts in men's involvement in parenting and childcare, media portrayals of fathers have remained static. Fathers still have precious little to do with their kids; they're incompetent and uncaring.

And if by some chance they do care, they're usually too dumb to figure out what to do. More often than not they're the objects of ridicule, and their children, their families, and their friends don't respect them.

Do these traditional, negative portrayals of fathers have an impact on anyone? The answer is an unequivocal yes. The media, says Todd Gitlin, have the power to "orchestrate everyday consciousness" and draw that power from what advertising professionals call framing. This involves nothing more complicated than "selecting some aspects of a perceived reality and making them more salient than the others," according to Scott Coltrane. Researchers say that media frames help define problems, diagnose causes, make moral judgments, and suggest remedies. "The repeated framing of events in specific ways contributes to the perception that what we are observing is 'natural' and inevitable," Coltrane adds. What we're being told is natural and inevitable is that fathers are absent or superfluous.

Nowhere are these stereotypes more blatant than in television sitcoms. Just think of the most prominent fathers on television: Homer Simpson (*The Simpsons*), Bill Cosby (*The Cosby Show*), Tim Allen (*Home Improvement*), Al Bundy (*Married . . . with Children*), Harry Anderson (*Dave's World*), and Paul Buckman (*Mad About You*). Every one of them is outwitted or shown up by his wife, ridiculed by his children (if they're old enough to talk), and in nearly every respect portrayed as parentally challenged.

This isn't to say that these fathers don't love their kids. But despite their good intentions, they're still unable to handle even the simplest child-related tasks. "Gee, honey," says the bumbling, inept but well-meaning father. "I'm incompetent. I guess you'll have to change those dirty diapers yourself."

When it comes to fathers and their roles in the family, rather than reflect reality television shows depict a kind of idealized world where people's dreams come true — at least women's dreams do. Take the very makeup of television families. Three times as many fathers appear on shows targeted to women as on those watched by men. Why? Because, Scott Coltrane explains, they're "focusing on mothers' desires for dads to be involved, tacitly acknowledging that the modern marriage bargain for women now includes consideration of men's abilities as parents, not just as breadwinners." And when women are watching shows like *Who's the Boss* (in which a man takes a job as a nanny) or *Full House* or *The Gregory Hines Show* (two other single-dad shows), they "can vicariously appreciate sensitive fathers, chuckle at their incompetence, and sometimes even fantasize about having a man who will do housework."

Producers have responded just as enthusiastically to other common female concerns. In 1991, Caryn James, a cultural critic for the *New York Times*, wrote an article about the increasing number of unmarried pregnant women on television shows. These shows keep women "in touch with the shifting realities of women's options." According to James, there are plenty "women who want children who do not need or necessarily want a spouse underfoot."

Only a year later, Murphy Brown (the main character in the sitcom of the same name) brought the "shifting realities of women's options" to prime time when she chose to have a child without a father. The then vice president, Dan Quayle, criticized Brown for "mocking the importance of fathers," and he was skewered in the media for his comments. But for one of the few times in his public career, Quayle was right. Almost immediately, Candice Bergen, who played Brown, became a feminist hero and would have been the ideal poster mother for a fathers-are-superfluous movement. Since then, many single female television characters have chosen to have babies without bothering to complicate their lives by having a husband.

Of course, television producers aren't only trying to appease women; they're constantly on the lookout for ways to get a laugh. And men seem perfectly willing to accommodate them. As a result, we end up with shows like *Men Behaving Badly*, which serves no other productive purpose but to demonstrate what boors all men are, and *Something So Right*, in which the lead actress has two ex-husbands: the dim-witted jock who barely sees his son and the rich jerk whose career and new trophy wife are more important than his daughter. Talk-show hosts David Letterman and Jay Leno, among others, routinely fall all over themselves to show us just how politically correct they are. If they ever poke fun at a woman, the audience usually rebukes them with a groan. But when a man is on the receiving end of a joke, everyone laughs heartily.

Fathers provide a facile and nearly endless source of humor. Take, for example, this scene from *Empty Nest*, starring Richard Mulligan as a single father whose adult daughter has moved back home with her baby. In one episode, Mulligan, who plays a doctor (implying, presumably, a certain level of intelligence and professionalism), has made some of his special French toast. The baby tosses it on the floor, where the dog sniffs at it but after some thought drops it into the garbage. Everyone knows dads can't cook.

One interesting byproduct of the search for the almighty laugh has been a tremendous overrepresentation of single fathers on television. According to media researcher Tom Skill, single dads on TV — who are usually widowed, rarely divorced — have always proportionally outnumbered their real-life counterparts. In the 1950s, when 1 percent of American families were headed by a single father, more than 17 percent of TV families depended on a single dad to head the household (*My Little Margie* and *The Rifleman*). In the 1960s it was 1 percent in real life and 28 percent on TV (*Bonanza, My Three Sons,* and *The Andy Griffith Show*); 2 percent versus 18 percent in the 1970s (*The Courtship of Eddie's Father* and *Sanford and Son*); and 3 percent versus 22 percent in the 1980s (*Benson* and *Empty Nest*).

"In the past, fathers dealing with domestic chores were funnier than mothers making headway in the business world," Skill says. "More and more real-life mothers were going through that struggle, and the programs didn't want to show that pain." So we're back where we started: even when they're going for a laugh, producers and their writers are trying to make women happy. And dads, as usual, make a great target.

Television commercials take up about 20 percent of a typical broadcast hour, and the average American is exposed to 500 ads per week (26,000 in a year), making their impact on how we see ourselves and each other especially great. Men are significantly overrepresented in commercials (85 percent of the voice-overs are done by males, and 54 percent of all roles are played by men), but when it comes to family life, things change in a hurry. Women are over 50 percent more likely than men to be shown as parents, 50 percent more likely to be shown nurturing or comforting their children, and six times more involved in teaching them.

When men are shown fathering, they're pigeonholed into one of two stereotypical categories. Most commonly they're shown as subservient to their wives and oblivious of their children's needs. Fathers who do take some parenting initiative do so in a manner that is often associated with mothers: serving, encouraging, and being emotionally supportive, as opposed to the traditional male style of playing and instructing. "This corresponds," says Scott Coltrane, "to the phenomenon of men continuing to feel like 'helpers' in their own home, and suggests that popular cultural symbols are not yet suggesting that men should assume half of daily responsibility for home and children." It's critical to remember that while "female" characteristics are extremely valuable, they are no more important to children's emotional, physical, and psychological development than the things men do. And there is, of course, some overlap between mothers and fathers, but each also makes unique contributions to their families.

In those carefully constructed families in commercials, however, only mothers really care about their children. Here are a few examples:

- In a spot for Post Raisin Bran, a father and his daughter are oohing and ahhing about their cereal. "Somebody must really love us," says dad. "Who do you think it is?" "Mommy!" yelps the child.
- Another breakfast cereal, Kix, is "Kid tested, mother approved."
- When it comes time to make lunch, "Choosy mothers choose Jif peanut butter."
- Robitussin cold medicines are "recommended by Dr. Mom," who in some ads drags herself out of her sickbed to keep an eye on her incompetent husband, who is haplessly trying to manage the house for a few hours.
- A Tylenol ad featuring a father-son fishing trip ends with the son saying that he got his smarts from mom.
- In a commercial for Aquafresh toothpaste, a father and child argue about whether fluoride or mouthwash is the toothpaste's most important ingredient. They probably would have argued all day if mom hadn't stopped in to tell them, "You need both."
- An MCI pager commercial showing a bunch of kids caught in a

sudden downpour tells us that a single call to mom's pager will ring her office and her cell phone and that "Mom rolls in right before the storm."

There are, of course, a small number of ads that portray fathers in a positive way, but they are the exceptions that prove the rule.

As with children's books, it's tempting to argue that these portrayals of mothers and fathers are nothing more than glimpses of reality. After all, mothers still do most of the shopping and feeding. But the problem is the obvious message contained in these ads, that fathers are mainly stupid and incompetent and don't have much to contribute around the house. Viewers, especially children, are left with the distinct impression that fathers just don't care. they don't feed their kids, don't clothe them, won't be there to take care of them when they're sick, and shouldn't be called in case of an emergency.

Again, the simple fact is that commercials, like children's literature, don't reflect reality. Instead, advertisers take advantage of the power of framing to create a kind of utopian world free of discrimination and full of hope and possibility — at least for women and minorities. Only about 70 percent of women are in the workforce, and a large portion of them work only part time. Nevertheless, women in commercials are twice as likely to be workers as mothers. Take, for example, an ad for Ford pickup trucks featuring "real-life action heroes." The spot shows volunteer firefighters and rescue workers — half of whom are female — on the job. But as we noted earlier, 98 percent of firefighters are men.

Given all that they know about framing, why don't advertisers reinvigorate the image of fathers as they've done for mothers? Why don't they more accurately reflect the changes fathers have made in their lives?

Part of the problem may be advertising's twisted version of affirmative action. "For years, women got the short end of the stick in advertising. . . . We had the dumb blondes, but now there's a role reversal going on," Dr. Joyce Brothers told the *Los Angeles Times.* "And when you make the man the butt of the joke, you will attract attention."

"Now there are so many women's advocacy groups that will come after you that you don't dare take a chance," one advertising executive

said. A recent survey of one thousand randomly selected advertisements found that "100 percent of the jerks singled out in male-female
relationships were male. There were no exceptions. . . . 100 percent of
the ignorant ones were male. 100 percent of the incompetent ones
were male."

This can be seen in commercials for two anti-diarrhea medications.
In one ad for Imodium, a man who clearly needs to find a bathroom
fast keeps his carpool waiting while he stops at a restroom. In another,
he makes a wiggling, squirming fool of himself on an airplane. Spots
for Koapectate, which feature a woman in need of a bathroom, are far
more respectful of her discomfort and her urgency. In two contrasting
Robitussin cough syrup ads, a woman watching her daughter perform
is helped through a coughing fit by a considerate and sympathetic
neighbor. But in another ad, when a man coughs in a movie theater,
the actors on the screen break out of their roles and demand that
someone give the boor a cough drop. The helpful, though in this case
disgusted, person in the adjoining seat does exactly that. In keeping
with the Dr. Mom philosophy, the saviors in both commercials are
women.

When it comes to anything having to do with health, women are
apparently the only ones to turn to. In the mid-1990s Advil ran a series
of six commercials featuring a hatmaker, a blacksmith, a photogra-
pher, several electricians, a hairdresser, and a TV production person.
In five out of the six spots, the person recommending Advil was a
woman. In a commercial for Rogaine, a balding man is told by his wife
that help is available. In a similar spot for Rogaine for women, a thin-
haired woman is told about the product by another woman. Really, of
all the things we should let men be knowledgeable about, hair loss
should be near the top of the list.

Advertisers use negative images of men and fathers because, quite
simply, they work. During each of the last three or four presidential
campaigns, poll after poll told us that voters were sick and tired of the
mudslinging and name-calling. Those same polls, however, indicated
that viewers remembered negative ads better than any others. And
while television ads are equal opportunity insulters of politicians, they
insult or make fun only of men.

The same applies, of course, to ads that bash fathers. In fact, consumers remembered the "You need both" Aquafresh ad better than almost any other in its category, said Donald F. Bruzzone, president of a research firm that studies hundreds of commercials each year. Sounds like an advertiser's dream, right?

Maybe. If you're a father, it's more like a nightmare. Not only are these ads extremely successful, they also reinforce the old stereotype of the absent, uninterested father. In the Aquafresh ad, Bruzzone found that consumers remembered that it was the mother, not the father, who solved the problem.

Taken together, these stereotypical, negative images of men and fathers are part of what one advertising executive calls the "nitwit-ification of American men." "Advertisers are trying to make women look smart because they know women do most of the shopping," he said. "If that has to happen at the expense of men, well, they figure that's okay." Or, as Bruzzone explains, these ads "seem to do more to turn females on than they do to turn males off." In a world where women make the overwhelming majority of family spending decisions, it makes sense for advertisers to worry more about keeping female viewers happy than about alienating male ones.

Of course, not all fathers are shown as boors. Johnson & Johnson has some wonderful spots featuring nurturing, caring fathers. And not long ago, *Boston Globe* columnist Anita Diamant identified one positive image of fathers that actually seems to be increasing in popularity. "The naked father is seen most often in magazine advertisements for baby powder, camera equipment, and faceless corporations, cradling a beautiful, naked baby against his sleek, muscular chest. The naked father may be black or white, but wherever you find him, this new icon of paternity is invariably handsome and obviously crazy about his kid."

Showing bare-chested or naked hunky men in this fashion might also be seen as another type of advertising's affirmative action — a gimmick designed to appeal to women — with the rationale going like this: we've used sexy women to sell all kinds of products for decades, so now let's give women something to drool over for a while.

What seemed at one point to be progress in getting fatherhood into the national consciousness has turned out to be short-lived. "The kinder, gentler image of men is losing momentum," said Ted Bell, president of Leo Burnett USA, a major advertising agency, in an interview in *New York* magazine.

Motion pictures theoretically have far more opportunities to develop character and explore the complexities of people's lives than commercials or television shows. Nevertheless, celluloid fathers fall into one or more of the following four broad categories:

The Bad Father (who pays the price)

This genre is glaringly exemplified by a movie that nearly became a political movement. In *The First Wives Club*, three bitter women abuse, kidnap, blackmail, and defraud their former husbands, ultimately turning them into "slaves." One of the mothers even manipulates her daughter into helping bring down her father. The men's crimes? Getting divorced. Films like *The First Wives Club* perpetuate the myth that divorce is all about loutish men abusing helpless women.

The Absent or Distant Father

In the early part of *Bambi* — nearly fifty years old but still one of the most popular children's movies of all time — Bambi enjoys a warm, nurturing relationship with his mother, presumably his only parent. It's only about halfway through the film that we are told he has a father at all. And when we finally do meet dad, he is a stern, authoritative, and at best fleeting presence in the young deer's life. At the end of the movie, Bambi himself has become a father and, like the only male role model he ever knew, does his fathering from a distant hill.

In Roald Dahl's classic book *Charlie and the Chocolate Factory,* young Charlie had both a father and a mother. But by the time it hit the big screen as *Willy Wonka and the Chocolate Factory,* dad had mysteriously disappeared, and no one said a word about it. Mom, though, was still there.

Falling Down generated a huge amount of controversy, including a cover story in *Newsweek* about "white male backlash." In the movie, divorced father Bill Foster, played by Michael Douglas, calls his ex-wife to get permission to bring his daughter, Adele, a birthday present. "How's Adele?" he asks. "She's doing just fine without you," says his ex. "*Falling Down* is about the violent decomposition of a man's life," wrote David Blankenhorn. Bill Foster "loses his balance — and finally his life — precisely because he loses his fatherhood."

The Irrelevant or Replaceable Father

The theme here is that since fathers are superfluous, anything positive that a man might offer to a child can be provided by pretty much anyone — or anything.

In *The Big Chill*, a single woman lawyer spends the weekend trying to decide which of her old male friends should inseminate her so she can have a child on her own. Further illustrating the sad fact that even fatherhood is a women's issue, one of the other women at the weekend finally offers her own husband to do the job.

In *E.T. the Extra-Terrestrial*, Elliott's father has abandoned his family and presumably taken up with a younger woman. But not to worry, because E.T. becomes a father figure to young Elliott.

In *Terminator 2: Judgment Day* yet another extraterrestrial replaces a real-life father. "It was suddenly so clear," muses Sarah, the mother of John Connor, who grows up to be the leader of the rebels. "The Terminator would never stop, it would never leave him, and it would never hurt him, never shout at him or get drunk and hit him, or say it was too busy to spend time with him. It would always be there, and it would die to protect him. Of all the would-be fathers who came and went over the years, this thing, this machine, was the only one who measured up."

And in *St. Elmo's Fire*, a man abandons his wife and baby daughter to pursue his musical career. "I thought about hanging around and being one of those 'I'll see you on the weekend' dads," he says. "But that's not what Melody needs. Besides, that would just confuse everybody."

The Improving Father

Fathers are allowed to grow somewhat as characters, but their developmental trajectory (or "arc," in film parlance) is fairly predictable.

In the beginning of the film, the father in question is usually emotionally or physically absent, mean, incompetent, or buffoonish. By the end of the last reel, however, he often becomes a reasonably nice guy, manages to hang on to his wife (or "get the girl" if he didn't already have one), and earn the respect of his children. The problem here is that while fathers develop somewhat over the course of the film, mothers rarely do — they don't have to. From first frame to last, Mom's skills as a parent and the respect and love she receives from her children are never in doubt, even if she is, in fact, a complete incompetent.

A Czech film, *Kolya*, the 1996 Academy Award winner for best foreign film, offers a wonderful example of this theme. The plot gets its main twist when the Russian mother of a small boy pays a man named Louka to marry her, ostensibly so she can get the Czech equivalent of a green card. A few days after the wedding, though, Louka is forced to become Kolya's primary caretaker when mom goes off to Germany to be with the man she really loves. Louka, stereotypically, has no interest in parenting and tries to palm the boy off on any number of friends and relatives. True to the predictable pattern, Louka comes to love Kolya and gives up his career, and nearly his freedom, to keep the boy from being taken away from him by the authorities.

Then, just when you think things can't get any cozier between Louka and Kolya, the mother returns. She mutters a perfunctory apology and demands her son back. Louka turns the boy over and watches helplessly as mother and child fade away.

Kolya is essentially a celluloid version of the Dr. Seuss book *Horton Hatches an Egg*, in which Mayzee the lazy bird tricks Horton the elephant into sitting on her egg while she takes an extended vacation. Like the mother in *Kolya*, Mayzee reappears after Horton has done all the hard egg-hatching work and demands her egg back.

Yet unlike Louka, who turns over his "son" and walks away, Horton "gives birth" to a creature that is clearly partly his: an elephant with wings. Whether in fun or motivated by some internal knowledge, Dr. Seuss understood, as few others did in the 1960s, that fathers matter. Horton's contributions to his child are not only permanent, they're every bit as important as the mother's.

In *Three Men and a Baby*, three hip bachelors unwillingly assume primary responsibilities for a baby abandoned at their doorstep. The message: not only does it take three men to raise a child, but months later mom can step in right were she left off without missing a beat.

In *The River Wild,* dad is emotionally and physically absent. His son hates him, his wife wants a divorce, and even the dog refuses to obey his commands. On a dangerous rafting trip with a pair of killers, dad proves his love, saves his family, and earns the respect of his dog.

And in the 1998 film *Armageddon,* one of the main characters, who is just about to be blasted into space on a death-defying mission, goes to visit his very young son, whom he obviously hasn't seen for quite a while. When he arrives, the boy is playing on the porch. They smile at each other and then the boy asks his mother, who has just come out of the house, who that man is. "He's a salesman," she says, rushing the boy inside. She then rather rudely tells the man that he isn't supposed to come around, that the "court says you can't, it confuses him." But at the landing strip where our hero lands after having helped save the world from total destruction, his ex-wife is there with her previously confused son to welcome him back into the family. Apparently, when dad was just a regular guy, he was wasn't a good enough husband or father. Now that he's famous (and rich), well, that's a very different story.

Kids' books and movies and television shows aren't the only places that negative images of fathers predominate. These stereotypes are so widespread that David Blankenhorn asks, "If you were an alien from another planet, curious about human factors but confined to the Current Periodical section of a leading university library, what would you conclude about fatherhood in late-twentieth-century America?"

The answer is clear to Blankenhorn as well as to anyone else who has ever opened up a newspaper. Our depictions of fatherhood largely assume "that fatherhood is superfluous. More precisely, our elite culture has fully incorporated into its prevailing family narrative the idea that fatherhood, as a distinctive social role for men, is either unnecessary or undesirable."

Every year on the third Sunday in June, the one day that is supposedly dedicated to appreciating fathers, just about all the print media have to offer are articles slamming fathers in the same old ways.

AT&T routinely reports that Mother's Day is the busiest calling day of the year, and Father's Day is "just another Sunday." Well, almost. The truth is that while the total number of calls on Father's Day is nothing special, the number of collect calls is the highest of the year.

Father's Day images are just a distilled version of the images Americans get the other 364 days of the year. But what's interesting is that on Father's Day there are usually more negative articles about fathers than on any other day. And each year, the coverage gets worse.

From 1990 to 1995, when the total number of Father's Day articles dealing with fatherhood increased about 75 percent, the number on fathers' absence from home went up 400 percent, to a total of 27 percent of all Father's Day coverage. "Media attention to this topic [in 1995] not only dwarfed 1990's press coverage, but it far exceeded the overall increase in attention to fatherhood topics in 1995," writes researcher David Brenner. Articles included "Disappearing Dads Disruptive to Society," "Where Have All the Fathers Gone?" "Happy Fatherless Day," and "Save the Fathers."

Adding to this fascination with the negative were numerous cartoons about absent fathers. For the most part they fit this theme: a mother and child are watching television or going shopping and see an advertisement for Father's Day. The child asks her mommy, "What's a father?"

Coverage of young, poor, unmarried (and, for the most part, black) fathers is especially harsh, with the Father's Day focus squarely on "cracking down on men who impregnate" or on the most recent attempts to improve child-support collections.

On Father's Day in 1997, a front-page article in the *Toronto Sun* asked, "Why do Parents Murder Kids? On Father's Day Michele Mandel seeks answers to a deadly question." The article went on to imply that men are the only parents who abuse and kill their children, an implication that flies in the face of data to the contrary: that a child is far more likely to be abused or injured by his or her mother than by the father.

Father's Day coverage hasn't gotten much better since. On June 17, 1998, President Clinton issued a Father's Day proclamation recognizing that "devoted fathers work day in and day out, not only to help provide their families with food, clothing, education, and a good home, but also to give their children the values, guidance, encouragement, and self-esteem to make the most of their lives." The proclamation, which called on "communities across the country and all the citizens of the United States to observe this day with appropriate ceremonies and activities that demonstrate our deep appreciation and abiding love for our fathers," was not reported in a single major newspaper.

To its credit, the *New York Times* ran an op-ed piece by Gail Sheehy, author of *Men's Passages*, which discussed with great sensitivity the discrimination faced by divorced fathers, and several positive articles about fathers appeared in smaller newspapers. But in other metropolitan areas the media opted for more traditional Father's Day fare, such as articles on fathers who batter their children and the like.

Some divorced fathers don't pay their child support, some men are emotionally absent, and some are abusive. But the overall impression one gets from the usual Father's Day coverage is that all divorced men are deadbeats and that the majority of fathers are emotionally absent and abusive. Can you imagine what would happen if the media covered Mother's Day the same way and newspapers, magazines, and television were filled with stories about welfare mothers, abusive mothers, drug-abusing mothers, mothers who don't allow their ex-husbands to see their children, murdering mothers, and the like?

These negative images have a decided impact on the way we — adults and children — come to see the world. First, we've essentially glorified the useless father, making him a role model. He doesn't really have to do that much around the house, he makes people laugh, and he's kind of endearing — in much the same way as women who don't know how to pump gas, change a fuse, or balance a checkbook were, and to some extent still are, considered endearing.

Second, "The seductively realistic portrayals of family life in the media may be the basis for our most common and pervasive conceptions and beliefs about what is natural and what is right," wrote George Gerbner, a leading media researcher, and his colleagues. And our children are buying into those beliefs as fast as they can. Sixty-two percent of children between ten and sixteen say that kids their age are influenced by what they see in the media, and 65 percent say that shows like *The Simpsons* and *Married . . . with Children* encourage kids to disrespect their parents. Even in television and movie families in which the father is more involved and more nurturing, such as those on *Family Ties* and *Cosby*, "with predictable regularity . . . these affable dads were taught some lesson about family life by their wives. They often boasted that men were superior, but the husbands and fathers on these shows were typically outdone by forbearing wives who proved them wrong without having to challenge them directly."

Third, men are having a hard time reconciling society's demands that they become actively involved, sensitive, supportive, and loving fathers with the role models society offers. "Men are being almost constantly told — and can see for themselves, if they look close enough — that their behavior does not square with the ideal, which means that they are being reminded on a regular basis that they are failing as fathers," writes sociologist and historian Ralph Larossa. "Failing not when compared with their own fathers or grandfathers, perhaps, but failing when compared with the image of fatherhood which has become part of our culture and which they, on some level of consciousness, believe in."

Finally, and perhaps most damaging, negative stereotyping of fathers may ultimately undo much of the progress we've made toward equality between men and women. "Stereotyped and conventional portrayals of gender on television [and, presumably, on the big screen] have some important impacts on children and adults," write Kenneth Allan and Scott Coltrane. "One of the most common findings . . . is that increased television viewing is associated with more stereotypical views, especially about gender. Children tend to learn about jobs and work settings from television, and more exposure leads to gender-stereotyped views of occupations among young people."

When media researcher Michael Morgan asked kids about sex-typed chores (doing the dishes, yard work, and others), she found that their TV watching affected the way they viewed those chores. Children who watch more television have more traditional views about the kinds of household tasks that are appropriate for men or women. Kids are obviously being subtly — or not so subtly — socialized into traditional gender roles in part by TV programs.

Television can be a positive force for changing attitudes and behavior, a fact that we sometimes tend to forget. In the 1980s, when women began to be portrayed in a wider range of occupational roles, girls who watched lots of TV had more positive attitudes and aspirations about the kinds of nontraditional occupations — lawyer, doctor, and the like — they saw on prime-time shows.

Freestyle, a public television series broadcast in the early 1980s that focused on counter-stereotyped portrayals (for example, women as engineers and doctors, men as nurses and secretaries), resulted in changes in attitudes in fourth-, fifth-, and sixth-grade children. Unfortunately, such programs have brief lives on the air, while other programs, with their myths and stereotypes, capture the ratings.

Since no one really expects the media to portray much of anything accurately, we have to ask ourselves whether they are helping us achieve our common goal of getting fathers to take on more responsibility and be more actively involved parents.

Sadly, the answer is a resounding no. In fact, the media are doing more harm than good. Hammering men over the head with — and so wildly exaggerating — their shortcomings only fills them with feelings of shame that serve to drive them further from their families and children. "Research on shame and guilt consistently finds that the subsequent behavior of shamed individuals is one of retracting and removing themselves from the shaming situation," writes researcher Nancy Heleno Obetz. "These actions are motivated by feeling a sense of shrinking, being small, worthless and powerless."

The media have a powerful role in shaming particularly young, poor men, who already have a difficult time living up to society's expectation that they support their children financially. "The stereotype of young, unwed fathers as irresponsible and cavalier, long on braggadocio and short on commitment, casts a deep shadow over young men who would be involved dads. It shapes expectations — among the new fathers' partners and families, the community resources that serve them, and the young men themselves. These expectations too often inhibit rather than foster a young man's relationship with his child, robbing both of the benefits of fatherhood."

*   *   *

It's important to sympathize with the rage some people feel toward their fathers for being physically and emotionally distant. And it's important to understand their sense of abandonment and empathize with the anger and resentment they feel when their fathers point to the monetary support and educational opportunities they provided and think these things somehow entitle them to be called good fathers.

It's also very important to understand that some of the fathers of previous generations brought much of this rage, resentment, and hate on themselves. Men, for the most part, were the ones who created the traditional stereotypes concerning work and family. They kept what they thought was the "good stuff" and left the women to take care of the house and kids. And after a while, the "good provider," as exemplified by the often emotionally distant fathers in *Leave It to Beaver* and *Father Knows Best,* became the norm.

It is only recently that men and women have felt able to speak out against the traditional role fathers have played in the family, only recently that society has finally come to terms with the fact that the distant father was not the ideal father at all. And, as with many things, we've found that one healthy way of dealing with our mixed feelings about fathers is to laugh at them. But in the midst of this newfound freedom to lash out against yesterday's absent, neglectful fathers, today's fathers are falling victim to cruel stereotypes. As Betty Friedan writes in *The Second Stage,* the men who are alive today "personally didn't create the system or conspire to dominate women."

If one looks solely at the conventional trappings of success — economic, political, and social power — men have certainly had more than their share. But society — men and women — must recognize that men have paid a very high price for their success. The average woman's life span exceeds the average man's by seven years, up from only one year just two decades ago. Men aged eighteen to twenty-nine are three times more likely to suffer from alcohol dependency than women in the same age group. Writer Ellis Cose speculates that part of the reason men are more self-destructive is that they have often failed to connect emotionally with others: co-workers, wives, children. Men commit suicide twice as often as women (despite the fact that more women than men suffer from depression), they are murdered in the workplace five times more often, and die sooner of all the major diseases. In their frantic pursuit of success, many men have denied themselves the joys of knowing their families. Many of today's fathers know perfectly well that the traditional measures of success are not all they're cracked up to be, and they are committed to being a strong presence in their children's lives, physically and emotionally.

Just as society can and must understand the rage sons and daughters alike feel toward the fathers of yesterday, it must also understand and empathize with the rage and anger of today's young fathers. Imagine their reaction to the cold, absent, or incompetent way they're portrayed in the books they read to their children and in the movies, television programs, and commercials they watch. And imagine their frustration when, even on Father's Day, there's no escaping the stories about deadbeat daddies and other neglectful, distant, and abusive men.

The feelings of futility and hopelessness young fathers experience when unfairly stereotyped are as strong and deep as those experienced by many young African-American men when whites, fearing for their safety, cross the street to avoid them. It's humiliating, degrading, and ultimately psychologically damaging. By perpetuating nothing but the most negative stereotypes and by ignoring the existence of millions of wonderful, nurturing, loving fathers, the media make it almost impossible for men to escape the roles society has foisted on them.

The media have gone a long way toward changing their portrayals of women and minorities, perhaps because society has at last recognized that by addressing their problems and needs instead of ignoring them, minority communities can be kept from feeling so alienated. Today's fathers, though, are still alienated from their children. Some fathers deserve the bashing they get. But many of them, victimized by a rigid and often reactionary society, have assumed roles they never wanted and can't shake. By refusing to acknowledge our complicity in forcing fathers into their present roles, and by ignoring fathers' importance in our lives and the lives of our children, we are sentencing ourselves to another generation of the status quo.

Part 3

The Barriers

6

Socializing Children: From Baby to Daddy

HROUGH THE BOOKS they read and the television shows and movies they watch, children develop ideas about the nature of fatherhood. Many of these ideas are wrong, but they nonetheless have a powerful influence on our children. It is, however, the way in which boys and girls are socialized — by their parents, their peers, and their teachers — that is most responsible for shaping their ideas about appropriate gender roles and, correspondingly, their expectations about their future roles as mothers and fathers.

This isn't to say that there aren't any inherent biological differences between boys and girls; there are. Male fetuses for example, are more subject to miscarriages and birth-related problems than females, says Carole Beal, author of *Boys and Girls: The Development of Gender Roles,* in part because boys at birth are physically heavier and longer than girls, and mothers spend almost one hundred minutes longer delivering them.

Within hours of birth, girls are much more interested than boys in people and faces; boys are just as happy looking at an object dangled in front of them as they are looking at a face, says Anne Moir, author of *Brain Sex.* In fact, at only four months, baby girls can tell the difference between photographs of people they know from those of strangers; boys can't. Boys also take in less sensory data than girls: they're less discriminating when it comes to food and less sensitive to touch and pain.

In contrast, the outward biological differences between boys and girls during the first eighteen months of life are so slight that when babies are dressed in nothing but diapers, most adults can't tell a boy from a girl. And recent evidence indicates that many of the remaining "differences" are based more on adults' preconceived notions about gender than on fact. When their babies are less than a day old, for example, parents are likely to describe their newborn daughters as small, soft, less attentive, cute, delicate, and fine-featured. Boys, on the other hand, are viewed as strong, hardy, firm, and well coordinated.

In one of the first studies of its kind, two Cornell University researchers, John and Sandra Condry, showed a group of more than two hundred adults a videotape of a nine-month-old baby at play. Half were told they were watching a boy, the other half that they were watching a girl. Although everyone viewed the same tape, the descriptions the two groups gave of the baby's behavior were incredibly different. The "boy" group saw more pleasure and less fear in the baby's behavior than the "girl" group. When the video baby displayed any negative emotions, the "boy" group saw anger and the "girl" group saw fear. In a later study, adults played in a more masculine way (that is, rough-and-tumble play) with a baby that they were told was a boy and in a gentler and more nurturing fashion with a "girl" infant — regardless of the baby's actual gender.

Parents apply the same kind of stereotypes to their unborn babies as well. Expectant mothers who know they're carrying boys routinely describe the babies' movements as vigorous, earthquake-like, very strong, and calm but strong ("the John Wayne fetus"). They described girls as very gentle, not terribly active, and lively but not excessively energetic. In point of fact, there are no differences between boys' and girls' fetal activity levels.

Babies and toddlers aren't the only ones who get stereotyped by gender. Men are stereotyped as, and are expected to be, independent, assertive, dominant, and competitive in social and sexual relations. Women are stereotyped as well, and are expected to be more passive, loving, sensitive, and supportive in social relationships, especially in their roles as wives and mothers. Expressions of warmth in personal relationships, anxiety under pressure, and suppression of overt aggression and sexuality are regarded as more appropriate for women than for men. Our culture has a very difficult time accepting the possibility that men as well as women can be nurturing, sensitive, and caring — important ingredients for successful fathering.

These stereotypes do, however, sometimes vary with ethnicity and other factors. African-American children, for example, are more likely to be socialized without strict gender roles. Early independence is valued for girls as well as boys, and there is less differentiation in assigned family tasks. Similarly, girls are encouraged to be assertive, and boys are encouraged to express emotions and nurture others.

Age and education can also alter gender-role expectations. In the United States, female students and college-educated women between the ages of eighteen and thirty-five are more likely than older or less educated females to perceive the feminine role as involving independence and achievement. Men, however, even young educated ones, maintain more stereotyped gender roles than do women. When it comes to parents, single-earner fathers have more traditional attitudes about gender roles than fathers in two-income families. Mothers' gender stereotypes are the same whether or not they work outside the home. But a mother's work situation does have an effect on her children. Children whose mothers work in skilled occupations and professions regard women's educational and vocational aspirations and men's assumption of housekeeping and childcare tasks as more appropriate than do children whose mothers are not employed.

Long before boys are able to aim their first play gun at a pretend foe and before girls sit their dolls down to their first tea party, their parents have already begun to affect the children's choices of toys, games, and activities. Parents actively shape children's tastes and preferences, and the way parents socialize and treat their children goes a long way toward determining the different gender paths that boys and girls follow. These paths, in turn, set the stage for parenting roles in adulthood.

The process starts early. Many parents who know the gender of their unborn babies decorate the nursery or bedroom accordingly. In 1975, psychologists Harriet Rheingold and Katie Cook carefully recorded the kinds of toys, decorations, furniture, curtains, and bedspreads that were in the bedrooms of boys and girls between the ages of one month and six years. The rooms were dramatically different. Boys' rooms were usually painted blue or red and contained vehicles, depots, machines, army equipment, soldiers, and sports equipment. Girls' rooms were more likely to be painted pink or yellow and contain dollhouses and ruffled furnishings. Girls had more floral-patterned curtains with lace, and boys had a more tailored look. Boys had more action-oriented toys, while girls' toys were more family-focused.

One might think that times have changed over the past quarter century, but they haven't. In 1990 another group of researchers repeated the children's-rooms study and found that boys still lived among red race cars and girls among pink ruffles, lace, and dolls.

The differences between boys' and girls' rooms may seem largely cosmetic, but they carry serious cultural messages. Boys tend to receive, from their parents and other adults, a wider variety of toys than girls. They get more trucks and cars, tools, sports equipment, balls, gardening and beach and construction toys — the kinds of playthings that subtly shape the stereotype of the macho, sports-minded male. Girls, on the other hand, receive more dolls, play kitchen appliances and utensils, toy furniture, and jewelry — objects that provide opportunities to begin practicing parenting and housework skills.

Parents also nudge their children toward desired gender roles by the way they dress them. On a trip to the local shopping mall you will find dozens of baby boys dressed in blue or red; girls are mostly in pink, with puffy sleeves, ruffles, and lace. Many infant girls also wear ribbons — usually pink — on their nearly bare heads so no one will mistake them for boys.

"Sex-typed clothing serves very well to announce the child's sex and thereby ensures sex appropriate treatment even from strangers," writes Beverly Fagot, a long-time gender expert. Even pacifiers come in pink and blue, and disposable diapers for boys come with a blue tab and "extra protection up front"; the pink version for girls is equipped with "protection down low." As a society that is supposedly struggling to recognize gender similarities, we seem to forget that for centuries parents somehow got by with unisex diapers.

It doesn't take children long to figure out that the way one dresses is an important clue to his or her gender. Sandra Bem, a Cornell University psychologist and the author of *The Lens of Gender,* recounts an anecdote involving her son Jeremy's experience of wearing barrettes to nursery school. "Several times that day another little boy insisted that Jeremy must be a girl because only girls wear barrettes. Jeremy finally pulled down his pants to make his point convincingly. The other boy was not impressed. He simply said, 'Everyone has a penis; only girls wear barrettes.' "

Do these subtleties matter to the way boys and girls grow up? And does it really matter whether a baby is dressed in ruffles and flowers or in a Dodgers uniform? The answer to both of these questions seems to be yes.

These hints at children's gender clearly alter the way that adults perceive and treat them. If a baby is adorned in pink ribbons and lace, she will more likely be seen as delicate and fragile. If a baby is dressed in a blue sailor suit, he will more likely be viewed as a budding tough guy. Needless to say, a tough-guy image is hardly compatible with the qualities associated with a sensitive and involved father. Although it is unlikely that dressing up a boy in a mini-version of a Miami Dolphins jersey is going to doom him to uninvolved fatherhood, choice of clothing is part of the early stereotyping that may, in conjunction with other cultural messages, help shape a boy's expectations about his future fathering role.

Signs of boys' and girls' differing attitudes toward parenthood are evident very early. By age four or five, girls interact more with babies than boys do. When asked to care for a baby, boys are more inclined to watch the baby passively, while girls actively engage in caretaking.

In one study, a group of three- to six-year-old children were watched for a week during their daily free-play period. On two "baby days" a thirteen-month-old baby visited and was placed in a playpen, and on "fish days" a tank with goldfish was placed in front of the empty playpen. As expected, girls spent more time in the area than boys did when the baby was present, but not on other days — children of both sexes apparently like goldfish equally well. Older boys spent significantly less time in the area than the younger boys did on baby days, which suggests that as boys get older they become gradually less attracted to babies.

This isn't to say that boys are completely devoid of nurturing behavior. They are, in fact, just as nurturing as girls when the task is helping a younger child pick up spilled game pieces, sharing cookies with a younger peer, or giving some of their candy to a poor child. Boys and girls are also equally emotionally responsive to the sound of a baby in distress: they both become upset and agitated. When interviewed later about their reactions to a crying baby, girls expressed more empathy than boys. "It may be that just as others believe girls to be more empathetic than boys," writes psychologist Phyllis Berman, "girls themselves believe they are particularly empathetic. This belief would have much support from widespread stereotypes about the natural proclivities of women, particularly when the empathy is directed toward babies."

This is all part of what Berman calls the "social scripts" that boys and girls develop long before they're five years old. "It is likely that parenting or caregiving scripts are assembled in a gradual but discontinuous manner throughout childhood," she writes. "And it is reasonable to believe that these early scripts may be precursors of and contributors to scripts generated in adulthood."

Parenting scripts are in turn related to what researchers call "self-efficacy," the feeling that we can successfully tackle a certain task. As our sense of self-efficacy in a particular activity increases, the more we're likely to continue investing time and effort in that activity.

In early childhood, girls play with dolls they can feed, burp, comfort, and dress. They have opportunities to baby-sit and assume responsibility for younger siblings who do much the same things. Girls get lots of practice in developing their nurturing skills. When they reach adulthood, they're already quite good at caring for burping, crying, and needy infants. They have, in effect, been practicing the maternal role throughout their growing years and will be more likely to embrace the tasks of parenting.

The time boys spend playing with trucks and throwing a baseball leads to a strong sense of self-efficacy in the mechanical and sporting spheres of life but leaves them ill prepared to tackle many of the demands of parenting. (Girls, it should be noted, are as a rule ill prepared for sports and the mechanical chores of life.) This does not mean that a man can't change or that he can't pick up parenting skills as an adult (or, for that matter, that a woman must always "throw like a girl").

Childhood socialization experiences leave boys at a disadvantage compared to girls when they become parents. For girls, childhood is an extended apprenticeship in parenting. But for boys it is an apprenticeship in sports and mechanics — wonderful training for the working world, perhaps, but not particularly helpful to the future father.

Parents aren't the only ones who enforce the rigid gender roles that our culture prescribes for boys and girls. Children themselves often operate as kind of junior gender police, "punishing" those who buck traditional gender roles. The consequences are especially severe for boys. Boys who play with dolls rather than trucks are criticized five to six times more often by their classmates than children who stick to gender appropriate toys. Girls who would rather play firefighter than nurse are not treated nearly as harshly. They are for the most part ignored and not criticized.

There's no doubt that peer feedback makes a big difference to children's behavior. A nasty glance or sharp word from another child can quickly lead a boy to drop his tea set and pick up a toy truck or baseball bat. The result is that children from preschool age onward choose to live in gender-segregated play worlds that encourage separate styles of interaction that are distinctly male and female. These separate worlds in turn influence children's interests, skills, and competencies as they approach adulthood and parenthood. And the messages they get aren't particularly encouraging for nurturing fatherhood.

When they begin to leave home and go to school, boys and girls are treated differently by teachers. And the messages kids get in school are often quite different from the ones they get at home.

In many ways, schools are "feminine." They value quiet, obedience, and passivity — the qualities that our culture deems appropriate for girls — and they discourage the boisterous, assertive, competitive, and independent qualities that boys are pushed toward at home and by their peers.

Given that the overwhelming majority of grade school teachers are women, this isn't too surprising. Teachers, for example, acknowledge and respond positively to girls' social initiatives, such as talking and gesturing, more than to the same displays on the part of boys. And teachers respond more negatively to boys' assertive behavior, such as pushing and shoving, than to that of girls. Boys are encouraged to engage in "feminine" quiet activities rather than in "masculine" aggressive and rough-and-tumble play.

Perhaps because of the conflicting messages that boys get about appropriate behavior, school for most boys is not a happy place. Boys view themselves as being less well liked than girls by their teachers. They have more difficulty adjusting to school routines, create more problems for their teachers, are criticized more and often perform well below their abilities. As boys move through school, they outnumber girls four to one in remedial reading classes. Attention deficit disorder and stuttering are essentially boy-only conditions. Despite the current concern about how schools shortchange girls, girls tend to like school more and perform better academically than boys.

There is one area in which parents', peers', and teachers' attitudes about boys' behavior coincide. Boys who engage in cross-gender activities, such as dress-up games and playing with dolls, are firmly criticized. Girls, however, are far less likely to receive criticism from teachers and peers for cross-sex play — building with blocks, say, or playing with trucks. The message for girls is clear: you can do anything. It's also clear for boys: stick to what you know best and leave the nurturing activities to the girls.

Even if parents, teachers, and children themselves suddenly stopped promoting certain types of behavior, another factor would still have a very positive or very negative impact on how children formulate their fatherhood-related images and desires: the model they get from their own fathers.

Canadian fatherhood expert Kerry Daly asked the fathers of young children about where they got their ideas about fatherhood. Some, of course, used their relationship with their own fathers as an example. "I think that much of what I base my parenting practices on are his model," said one young father. "The type of father that he was, I am trying to emulate. He was very solid, always around, and was never not there."

Sadly, this contemporary father is in the minority. Most of the men in Daly's study either did not view their fathers as a model or wanted to do better than they did. "I don't want to be like him as far as fathering goes," one man recalled. "He feels the children are to be seen and not heard. We don't have the same feeling." Another father commented on how things are different for fathers today than they were for his father. "If I could fault my dad in any way, he didn't spend time with us; he was always working. I told him that I regretted that we didn't get to spend enough time together when I was little. He feels bad about that, but I think we have a lot more freedom to spend time with our kids today than maybe our parents did." This father sees society's changing expectations in the light of his own father's circumstances. "And maybe it was the values of society at the time but dad was supposed to work and mom to look after the kids. And that has sort of changed; nowadays, dads are also supposed to participate in raising a kid."

Many fathers in Daly's study adopted a piecemeal approach to defining fathering. Instead of emulating one person, these men tried to assemble a cohesive image from a variety of sources. Here is how one dad expressed this "multiple models" approach: "No, I don't think I try to emulate anybody saying, 'This is a good father, I want to be more like him.' You know, I look at people I know and I say, 'Well, he does that well with his kids,' or 'He handles these sorts of situations well with his kids.' Maybe I'll draw on that and someone else."

As men become fathers, they appear to be struggling to reconcile old images and models of fathering behavior with the new ones that face modern fathers. Even if they choose to emulate their own fathers, the rapid changes in our society make it difficult for current fathers to apply lessons from the past in any simple way. This lack of good role models is yet another barrier to moving men toward greater involvement.

The question, then, is whether children's gender-role stereotypes can be modified. Can children learn that a fashion model or a firefighter can be either a male or a female? Recent research suggests that the answer to these questions is yes. In one study, two groups of children were presented with ten occupations that they would view as typically masculine (dentist, farmer, construction worker, etc.) or feminine (beautician, flight attendant, librarian, etc.). The children in one group were taught that gender is irrelevant and learned two other ways of conceptualizing these jobs — namely, a person's liking of some part of the job (construction workers must like to build things) and the skills needed to learn to do the job (construction workers must learn to drive big machines). The children in the other group participated in a discussion about the role of specific occupations within the community, with no emphasis on reducing gender stereotyping.

Later, when asked who could do various jobs, the children in the group designed to reduce gender stereotypes gave more "Both men and women" responses than the other kids — not only for the occupations involved in the "lessons" but for a range of other occupations as well (for example, police officer, nurse). Children in the control group still said that "girls can't be firefighters."

Unfortunately, this kind of social engineering is a lot harder to accomplish than it might seem. A psychologist colleague overheard the following exchange between her son and a friend, which nicely illustrates this point:

> Son: My mother helps people. She's a doctor.
> Friend: You mean a nurse.
> Son: No. She's not that kind of doctor. She's a psychologist. She's a doctor of psychology.
> Friend: Oh. She's a nurse of psychology.

Still, some parents have taken significant steps to change their lifestyles in order to increase the equality between the sexes. Anthropologist Tom Weisner studied children living in countercultural communes and found that six-year-olds reared by these unconventional parents were more flexible in their views about appropriate occupations for boys and girls than children in more traditional families. The children in communes were more likely to assume that girls could be engineers and firefighters and boys could be librarians or nursery school teachers. More than 70 percent of these children gave non-sex-typed answers, compared to only 40 percent of the children in the conventional group.

Some family lifestyles can make children more rigidly sex-typed. Children reared in devotional communes that strongly emphasize conventional gender typing, for example, tend to see greater distinctions in male and female roles than children in conventionally married families.

If there's one thing that's clear from all of this, it's that gender roles and attitudes can be modified. And while it's going to be very hard to do much to change most of today's fathers, there's plenty we can do to make sure this pattern doesn't repeat itself in the next generation.

7

Socializing Adults:
From Husband to Father

L ARGELY BECAUSE OF the lessons boys and girls learn when
they're young, by the time they marry or begin to form adult relationships of their own, their attitudes about gender and parenting are already firmly in place. After years of training, for example,
women have bought into the dominant view that mothers are biologically predisposed to nurture children. As a result, they have no trouble
seeing themselves as mothers, whether they're married or not. Men,
too, have internalized the myth of the superior mother. But for them,
fatherhood and fathering are inextricably linked with marriage, or at
least with being in a committed relationship.

Not surprisingly, family researchers have discovered in recent years
that men's satisfaction with their marital relationships is a major factor in determining how involved they will be with their children. The
more satisfying men's marriages are, the more involved and happy
they are in their fathering roles, and the more unhappy and volatile
their marriages are, the less involved they become and the lower the
quality of that involvement.

This marital satisfaction/father involvement connection may actually start before men become fathers. Researcher Shirley Feldman and
her colleagues found that expectant fathers whose marriages were
rated as "satisfying" during the third trimester of their wives' pregnancy were subsequently more involved in caregiving and play with

their six-month-old infants. In addition, psychologist Martha Cox and her colleagues have found that the quality of a father's parenting is better when his marriage is better and that a supportive marriage can help to overcome his lack of preparation for parenthood.

Even babies sense when their fathers aren't happy in their marriages. Eleven-month-olds, for example, are less likely to look to their fathers for help in novel situations (such as seeing an unfamiliar person) when their fathers are in distressed marriages. As John Gottman found, men in unsatisfying marriages tend to withdraw from their wives and perhaps from their children. Children whose fathers are unhappy or under stress "act out" more and suffer more from depression than children whose parents are in less stressful marriages. And kids who watch their parents fight are frequently more aggressive, feel more guilty, and tend to be more withdrawn.

Does the quality of a marriage have as much impact on mothers as it does on fathers? Not according to psychologist Jay Belsky and his colleagues, who conducted a series of home observations of mothers and fathers when their infants were one, three, and nine months of age. Other studies confirm Belsky's results. Adolescent fathers, for example, have more positive interactions with their infants in families where there are high levels of mother-father engagement. Mother-child interactions, however, were completely independent of the mother's relationship with the father. Overall, said one group of researchers, the quality of the marriage, whether reported by the husband or the wife, is "the most consistently powerful predictor of paternal involvement and satisfaction."

Given the connection between marital satisfaction and paternal involvement, it shouldn't come as a surprise that fathers who are in supportive and satisfying marriages bond more securely with their infants and toddlers. What is somewhat surprising, though, is the way mothers benefit from the additional support their happy husbands provide them. Studies in both the United States and Japan have found that the more emotionally supportive a father is, the more competent a caregiver his wife is and the better her relationship with their children.

Even in the happiest relationships, there's little argument that fathers aren't always as involved as they could and should be. Some fathers, of course, have no desire to be involved. Most, however, do. But the mixed messages that fathers get from the media and from their employers (which we'll discuss in detail in the following chapter), and the lack of support they get from society in general, make it especially difficult for fathers to do anything to substantially change their lives. What holds fathers back most from getting involved is their partners, many of whom are reluctant to give up their control of an area in which they've been dominant: the caregiving role, which historically and culturally has been central to women's identity.

In truth, women have been children's primary nurturers for a relatively short period of time. Before the Industrial Revolution, when they left their wives and the family farm to work in cities and factories, men were the central figures in their children's lives. But rather than consider the historical precedent for men's involvement, too many people — especially women — have seized on the past two centuries and insist not only that women naturally do a better job of raising children, but that they don't even need men to help out. A 1994 National Opinion Survey confirmed this view. In response to the question "Can one parent bring up a child as well as two parents together?" 50 percent of women said yes. In contrast, men disagreed by more than a two-to-one margin.

These conflicting messages about how involved to be ("You need to take a more active role around the house" versus "I don't really need your help anyway") ultimately reinforce fathers' negative self-image and lack of confidence in their parenting skills and abilities. Whether they pull back by themselves or they are made to feel unwelcome in their own homes, the result is the same: far too many men are unable to participate as actively as they would like in raising their children.

Men do, of course, bear some of the responsibility for this. They could, for example, not hand over their crying babies to their wives; they could put in a little extra time learning how to parent the old-fashioned way: on-the-job training. Still, most researchers who have studied men's and women's roles and responsibilities in the family agree that mothers play a "gatekeeping" role, either supporting or inhibiting fathers' involvement with their infants. Fathers, they say, are precisely as involved at home as their wives will let them be.

Maternal gatekeeping comes in a variety of forms. To start with, many women view men as inherently incompetent when it comes to parenting or caregiving. Others resent men's intrusion on the traditional feminine turf of mothering and restrict men's access. However it happens, mothers have great influence on the type of relationship a father can have with his children.

Among the factors that most influence mothers' gatekeeping behavior — and which in turn most influence fathers' levels of involvement — are their attitudes about the father's and their own caregiving roles. Psychologists Ashley Beitel and Ross Parke found in 1998 that men whose partners believe that women are innately superior to men in their caregiving abilities and who do not value their husbands' involvement are, not surprisingly, less involved with their infants than men whose partners had more supportive attitudes. Mothers who view their male partners as competent actually boost these men's competence by encouraging them to take on more responsibility and practice their caregiving skills. At the same time, the more competent a father is, the more involved he tends to be and the more his wife will think he's competent. As it turns out, mothers' attitudes about fathers' competence are important in predicting fathers' involvement with their children — even after taking into account fathers' own attitudes.

If fathers in intact families sometimes find it hard to be as involved with their children as they would prefer, for divorced fathers it's even harder. Sociologists Graham Spanier and Linda Thompson found that only about a third of divorced fathers saw their children at least once a week — a figure that decreased steadily with time. Two years after divorce, fewer than 20 percent of fathers had weekly contact with their offspring, and another 20 percent saw them less than that. In a similar study, the demographers Judith Seltzer and Suzanne Bianchi found that 37 percent of divorced fathers saw their children once a month, and 35 percent never saw them at all. Interestingly, studies of mothers who don't have custody of their children show a slightly different trend: only 19 percent of noncustodial mothers don't see their children at all, and 46 percent have at least monthly contact.

One of the root causes for this steady decline in divorced fathers' contact with their children is societal: we define women as mothers even when they no longer live with their children, but when men stop living with their wives and children, "they no longer see themselves (or are seen by their former wives) as full-fledged fathers. It is as if their license for parenthood were revoked when their marriage ended," write sociologists Frank Furstenberg and Andrew Cherlin. So it is no wonder that our legal system awards mothers sole custody of the children 82 percent of the time, compared to about 11 percent for fathers (only 7 percent of fathers have some form of shared custody).

There are, of course, other factors that contribute to fathers' "retreat from parenthood": geography, economics, and remarriage are among the leaders. Generally, the farther a man's children live from him, the harder it is to maintain contact and the less likely it is that he will visit regularly. When divorced parents remarry, mother-child bonds tend to be strengthened while father-child ties are strained (second wives are less likely to want to raise someone else's kids than second husbands). Actually, it doesn't seem to matter much which biological parent remarries. Either way, fathers decrease contact with their biological children.

But as in intact families, one of the most important factors in determining and setting the tone for divorced fathers' involvement with their children is maternal gatekeeping. As many as half the mothers with custody have refused to permit their ex-husbands to see the children at least once — and the children's health, safety, or wishes had nothing to do with the refusal. Some of these single mothers claim they are trying to "protect" their children from supposedly inept or incompetent former husbands or boyfriends; others want to punish their former partners; some are using access to children as a way of extracting support payments; and still others view the father's involvement as nothing more than "bothersome, empty rituals," say Judith Wallerstein and Joan Berlin Kelly, authors of *Surviving the Breakup*. It's no wonder, then, that many fathers lose contact with their children after divorce.

If women assume that men are incompetent and put up barriers to their involvement, what happens if men improve their skills? To find out, researchers Jane Dickie and Sharon Gerber studied a group of couples with infants between four and twelve months old. Half of the couples attended eight classes that taught them how to interpret and respond to their infants' signals. The other half received no training at all. After the classes were over, Dickie and Gerber observed all the couples in their homes as they interacted with their babies.

To start with, the "trained" parents — of both genders — had a higher opinion of their spouses' competence than the untrained parents did of their spouses. Trained fathers touched, held, and looked at their infants more, and they were more likely to smile and talk in response to the babies' behavior. The babies seemed to appreciate their newly trained parents' skills too: babies with trained fathers tried to play with their dads more than those with untrained fathers.

For a small but growing number of fathers, parenting classes are just the beginning: they're taking their commitment to their families far beyond the traditional, assuming an equal role with mothers at home. Others are reversing roles and becoming full-time caregivers. These pioneers serve as a valuable illustration of at least one way that men and women can work together to help fathers break through the "glass wall" that keeps them from achieving their full potential outside the workplace.

Here's how *Boston Globe* reporter Barbara Meltz described Robert D., one of about two million fathers who stay at home to look after their children while their partners work. "For almost an hour, / month old Sam D. has played happily by himself in his infant walker. Now he's fussing. Robert D. scoops up his son onto his lap which works for about three seconds. In quick succession, Dad D. tosses Sam in the air, slings him over his shoulder and finally paces with him in his arms. His next trick is lunch. That's magic."

Kyle Pruett, the author of *The Nurturing Father,* has identified no negative effects of having the father as the primary caregiver. In fact, Pruett found that infants reared primarily by their fathers scored high on tests of problem-solving, social, and personal skills. When he followed up with these children two and four years later, he found that they were generally more curious than children raised primarily by their mothers, and he attributed much of the difference to fathers'

more robust, stimulating parenting style. The children were also significantly more flexible. "They learn that love, discipline, just about
everything comes in several flavors. They see there isn't just one way
to do something." Their adaptability makes them better equipped to
deal with disappointment and frustration in social and academic
situations.

Norma Radin, an expert on families in which the father is the primary caretaker, has seen similar results. Children whose fathers stay
at home, Radin found, have higher levels of what she calls "internal
control" — a belief in their own ability to control their fate — than
children in more traditional family arrangements. She speculates that
since at-home fathers are, almost by definition, "take charge" types,
they provide very positive models of self-determination for their
children.

Perhaps the biggest benefit of all is the improvement in fathers' relationships with their children. Primary-caretaker fathers often report
understanding their children better and taking more pleasure in them.
According to Loyola University researcher Robert Frank, reverse-
role fathers spend more than twice as much time nurturing their
children — playing with, comforting, and talking to them — than
traditional working fathers. (In contrast, stay-at-home mothers spend
about the same amount of time nurturing their children as working
mothers.) Consequently, kids with stay-at-home dads seek out their
fathers in times of distress three times more often than children in traditional families.

At-home fathers also tend to be much less rigid in their attitudes
about men's natural parenting abilities. Australian researcher Graeme
Russell has found that about 80 percent of fathers and 90 percent of
mothers in role-sharing families believe that fathers are capable caregivers (although some still thought that mothers were better suited to
the task). In traditional families, though, only 49 percent of fathers
and 65 percent of mothers felt that men were capable of taking care of
children.

Children in role-sharing families are also a lot less likely to pigeon-
hole their parents according to stereotypical gender roles. When researcher Norma Radin asked preschoolers, "Who does what around the
house?," the children in nontraditional families gave less-stereotyped

answers (mom wasn't viewed as the only one to use the vacuum cleaner or dishwasher, for example). This open-mindedness about gender roles lasts a long time. Adolescents who grew up with dad as the primary caregiver are consistently more accepting of nontraditional employment arrangements. They prefer dual-earner families over single-earner ones, and they're also a lot more supportive of parents who share childcare than of those who don't.

Fathers who share more equally in the home reap other benefits as well. Many are genuinely relieved to be out of the business fast track. "I enjoy the freedom from the routine pressures and hassles of work," said one father in Graeme Russell's study. Other research indicates that role sharing fathers tend to be more open and emotionally expressive.

Women, too, benefit from fathers' increased presence in the home. Mothers with stay-at-home husbands have a greater chance to pursue their own careers and, consequently, report increased self-esteem and greater independence. As one mother said, "After going back to work, I started to value myself more. . . . I have also become more pleasant."

But men who buck social norms in American culture face some serious consequences. "They get teased by the men they know, shunned by mothers at the playground and turned into a symbol, even when they don't want to be," says Scott Coltrane. Others get bored, miss the contact with other adults, and regret the loss of status that comes with not holding a regular job. As one dad observed, "I had a lot of difficulty adjusting to the idea of not having a job. I didn't realize how important that was to me."

There are also some drawbacks for mothers. Some feel jealous, guilty, and resentful of the special relationship that their husbands develop with their children. "It still stings when the kids go to their dad when they're hurt or needy," lamented one mother — and she's not alone. "Even though a wife may be comfortable sharing what has traditionally been a mother's role," says Kyle Pruett, "she may feel pressure from friends, family and society that makes her wonder, Am I less of a mother? Am I a bad mother?"

For many trend-bucking families, these drawbacks are so significant that they end up outweighing the benefits. Following up with his role-reversal families after two years, Graeme Russell found that only about one-quarter of the families still maintained their nontraditional ways. This telling statistic, researchers say, is a clear affirmation of the power of our attitudes about gender roles, especially in the area of childcare. These cultural attitudes are extremely difficult to change, but unless we do — and unless men, women, employers, and policy makers can come together to support men's changing roles — we'll continue to be locked into traditional roles that just don't work.

8

The Workplace

W E'RE ALL FAMILIAR with the "glass ceiling" that women often confront as they pursue advancement in the business world, but they are not the only ones whose goals and dreams are hindered by subtle, nearly invisible barriers. Millions of men who have tried to challenge society's deep-seated belief that their place is at the office, that work-versus-family concerns are "women's issues," and who have tried to make family a priority also find themselves trapped.

Just as women have struggled for decades to get work-family conflicts out in the open, a growing number of frustrated fathers have recently taken up the cause. As a result, a few small cracks have appeared in the barriers that keep men from their families. Recently, for example, the actor Mandy Patinkin made a choice that would have been unthinkable even five years ago: he gave up the work he loved in order to spend more time with his family. "I will not lose my family for this job," he said. And former Secretary of Labor Robert Reich recently gave up "the best job I've ever had and probably ever will" to spend more time with his family and to pursue the elusive solution to the work-family dilemma.

Of course, television actors and cabinet secretaries aren't the only ones who are reexamining their commitments and priorities, nor are they the only ones who are unhappy devoting only leftover time to their children. In fact, the majority of men fighting to make the workplace more family friendly for fathers are people you've never heard of. Here's how a U.S. Postal Service worker, for example, reacted when he was told he'd have to work nights: "I told them I could not work nights because I had a ten year old son and I am a single parent. I cannot afford child care on one income, plus I would not be able to be a parent for my son. Being with my son two days a week is not a good way to be a parent."

Part of the reason work-family concerns have been seen as a women's issue is that our society tends to view the workplace as "the arena in which men struggle to establish their identity and by which they measure their success and failure." In contrast, we see the home as "the place where 'man the worker' returns daily to heal the wounds received on the job." James Levine, director of the Fatherhood Project at the Families and Work Institute, recently asked a group of workers at a health and eye care company to indicate "what percentage of working mothers and fathers experience a significant amount of conflict between work and family life." These workers put the figure at 80 percent for women and from zero to 20 percent for men. According to Levine, these views reflect the inaccurate but "prevailing assumption that men do not feel that tug-of-war between their 'job selves' and their 'parent selves.' "

No matter how prevalent these assumptions are, however, they don't have much to do with reality. In 1993 the Families and Work Institute conducted a nationwide study of the changing workplace. They found that in dual-career families, nearly 61 percent of families reported either "some" or "a lot" of work-family conflicts. Fathers and mothers reported the same level of concern about balancing work and family. And even in the more traditional, mom-stays-home-while-dad-goes-to-work families, 56 percent of fathers said they experienced some or a lot of conflict.

"You work longer hours because of the fear that you're not providing enough," said one father. "Then there's the guilt that you're not spending enough time with your family. It goes around and around. You work harder for stability and it gives you less stability than you think." Other dads agreed: "There's always conflict. . . . I often feel guilty because I probably missed a Boy Scout meeting or whatever." And: "At the end of the day I get half an hour with them before they go to bed. . . . I love what I do but if I'm going to make any more money it will be at the same pace. There's no getting around that in this day and age."

Besides just complaining about work-family conflicts, men are beginning to make changes at the office that may ultimately help them achieve a more satisfying family life. In a 1995 poll of eighteen thousand DuPont employees, men and women, workers not only worried about balancing work and family; many declined transfers, promotions, and overtime work because of family obligations and responsibilities. Among managers and professional-level employees, 47 percent of women and 41 percent of men refused to relocate, and 7 percent of women and 11 percent of men turned down promotions.

Again, white-collar yuppies aren't the only ones willing to put their careers on the line for their families. A growing number of blue-collar workers, males as well as females, also refuse overtime, promotions, and night-shift reassignments that might interfere with their family life. "This is a message we're hearing from employees at lots of companies. Men and women are consciously making these trade-offs and a big part of it is concern for their families," said Catherine Popper, managing director of the company that conducted the DuPont survey.

So do companies really care about families? Yes and no. In 1995, only 36 percent of the employees at Eli Lilly, a progressive, family-friendly company, agreed that it was possible to advance on the job while still devoting adequate time to family and children. "Today in corridors of business and elsewhere, families are getting more lip service than ever. Being on the right side of work and family issues — having the proper programs, letting mom or dad slip out to watch a t-ball game — is very politically correct," writes Betsy Morris in *Fortune*. "But corporate America harbors a dirty secret. People in human resources know it. So do a lot of CEO's, although they don't dare discuss it. Families are no longer a big plus for a corporation; they are a big problem. It's fine to have the kids' pictures on your desk — just don't let them cut into your billable hours." A 1993 study by management professors Joy Schneer and Frieda Reitman further illustrated corporate America's subtle distaste for families. Schneer and Reitman interviewed 236 male managers, all with MBAs from well-known East

Coast universities, and found that if the manager's wife worked —
which, as research has shown, leads to increased family time for men
— he suffered greatly in terms of salary and promotions. In that year,
managers whose wives worked made a very respectable $95,067 a year.
But if their wives stayed home, the men earned an average of $125,120
— what amounts to a $30,000 bonus for spending less time with the
family.

Men whose wives worked also found themselves butting their heads
against the same glass ceiling that has confined their female colleagues: the men were promoted to top management positions 10 percent less often than their colleagues whose wives stayed home. Betsy
Morris suggests that corporate employee manuals should be revised to
include the following warning: "Ambitious beware. If you want to
have children, proceed at your own risk. You must be very talented or
on very solid ground to overcome the damage a family can do to your
career."

Not surprisingly, many men feel that they need to keep secret their
desires to spend more time with their families. A court reporter recently had a particularly telling experience. "Both opposing male attorneys asked her separately if she could come up with an excuse why
she couldn't stay after 5 P.M. They both had to leave to pick up their
kids, but were too afraid of losing face with their opponent to make
the request themselves." This need to save face has led to what is essentially a conspiracy of silence, or what James Levine calls "the invisible
dilemma of Daddy Stress," where fathers feel the tension created by
the competing demands of home and work but don't want to tell
anyone about it — especially their male work colleagues or super-
visors. "I find guys doing all kinds of strange things to avoid publicly
acknowledging that they have parental responsibility," says Levine.
"They'll sneak out to pick up their kids at daycare, or wait just a few
minutes after their boss leaves to go themselves. People need to break
this pattern."

For the average father, breaking this pattern is a lot harder than it
sounds. As more and more companies enter the global marketplace,
they're finding that they can no longer close their doors at 5 P.M. Instead, they're running twenty-four hours a day, meaning that only a

third of employees can work the more desirable day shift. The rest are stuck working nights or evenings or, even worse, in rotating shifts that change every week or month — all schedules that drastically cut into the time workers can spend with their families. In one company, Amerco, nearly half the employees work rotating shifts. As one employee says, "In all this talk about family-friendly policies, we are the forgotten people." In addition, factory workers are putting in more hours on the job than ever before, according to the U.S. Bureau of Labor Statistics. In 1994 these workers averaged four hours and forty-two minutes of overtime each week — the most in the thirty-eight years that the agency has tracked overtime hours.

In the face of all this, men continue to push their employers, albeit gently, to make the workplace more father friendly. A small number of companies have responded, offering men paternity leave, flextime, job sharing, or telecommuting. Progressive employee policies make for good news stories, and the companies offering them are frequently written up in such books as *The 100 Best Companies to Work For in America,* by Robert Levering and Milton Moskowitz. But how prevalent are these changes?

Despite the decades-long debate on "family values" and the recent passage of the Family and Medical Leave Act, only about 10 percent of U.S. worksites and slightly fewer than half of employed fathers are covered. Under the act, eligible employees can take up to twelve weeks of unpaid leave per year after the birth or adoption of a child or for any other personal or family medical problem.

Offering paternity leave is only half the battle, however. The real problem is getting men to actually take it. The Commission on Family and Medical Leave found that men are far less likely than women to avail themselves of most types of family leave. And when it comes to caring for a newborn, or an adopted or a foster child, men are nearly seven times more likely to need, but not take, family leave. Those men who do buck these trends take far less time off than women do.

One reason for men's rather anemic participation in family leave is that in most cases it isn't paid time off. Only 1 percent of fathers in either the public or the private sector are eligible for at least some paid paternity leave. (For mothers the rates aren't a lot better: 3 percent in the private sector and 1 percent in the public sector.) And since the average working woman still makes less than the average working man, many families conclude that they can better survive the loss of the woman's salary.

"The primary reason people were not taking advantage of the [Family and Medical Leave] Act was because they could not afford to," says Terry Neese, a member of the U.S. Commission on Leave. He may be right. According to a survey of 1,206 worksites by the University of Michigan, of those who were aware of their options and who needed to take time off, 64 percent chose not to take it because they could not afford to go three months without a paycheck.

Financial pressures aren't the only consideration, however. A lot of men who might otherwise be interested in breaking through the glass wall that separates them from their families are hindered by the fear that getting on the "daddy track" will hurt their careers. As one young father who elected not to take advantage of his law firm's family leave plan put it, "I wanted to take the leave, but I knew I'd never make partner if I did. All the male associates knew it would be career suicide." The late Malcolm Forbes had this to say about the Paternal Leave and Disability Act of 1985: "New daddies need paternity leave like they need a hole in the head."

In 1986, when Catalyst, a not-for-profit research and advisory group in New York, asked human resources directors and CEOs at fifteen hundred large corporations how much time would be reasonable for men to take as paternity leave, it found that most agreed with Forbes: 63 percent said "none." Even at companies that offered it, 41 percent said no amount of paternity leave was reasonable. Ten years later, nothing had changed. "There's been a lot more discussion about family leave recently, especially since the Family Leave Act was passed," says Marcia Brumit Kropf, Catalyst's research group leader. "But we've found that there hasn't been any significant change in most employers' acceptance of men actually taking the leave." As if to prove the point, when Houston Oilers football player David Williams missed one game during the 1993 season so he could be with his wife while she delivered their baby, he was fined $125,000.

*   *   *

At least some of the responsibility for creating the fear of taking a leave rests with the prevailing corporate view that men who want to spend time with their families are somehow less serious and less devoted than those who don't take advantage of existing family-oriented programs. Here's how a manager at one of America's most family-friendly companies described dealing with an employee who applied for paternity leave. "I took him aside and said, as your boss I have to grant you this leave. But as your friend, I'm advising you not to request it. Just take vacation time if you want to be with your family. Applying for paternity leave will send the wrong message around here about your commitment to work."

Some companies don't even let their employees know they're eligible to take paternity leave. A 1996 report from a bipartisan family-leave commission reported that only 58 percent of covered employees had heard of the Family and Medical Leave Act. It's pretty hard to exercise your options when you don't know what they are, and for many employers, that seems to be just fine.

And even if they do tell their employees that leave is available, many employers aren't interested in going along with the program. Here's how Arlie Hochschild, author of *The Time Bind,* described a typical case:

> One worker found himself in a fierce struggle with his boss over his request for a single week of paternity leave.
> "Call it vacation," his boss suggested.
> "I'd like it in addition to vacation," the worker said. "Can you deduct it from my pay?"
> "Take it for free then," his boss replied, irritated.
> "I'm not asking for something free," came the response.
> "Well I can't give you paternity leave. It's too much paperwork. Why don't you just take it unofficially?"

In an even more glaring example, the in-house legal counsel for a regional stock exchange described a conversation he had in 1998 with one of his division managers. "He actually asked me whether there was any way he could legally fire a male employee for taking time off under the Act," he said. Employers aren't the only ones who make it hard for men to take advantage of family leave. Co-workers often put pressure on each other not to leave them with the extra burden. As one man put it, "It's great that Harry wants to be with his wife and baby, but it means more work for the rest of us. I've got a family too, and it just isn't fair to the rest of us who are left to pick up the slack." Taunts by fellow workers, like "Mr. Mom" and "Baby-sitter," reflect the attitude that taking paternity leave is not something a "real man" would do. For women, sure, but not for men.

Fathers who take paternity leave frequently have to deal with male co-workers' suspicions that the time off is not much more than a vacation. Here's what one man said after returning to work from a two-week leave: "To the women in the office, I was a great hero. Sam cooks! Sam does laundry! Sam takes paternity leave! But most of the guys I'm not close to ignored you. They all knew, but they acted as if they weren't supposed to know. They were thinking, 'Where were you, on vacation?' My close friends teased me. 'It must have been fun, what did you do? Did you change diapers? Come on, it must have been a great time. You just sat around and watched TV.' They thought I was using this time as an excuse to get away."

Recently, Joseph Pleck, a close observer of shifting policies for men, found that despite all these societal and workplace obstacles, the percentage of family-leave-taking fathers was growing. Ten percent of the employees who take family leave at IBM, for example, are men — a small but significant increase over just five years ago. And in a study in four states in which laws granting parental leave have recently been passed, 75 percent of fathers took off some time after the birth of a child — a modest but clear 5 percent increase from pre-statute levels. Men took off an average of 4 days after the birth of a baby.

In another study, Pleck interviewed 142 fathers of preschool children and found that 87 percent had taken some time off when their infant was born — an average of 5.3 days. "An allotted span of time for a young father to be around the house and enjoy the first weeks of his son's or daughter's life is beginning to be thought of less as an eccentricity, and more as a personal necessity," Maureen Green notes in *Fathering*. But neither the men in the four-state study nor those in Pleck's study referred to the time they took off to be with their newborns as "paternity leave." In fact, about half of the leave was taken as vacation or sick days.

Interestingly, the more days that fathers took off from work, the higher the level of involvement in childcare. "Although these associations do not necessarily show that taking time off from work at birth causes higher levels of later paternal involvement, they do indicate that leave taking is consistent with a broader pattern of greater paternal involvement," says Pleck.

Whatever it's called and however long it lasts, paternity leave has some significant and very positive results. "Thanks to the Family and Medical Leave Act of 1993 here I am changing my daughter's diapers and enjoying her first gurgles and giggles," says Tom McMakin, a writer who lives in Montana. "Because of this legislation my life is richer. . . . Because of my time home with Valerie, I'm also much more understanding of children and parents. I rush to help a mom with a stubborn car door or a dad whose youngest is on the verge of straying. I smile at mischievous kids, happy to see them speeding off in this direction or that, ruining their parents' best-laid plans."

The positive impact on companies of encouraging family leave are equally impressive. In 1991, for example, the Los Angeles Department of Water and Power, 78 percent of whose employees are men, started a comprehensive fathering program called Doting Dads. The program, highly publicized internally, includes a four-month paternity leave plan, a father mentorship program, a childcare referral service, even breast-feeding classes for both spouses. Since launching Doting Dads, L.A. Water and Power noticed a significant reduction in turnover and absenteeism. Executives at IBM, which also encourages use of its family leave plan, reported that any costs incurred to keep a job open for a man on leave or to redistribute his workload while he's gone are more than made up for in improved morale and increased productivity.

Although paternity leave is one of the most widely recognized father-friendly workplace policies, it is not the only one that counts. "It is what most people think of, in part because the media has so consistently made paternity leave the focus of any discussion of fathers and the changing workplace," notes James Levine. "It is as if there is a tele-photo lens that automatically goes from its widest angle to its narrow-est, without anybody noticing." As Levine goes on to say, new fathers are new fathers for only a short time, and children need their fathers as much when they're older as they do when they're infants. Recent re-search has debunked the popular notion that there are prescribed critical periods for social and cognitive development, usually early in life. Current theories suggest that dads and moms play a continuing and influential role in shaping their children's development through-out childhood.

But thanks to ignorant and insensitive employers, most men aren't able to fully realize their potential influence. "My husband missed our children's birthdays! He missed their games!" lamented one mother. "He missed father-daughter banquets! Didn't the company get enough of his time? Because we saw nothing of him!" Many fathers agreed. "I don't want to be like my dad, who worked his way through my child-hood," said one. "I want to be a part of my child's growing up. And companies ought to recognize that!" No video camera can ever make up — to either the child or the father — for a father's absence at his son's first violin recital or his daughter's first soccer game.

In addition, policies that permit fathers to care for a sick child can no longer be considered extras or frills; from the point of view of the child, the father, or the mother, they are neither. Parents have to deal with a sick child between six and nine times a year, with illnesses last-ing from a day to a week, according to the American Medical Associa-tion. The bottom line is that successful fathering requires more than a few days of paternity leave.

Flextime and job sharing are options that can allow men more time with their families. A father who can start his workday a few hours later can get his children ready for school. Or if he goes in a few hours early, he can spend some of the afternoon with his kids. "Flexible use of time is the single most important element in creating a workplace that is friendly to fathers, mothers and all employees regardless of parental status. This does not mean asking employees to work less, but giving them more control over when and where they get their jobs done," writes James Levine.

It's important to understand that there are various types of flex-time. Changing from a 9 to 5 schedule to 7 to 3 is perhaps the most common, and allows working parents to pick up their children after school. But it's still kind of rigid. Another option (and one that may offer more benefits to both individuals and companies by allowing workers greater control) is to give employees more day-to-day sched-uling flexibility—as long as they're in the office during certain "core" hours, say 11 A.M. to 2 P.M.

Men are increasingly clamoring for this kind of flexibility. One study, for example, found that 56 percent of men — up from 37 per-cent five years earlier — wanted flextime. In the same year, the Ameri-can Management Association polled five thousand workers and found that flexibility in scheduling their time was the top issue for an as-tounding 87 percent of them. And in its National Study of the Chang-ing Workplace, the Families and Work Institute found that having flexible work hours was a higher priority even than reducing total work time.

Recent as well as earlier evidence, such as studies conducted at Volvo plants in Sweden, at Hewlett-Packard in the United States, and of U.S. government workers indicates that flexible hours are economi-cally feasible and may have positive benefits for both families and em-ployers. A British study of male scientific workers found that flextime fathers spent more time in socializing and caring for their children when their wives were also employed. In the United States the results were similar. Government workers in Washington, D.C., increased their family time by more than half an hour a day after the introduc-tion of a flextime option. (Workers who did not participate in the pro-gram showed no change.) Most of this newfound time was spent with children.

In other studies, however, parents with flexible schedules don't spend any more time with their children than their co-workers with regular hours, and that shouldn't come as much of a surprise: "Free time won't and can't be used by all men or women to attend to their children; there is shopping, community and church work, bowling, and so forth," Levine writes. "In many cases, free time will mean a sec-ond job in order to meet family expenses in an inflationary economy.

What's important here, however, is not only the possibility for new relationships, but recognition of the fact that men too have a family
stake in job restructuring." Although the jury is still out on flextime's
value for fathers and families, it is still a growing trend in the United
States. Between 1990 and 1995, the percentage of companies offering
flexible hours rose from 54 percent to 67 percent.

Resistance to flextime in the workplace is often based on the erro-
neous assumption that it is a concession to families at the expense of
the company's goals. In the DuPont study cited earlier, Elizabeth Sheley found that workers who were using or were aware of the flextime
program were the most committed workers and the least likely to suffer burnout. At Hewlett-Packard, 12 percent of employees took advantage of flextime, and again the outcome for the company was positive:
lower absenteeism and higher productivity. In short, flexible scheduling is not just good family policy but apparently good business policy
too. Far too often, though, benefits such as flextime are available only
on paper, as part of PR campaigns that allow a company to appear
family-friendly.

Not surprisingly, flextime, like paternity leave, is drastically under-
utilized. In a 1990 study of Fortune 500 companies, for example, 45
percent of the top corporations offered flextime but only 10 percent of
eligible employees used it. This rate was even lower for men, who shy
away from this family-friendly policy for fear that their employers will
question their loyalty, commitment, and ambition.

Fathers aren't the only ones who don't use flextime as often as they
should. Minorities, particularly Latinos, Native Americans, and Asian
Americans, are more than twice as likely to be unaware of the availability of flexible work arrangements — and, consequently, not utilize
them — as white or black employees.

If persuading men to take paternity leave or work a flexible schedule is
difficult, getting them even to consider working part time is nearly
impossible. It's also pretty hard to get women to consider it. In one
study, fewer than 20 percent of the women and 2 percent of the men
who claimed to be interested in part-time work actually made the
change. And in *Fortune* magazine's 1990 study of manufacturing

firms, although 88 percent informally offered employees the chance to do part-time work, only 3 to 5 percent of them switched. Clearly, having one parent working part time is not an option every family can afford.

For those who do cut back their hours, there are other fears. First, as with paternity leave and flextime, many workers (this time including women) worry that at best their bosses will interpret a limited schedule as limited commitment to the job and at worst that they'll be passed over for promotion. Remember the infamous "mommy track" of the late 1980s, which was proposed for women who wanted to move at a slower pace? Although Felice Schwartz, the author who coined the phrase, hoped that it would allow women more time with their families, it quickly became synonymous with lack of ambition. The "mommy track," it turned out, was really a dead-end road. Second, for too many people, part-time work — especially in a job without a clearly defined structure — often turned into full time work at part time pay. "The only way to keep a part-time schedule without violating the unspoken rules of the workplace was, in effect, to work full time," writes Arlie Hochschild.

Job sharing offers another version of part-time work, in which two part-time employees share a single job. In some cases the employees are simply colleagues. In other cases, particularly in academia, they are married to each other.

In Norway, the researcher Erik Gronseth found that couples who either shared a single job or both worked part time had tried these nontraditional arrangements out of a desire to improve their relationships with their children. In the families in Gronseth's study, mother and father shared equally in childcare but the wife still did most of the housework. Many aspects of family life improved as a result of these shifts in work and childcare responsibilities. Fathers reported that they had "better and more open contact" with their children, felt closer to them, and understood them better. Mothers benefited too, and enjoyed their children more because of their reprieve from full-time caregiving. Nearly everyone in the study thought that "the children are the ones whose interests are best served by the work-sharing pattern." Marital relationships of these work-sharing couples improved as well.

Couples reported fewer conflicts, improved solidarity, and more mutual understanding. This effect may have been good for the children too, of course, since the way parents feel about each other can influence their relationships with the children. This way of organizing work and family life is likely to remain rare, but its advantages for both parents and children may make it attractive to more couples in the future, especially during the years when their children are young.

A four-day work week could also be used to help men break through their glass wall. The researcher David Maklan found that men who worked four ten-hour days a week devoted nearly four more hours a week to childcare than men who worked five eight-hour days. There were, however, no differences in the amount of time they spent on housework. A father who takes on a larger share of childcare tasks will undoubtedly improve his relationship with his children and may also, by relieving the mother of some of those tasks, make her relationship with the children more enjoyable too.

Of all the workplace innovations that could help fathers reconnect with their families, telecommuting may be the most practical. Ten years ago, fewer than 1 million people worked from home at least eight hours a week during normal business hours. By 1996 there were 8.7 million. By the end of the century there will be 11 million telecommuters, and by 2005 that figure will exceed 17 million, estimates Charles Grantham, CEO of the Institute for the Study of Distributed Work.

Originally designed to accommodate the family needs of employees, telecommuting has become the darling of some of America's largest and best-known corporations, including IBM, Aetna, American Express, JC Penney, Pacific Bell, and Apple Computer. As the cost of office space rises and the cost of telecommunication equipment falls, more and more companies are finding that they can save money by having their employees work elsewhere at least some of the time. There are other benefits as well. Employees who telecommute are more productive and get more and faster promotions than their office-bound co-workers.

Although many work-family experts support the "virtual office" as part of a package of family-friendly work policies, telecommuting is far from a panacea for fathers and families. In the eyes of some critics, telecommuting has the potential to become "a cyberspace sweat shop that blurs the boundaries between work and home life." IBM account representative Jeffrey Hill and psychologists Alan Hawkins and Brent Miller recently studied the perceptions of 246 IBM employees, some of whom were teleworkers and others who were scheduled to become teleworkers but still worked in a traditional office. Despite optimistic predictions, teleworkers were not any more likely to report that they had sufficient time for family life than office workers. One teleworker said, "This has been a definite plus for me and my family. There is a better balance and more flexibility," while others commented, "I tend to work more hours instead of taking time to enjoy the family," and "It is as hard or harder to balance home and work." And another lamented, "Even vacation time blends into work time unless I go somewhere."

Overall, the majority of teleworkers in the IBM study reported having a "difficult" or "very difficult" time balancing work and family. One group of teleworkers who seemed to benefit most were parents with preschoolers. As the authors of the IBM study noted, this "is not surprising in view of the increasing number of dual-earner couples with young children for whom the flexibility of mobile telework provides new ways to meet the difficult challenge of providing quality child care." As one satisfied teleworker said, "I can take care of the sick child and get my work done. A win-win situation." Another noted that "I can easily start work early and take a few minutes to drive my child to school."

Clearly, telecommuting isn't for every father. But in the struggle to give men more time with their families, every hour is important. And telecommuting certainly gives men the power to spend less of their day at work (or getting there and back) and more at home.

Another way companies can help fathers (and mothers) spend more time with their children is to provide on-site daycare, an option that is usually offered only by fairly large employers. The federal government provides daycare at many offices and so do such private employers as Ben & Jerry's Homemade and John Hancock. One Alabama construction company even designed mobile childcare facilities so workers could bring their children to construction sites with them. And, as is the case with other father-friendly workplace policies, providing on-site daycare offers many benefits to fathers, children, and employers themselves.

In 1994, the daycare giant Kindercare surveyed fathers with children in work-site childcare programs and found some very positive effects on the men's job performance. Sixty-eight percent of the men reported an increase in job productivity, and 73 percent cited improvements in their ability to concentrate at work. Seventy-four percent said they were less anxious about their children as a result of being close to them while at work. Fathers often visit at lunchtime for half an hour two or three times a week, which increases the time they get to spend with their kids by approximately fifty hours a year. That's not even counting commuting time.

Clearly, the glass wall that fathers face in the workplace makes it extremely difficult for them to "have it all" — a fulfilling family life and a productive career at the same time. But it can happen. The state attorney general's office in Bismarck, North Dakota, for example, seems to offer its employees a kind of work-family utopia. According to one employee, "Most of the workers go home at noon — they get in their cars and drive home and have lunch with their kids." And they don't have to hide behind non-family-related reasons, either. "If you look at the computer bulletin board [where the attorneys sign out when leaving the office] you'll see people have down things like 'car pool.' They leave at 3 P.M. to pick up their kids from school and take them home. The building generally empties out at 5. The men are eligible for the same family leave as the women and they take it. They take flextime as much as the women. There's total acceptance of the fact that you'll take time off to go to your child's school conference. It's not free — they expect you to make it up — but you can openly say where you're going."

Unfortunately, cases like this are few and far between, and work-family issues are still nearly universally considered women's issues. This can change, though, if we're willing to make the effort. First, we must dispel the notion that men spend less time with their children because they're less interested in them. That argument is far too simplistic and overlooks the other factors at work here, not the least of which are the social and economic pressures that force men into the workplace, leaving them little time for anything else. Just as liberals and conservatives alike have come to appreciate the role that socioeconomic pressures play in crime and drug addiction, we need to see that identical pressures are at least partly responsible for fathers' perceived indifference toward their children. Second, we must also recognize that men's and women's glass barriers are inextricably related. As Karen DeCrow, a former president of the National Organization for Women (NOW) has said, "Until men are valued as parents, the burden of child rearing will fall primarily to women and frustrate their efforts to gain equality in the workplace."

We've removed a good deal of women's glass ceiling, but progress in allowing men to become equal participants in the family has been virtually nonexistent. The remaining barriers affecting women can be removed legislatively, but eliminating most of the impediments faced by family-oriented men can be achieved only through individual and collective effort. We will have to part with our cherished stereotypes about men — as we have with women — and their roles in the family and the workplace. And we'll have to work together to create an environment in which men can openly say what women — and some men — have said for years: our families and our children are important, for many of us even more important than our jobs.

9

The Men's Movement

FOR MILLIONS OF MEN, the men's movement has been enlightening and empowering, but for fathers the overall impact may actually have been more negative than positive. Some branches of the movement stress the importance of blind acceptance of our own fathers and ignore the necessity of learning to be a good father. Other branches emphasize traditional male and female roles and end up promoting the same negative behavior and socialization that contemporary fathers are struggling to shake off. Still others are so hostile to women that they can't possibly be taken seriously. Several branches of the movement do, however, offer some hope and support to fathers.

Unfortunately, though, "movements of all sorts tend to be dominated by their most extreme fringe," writes Ellen Frankel Paul in her deadly accurate critique of the men's movement, "Silly Men, Banal Men." And what dominates the men's movement, and the corresponding media coverage, Paul says, is "its kookiest element." For that reason, when most of us hear the phrase "men's movement" we immediately think of a bunch of guys running around in loincloths, beating drums and smoking cigars. Or a man who is, as *Playboy* columnist Asa Baber puts it, "a crybaby–tree hugger–softhearted white boy–wussie who sometimes dances around an open fire at night and pretends he was a caveman."

It's easy to see why the media and the public have turned the men's movement into fodder for endless satire, but the truth is that there's no such thing as a monolithic men's movement. Instead, there are a variety of movements, often working at cross purposes, focusing on such diverse issues as sexual politics, divorce reform, equal rights for men, support of feminism, and men's health.

While there's much disagreement over which of the many men's movements was born first, there's little question that they owe their existence in part to the women's movement. "The women's movement drew the lines of distinction that made it possible, no, made it inevitable that men would need to respond," writes Bob Matthews, a social critic. And in 1966 Myron Brenton, author of *The American Male,* noted that "when the plight of woman is given such intense scrutiny, a curiously distorting effect tends to be created. Suddenly the world is seen only through the feminist prism." Ellen Frankel Paul takes this idea one step further: "The men's movement," she writes, "is largely a reaction to a quarter-century of flagellation of men by radical feminists."

Some social historians feel, however, that the men's movement predates the modern women's movement. In *Hearts of Men,* Barbara Ehrenreich asserts that today's men's movement is an outgrowth of men's ongoing revolt against the confines of what she calls the breadwinner ethic. "The collapse of the breadwinner ethic had begun well before the revival of feminism and stemmed from dissatisfactions every bit as deep, if not as idealistically expressed, as those that motivated our founding 'second wave' feminists."

The men's movement can be seen as having seven main strands: four that deal with issues of concern to all men, including fathers, and three that concentrate their efforts almost exclusively on fatherhood. We'll take a look at all seven, focusing on their philosophy and their approach to fathers and fatherhood.

General Men's Movements

Men's Liberation Movement

This movement is essentially the flip side of early feminism and owes a great debt to the women's movement. In fact, Dr. Warren Farrell, one of the movement's most visible founders, is the only man ever to have been elected three times to the board of the National Organization for Women. The Men's Liberation guys strongly believe that men, like women, have been victimized by our social and legal structure and thrust into roles they neither asked for nor wanted. "Men and women have cooperated in the development of contemporary male and female sex-roles," wrote Richard Haddad in *Concepts and Overview of the Men's Liberation Movement*, "both of which appear to have advantages as well as disadvantages, but which are essentially restrictive in nature, growth inhibiting, and, in the case of the male, physically as well as psychologically lethal." High-priority issues for Men's Libbers include men's health concerns, divorce and custody laws, fighting false accusations of child abuse and domestic violence, ending the all-male draft, establishing reproductive choice for men, and men's work-family issues. Farrell's *Why Men Are the Way They Are* and Herb Goldberg's *The New Male* were among the first books to voice these concerns, and both became bestsellers.

While similar to feminists in their approaches to such issues as gay rights and equal opportunity in the workplace, Men's Libbers adamantly reject one of feminism's central tenets: that we live in a patriarchy and that women are the victims of male oppression. It is perhaps because of this rejection that so many feminists have labeled the Men's Liberation Movement as reactionary and misogynist. But according to men's rights pioneer Fred Hayward, this isn't true. "We must not reverse the women's movement," Hayward writes. "We must accelerate it. . . . [Men's liberation] is not a backlash, for there is nothing about traditional sex roles that I want to go back to. . . . We must give full credence to the seriousness of women's problems and be willing to work toward their solution, but if the others do not return the favor, it is they who are the sexist pigs. It is they who are reactionary."

The Men's Liberation Movement (sometimes also called "masculism") also shares with feminism an occasional reliance on inaccurate information and statistics. And in its pursuit of true gender equality, this movement sometimes spends a disproportionate amount of time and energy on minor issues. Nevertheless, this is really the only group that actively acknowledges, and struggles to educate others about, the obstacles and discrimination faced by men in a variety of areas of their lives.

New Misogynists

There is one small group of men who are to the Men's Liberation Movement what radical feminists are to the larger women's movement. Like their radical feminist counterparts, these men have all but forsaken an egalitarian attitude toward gender and seem content to blame everything on the opposite sex.

For the radical feminists, men are what's wrong with the world. For the New Misogynists, it's women. Essentially, it's a biology-is-destiny argument. Men, they say, by virtue of their greater size and strength, are supreme, while women, who are smaller and gentler, should be at home with the kids. Men who prefer egalitarian relationships with their female partners are really nothing more than "pussywhipped" (their term) by the women in their lives. These types of disturbing and ultimately damaging messages are articulated in Rich Zubaty's *Surviving the Feminization of America* and R. F. Doyle's *Rape of the Male* and are disseminated all too widely on the Internet by discussion groups run by John Knight and others.

Feminist Men's Movement

At the other end of the spectrum from Men's Liberation is the Feminist Men's Movement, made up of radical feminists who happen to be men. They are very political, believing that women are the victims of a patriarchal society dominated by men who oppress and exploit women. They don't much care for traditional religions (because they believe they're patriarchal) or for the kind of family in which a father might play an important role.

Dominated by academics and political theorists who can seem apologetic about having been born male, the Feminist Men's Movement (also called the Academic Men's Movement) got its start in the 1970s, when it began dictating the content of men's studies programs at college campuses across the nation. "They may feel only a vague pricking of conscience about their own complicity in the imbalance," writes Anthony Astrachan in *How Men Feel.* "Or they may openly acknowledge that men as a class (which does not mean all men) oppress women as a class (which does not mean all women). In either case, what they feel is guilt." Having so completely bought into what Ellen

Frankel Paul calls "feminism's bill of indictment," pro-feminist men are the darlings of the women's movement.

The Feminist Men's Movement is, in fact, hardly a movement at all: it simply refuses to acknowledge that men might have some special concerns and needs. Instead, it holds up women as the model for all that is good in the world and invalidates nearly everything men do. "For these men, the question of unfair divorce settlements, child-custody cases, and the like are a ruse used by some men who favor perpetuating their own dominant status in society," writes James Doyle, in *Sex and Gender*.

Pro-feminist men do talk about how fathers need to nurture their children and how men need more intimate friendships in their lives, but they insist on a purely female model. In short, this "stillborn off-spring of radical feminism" is trying to make men into women — an option that isn't healthy for anyone.

Mythopoetic Men's Movement

This branch of the men's movement has been around for decades but was propelled into national prominence by Robert Bly's 1990 best-seller *Iron John*. Far more spiritual than political, the mythopoets believe that in many ways men have been damaged by negative socialization and trapped in harmful sex roles. One of the worst injuries men have suffered is what the mythopoets call the "father wound." "Not seeing your father when you are small, never being with him, having a remote father, an absent father, a workaholic father, is an injury," Bly claims. By using stories, myths, gatherings of men, and some "new" rites of passage and initiation rituals — including, yes, the occasional drumming session — the mythopoets hope to encourage the bond between men and help heal their father wound.

Leaders of the Mythopoetic Men's Movement acknowledge a debt of gratitude to other men's movements, in particular the Men's Liberation Movement. "I don't want to omit people like Warren Farrell and Herb Goldberg who are doing men's stuff," said John Lee, another mythopoetic leader. "They get omitted far too often when the men's movement is discussed. If Robert [Bly] is one of the leaders and perhaps the father of the Mythopoetic Men's Movement, then Goldberg and Farrell . . . are the grandfathers."

Ironically, a respected poet, Bly, never set out to become the father of a movement. "What I'm interested in is the return of mythology, and the importance of initiation," he said in an interview just after *Iron John* was published. "I'm not interested in all the men having opinions on men's rights, and attacking women. I'm not interested in a national men's movement."

Bly and other mythopoetic leaders believe that for men to fully heal they must seek a definition of themselves, from within themselves and with other men. Men, Bly said, must learn to heal themselves and stop relying on women for the answers to their problems and needs. This rather benign separation from women has been interpreted as somehow maligning women, or furthering an "old boys' network," or downright anti-feminist. It is none of these.

What the mythopoets believe is that men and women make different contributions to their growing children and that boys especially need a strong male role model to help them develop into healthy, well-adjusted men. Not having one can make them into "soft males," the men Bly describes as "lovely, valuable people — I like them. . . . But many of these men are not happy. You quickly notice the lack of energy in them. They are life-preserving but not exactly life-giving." Part of the problem comes from men's remoteness from their fathers, but another part comes from the troubles men experience in their relationships with women. "They had learned to be receptive, but receptivity wasn't enough to carry their marriages through troubled times. In every relationship something fierce is needed once in a while: both the man and the woman need to have it. But at the point when it was needed, often the young man came up short. He was nurturing, but something else was required — for his relationship and for his life."

Feminists and other critics have taken Bly's call for "fierceness" as an attack on women. But what he's really saying is that some of men's problems come from the growing societal message that there's something wrong with masculinity. According to the mythopoets, masculinity is okay — but not violence or oppression, which are not natural components of masculinity. However, as Scott Coltrane, author of *Family Man*, comments, "Bly portrays men and women as different. . . . He elevates whatever differences might exist to the level of spiritual essence and violent opposition. He appreciates this difference only as opposites, as nations defending their borders, and implies that the male is the active principle, the fierce initiator, fighting to penetrate the receptive female."

This celebration of difference may inadvertently reinforce outdated notions about the differences between fathers and mothers — that fathers are incapable of being nurturing, sensitive parents and therefore lack important ingredients for successful relationships with their children.

The Fathers' Movements

Fathers' Rights Movement

The Fathers' Rights Movement may be the oldest — and by far the most disjointed — of the men's movements, tracing its origins to Divorce Racket Busters, a group founded in Sacramento, California, in 1960. By 1963 the group, which had changed its name to United States Divorce Reform, Inc. (USDR), boasted two thousand members.

Members of Fathers' Rights groups are sometimes thought of as the "warriors" of the men's movement, fighting for a fairer shake in such areas as divorce, child custody, child-support awards, and the rights of unmarried fathers. They tend to be politically conservative but share no single set of political or social views. What they do share, however, is a powerful desire to be allowed to have strong relationships with their children and to be more actively involved in their lives. Many are angry and frustrated at the legal system and their ex-wives, who they believe are denying them those relationships. Fathers' Rights groups also tend to be somewhat anti-feminist. But given NOW's and many other women's groups' position on divorced fathers, this is hardly a surprise.

Taking a page from the early women's movement, Fathers' Rights groups have tried to "make the personal political," lobbying (though largely unsuccessfully) local, state, and federal agencies to revamp a biased divorce and custody system and to acknowledge and support the importance of fathers in children's lives. Now that the Mythopoetic Men's Movement has stepped out of the media limelight, the Fathers' Rights Movement is gaining more media coverage, although little to none of it is favorable.

Fathers' Rights groups have gotten even more attention from NOW and other women's groups, which have tried to portray them as a threat to women everywhere. But there's really nothing to fear. Unlike women's groups, which see the value of putting aside their own differences in the pursuit of a common goal, Fathers' Rights groups suffer from a kind of "tower of Babelization." Here's how one Fathers' Rights historian described USDR: "Themselves seemingly afflicted with the divorce syndrome, various factions began feuding and broke off to form their own splinter groups. Separate organizations sprung up everywhere. There are now several hundred, with varying degrees of legitimacy. Most are mere mutual commiseration societies, without strong leadership."

Very few Father's Rights groups have more than a handful of members or more than a handful of dollars in the bank. And attempts to unite these groups under a single, presumably more powerful banner have generally failed. One notable exception was the 1997 protest against the movie *The First Wives Club*. Complaining that the movie furthered the traditional stereotype of men as louts and forgave women's illegal and immoral behavior, men's activist David Usher got men in dozens of cities across the country and overseas to picket their local movie theaters. "We organized it in just ten days," Usher says. "A ragtag but ebullient bunch of guys who finally experienced the rewards of putting aside our silly disagreements to work toward a common goal. We had all sorts of groups, ranging from the hard core to the more 'touchy-feely' groups participating."

As with the general men's movement, the New Misogynists have taken roost here as well. They rail blindly against the evils of households headed by single mothers and quite seriously propose that giving child custody to divorced fathers 100 percent of the time would eliminate the need for AFDC payments to single mothers and would, as a result, save the government $50 billion a year. The fact is that if men suddenly started getting full custody in the same proportion as women do now, children would undoubtedly suffer many of the same problems that are associated with growing up in homes without fathers.

Good Fatherhood Movement

The Good Fatherhood Movement focuses primarily on the problem of absent fathers and can trace its beginnings, in part, to David Blankenhorn's 1995 book, *Fatherless America*. In it, Blankenhorn eloquently promotes the idea that fatherhood — and, more important, the role of the father — is important to our society, and he artfully excoriates researchers and politicians who suggest it is the lack of money, rather than the lack of a father, that is the reason children growing up without fathers are significantly worse off than kids with them. At the same time, though, the Good Fatherhood Movement is critical of deadbeat dads and other men who disappear, emotionally or physically, from their families.

Demographically, this movement is different from many of the other men's or fatherhood movements. It comprises, among others, academics, writers, policy makers, and well-connected personalities, such as the former Secretary of Education William Bennett and the actor James Earl Jones. While predominantly male, the Good Fatherhood Movement welcomes and encourages the participation and policy advice of such prominent women as writer Barbara Dafoe Whitehead and divorce expert Judith Wallerstein. Philosophically, however, the movement has much in common with the conservative Christian Men's Movement.

To deal with the growing problem of fatherlessness, Blankenhorn proposes the Good Family Man, the kind of man every father should aspire to be, and offers twelve proposals that together would guarantee a father for every child. But in doing so, he's come up with something to offend nearly everyone. Feminists who had fought hard for freedom of choice and no-fault divorce laws will see as reactionary attempts to limit sperm bank withdrawals to married women only and calls to make divorces harder to obtain. Divorced fathers will decry his rejection of joint custody as a way to keep single fathers involved with their children. Liberals will object to the suggestion that unmarried women be encouraged to give up their babies for adoption by married couples. Never-married fathers will complain that their concerns have once again been ignored by people in a position to do something about them. Many others will take umbrage at the condemnation of absent and walk-away fathers and at the nearly complete lack of attention paid to the factors that drive so many men away from their families.

But the biggest complaints will come from the growing number of men who have rejected the traditional breadwinner role and assumed a fully involved, co-parenting relationship with their partners. To the Good Father Movement, these men are denying their masculinity and need to be reminded that a father's role in the family should be as junior partner to his wife. Blankenhorn refers almost derisively to the fully involved father as the "New Father," who, he says, is really "a mirage. It purports to be about fatherhood, but it is not. There is no father there."

In fact, it's Blankenhorn's Good Family Man who is the mirage. On the surface, he's a full parental partner, more nurturing and available than his father before him. But in reality, the Good Family Man is the old father with a new coat of paint — one who embraces the breadwinner role and defers to, and learns from, his wife's domestic authority. As one woman Blankenhorn interviewed puts it, "I run the train and I let him blow the whistle every now and then."

Christian Men's Movement

There are dozens of evangelical Christian men's groups, but the dominant one by far is Promise Keepers (PK), which was founded in 1990 by Bill McCartney, a former University of Colorado football coach. The group jumped into the national consciousness in October 1997 when half a million Promise Keepers from across the country and around the world attended a rally in Washington, D.C.

While ostensibly PK was formed to deal with climbing divorce rates and decaying family values, its basic message is that men, and especially fathers, need to reclaim their role in the family. "I can hear you saying, 'I want to be a spiritually pure man. Where do I start?' writes journalist Tony Brown in the group's manifesto, *Seven Promises of a Promise Keeper.* "The first thing you do is sit down with your wife and say something like this: 'Honey, I've made a terrible mistake. I've given you my role. I gave up leading this family, and I forced you to take my place. Now I must reclaim that role.' Don't misunderstand what I'm saying here. I'm not suggesting that you ask for your role back, I'm urging you to take it back." Brown insists that men should make "no compromise" on authority, and that women should submit to their husbands for the "survival of our culture."

This message was seconded in 1998, when the Southern Baptist Convention, this country's largest Protestant denomination, amended its statement of beliefs, adding that "a wife is to submit herself graciously to the servant leadership of her husband." Despite immediate criticism from other Protestant branches, Southern Baptist leaders stuck to their guns. "It doesn't take a scholar to be able to interpret what is clearly laid out in God's blueprint for the family," said Mary Mohler, who helped draft the amendment.

Like the Southern Baptists, Promise Keepers is no fringe group. It has an annual budget of $48 million, a paid staff of 260, and since its inception has reached 2.6 million men at gatherings in stadiums around the country. And although it purports to be doing "God's work," Promise Keepers is becoming quite political. McCartney, for example, has frequently — and publicly — opposed reproductive rights and was a staunch supporter of Colorado's 1992 Amendment 2 initiative, which would have denied certain basic rights to gays and lesbians.

PK's undeniably conservative views have angered many women's groups, which feel threatened by the group's rhetoric. And it has angered many, many others — non-Christians particularly — who are concerned about PK's lack of tolerance for anyone who doesn't fit the PK mold. Even within the organization, dissent is discouraged. "Promise Keepers urges men to form 'accountability' groups of no more than five members, within which they are expected to submit all aspects of their lives to review and rebuke. Each member must answer any probes concerning his marriage, family, finances, sexuality, or business activity," writes Russ Bellant.

Despite some very conservative social views, there are many positive things to say about the Promise Keepers. First, unlike some of the other men's movements that talk about racial inclusiveness, PK has successfully recruited large numbers of minority men into their membership as well as their leadership. (At the October 1997 rally, 14 percent of the attendees were African Americans, 2 percent were Asian, and 5 percent were Hispanic.) Second, PK acknowledges that many men are unhappy with the way their lives are going. "There is a growing number of men today who are recognizing that success in business, achieving all their goals, and making huge amounts of money are not going to satisfy them," says James Dobson, founder and president of Focus on the Family, a group aligned with PK. Third, while the mythopoets spend much of their time on woundedness and healing, Promise Keepers emphasizes changing men's behavior and getting them more involved with their families. "Here are men who, far from claiming to be saints, confess their sins and amend their lives . . . ," writes *Washington Times* columnist Joseph Sobran. "You'd think this movement would be beyond controversy. Think of it: People actually blaming themselves! admitting failure and guilt! making no claims of others! taking no government money! committing themselves to take care of the women and children who need them." And finally, Promise Keepers, like no other group before, has succeeded in getting the public and the media to look at the father's role in the family a little more seriously.

PK has taken nothing but flack from the left, and much of the criticism has been harsh. Patricia Ireland, the president of NOW, has accused PK of being a "feel-good form of male supremacy" that will lead to a society where women are only good for cooking and making babies. But, as Joseph Sobran asks, who is more interested in getting men more involved with their families, Promise Keepers or NOW? "Since the Promise Keepers was founded for the express purpose of dealing with it, the answer is obvious." However, the group must focus its efforts on accepting responsibility and getting involved rather than on taking charge. Insisting on women's submission to men does nothing more than set the father-involvement clock back twenty years.

Do men really need a movement at all? In a recent national poll, nearly half of Americans agreed that "the time has come for a men's movement to help men get in touch with their feelings and advance men's causes." Even some feminists agree. Betty Friedan, for example, writes that men's liberation is the other half of the struggle that began with the women's movement for equality. "Men, it seems, are seeking new life patterns as much as women are. They envy women's freedom to express their feelings and their private questions and the support they got from each other in those years of the women's movement."

What *kind* of movement men need is a different matter altogether. Ideally, there should be a powerful national movement devoted to achieving equal rights for both men and women. This may sound like what the women's movement is supposed to be about, but feminism's goal is actually "solidarity with women" rather than fairness for everyone, writes Cathy Young. And the result has been unfairness to men.

There is no single men's movement, no movement remotely as strong and seemingly focused as feminism, and there isn't likely to be one anytime soon. But even if there were, it's not clear that a single men's movement should be based on a feminist model. "If one could imagine such a thing, one would have to be dismayed by the prospect of a male counterpart to the women's movement of today, each trying to outshout and outwhine the other," writes Young.

But a movement that encourages men to talk, and then supports them when they do, would be a good thing. "I found myself in a tent with ninety guys, all opening up and speaking from the heart," said a fifty-year-old teacher who participated in a five-day wilderness retreat. "I was really surprised. We weren't holding out the way we men normally do with one another. And guys were saying things about themselves that I was holding inside myself as my darkest secrets! It was hard to believe. And it made me feel eager to participate and go further."

And, like it or not, the way to do this is in single-sex groups. "Men may best discover their authentic selves through intimate connections with other men," writes therapist John Guarnaschelli. "For decades this was precisely the theory behind women's groups — and no one has raised any real objections. This makes sense, doesn't it? In single-sex groups participants can more easily open up and express their vulnerabilities, without fear of whether the opposite sex will see them as weak or silly."

Ronald Levant, the author of *Masculinity Reconstructed,* offers a vigorous defense of male-only gatherings. "At their best, they serve two purposes. First, they offer a man an opportunity to learn from other men that he's not the only one feeling demoralized and confused — and this discovery alone can do much to alleviate the secret shame men attach to their feelings. Second, these gatherings offer men a safe place in which to begin re-examining their beliefs about manhood" — and, of course, fatherhood as well.

What the Men's Movements Do — and Don't Do — for Fathers

Fatherhood is a central part of most men's experience. What, if anything, do the various men's movements do for fathers? The answers are as varied as the men's movements themselves.

Feminist Men have little to offer fathers. They pay lip service to the importance of fathers in children's lives and even use the word "nurturing" from time to time, but they use a feminine model of parenting, saying essentially that "mother" is a verb, not a noun, and that men, too, can mother. In their quest for gender neutrality, they ignore the male-specific contributions — psychological, emotional, physical, intellectual — that fathers make to their children and provide little if any support for fathers who want to be more involved.

Men's Libbers are much better, acknowledging many of the obstacles that keep men away from their families, including work-family issues and women's gatekeeping, and seeking to break them down. But the efforts of Men's Libbers rarely make it into the media. And when they are given airtime or print space, it tends to be dominated by the New Misogynists, whose messages are often so unpalatable that even the occasional reasonable statement about the importance of fathers is ignored.

Unfortunately, the various fathers' movements aren't much better. Promise Keepers is devoted to reestablishing respect for fathers in the family, but its emphasis on traditional gender roles — dad goes to work and mom stays home with the kids — might make it even harder for men to be active fathers. In addition, there's evidence that

PK is more interested in bringing men back into the church than in bringing them together with their children.

A number of Fathers' Rights groups are also doing good work: using the press, they're able to show anyone who will listen that fathers are not as bad as they're made out to be. But they address mainly divorced and never-married fathers, leaving out the millions of men still in intact families who, for many reasons, are not able to be as involved with their children as they'd like to be.

Most disappointing of all, when it comes to fatherhood, is the Mythopoetic Men's Movement. On the surface, it has more to say about fathers than just about anyone. Boys who have not had enough fathering, warns Robert Bly, will suffer from "father hunger" for the rest of their lives. Despite all the talk about father hunger and father wounds, however, the mythopoets have taken a backward approach to fatherhood. Their emphasis is on finding role models and on coming to terms with one's own father instead of on the importance of being a good father. "Could it be, then, that [the mythopoets] are more concerned with proving their 'fierceness,' which, as they see it, differentiates them as 'real men,' than they are with encouraging good fathering?" asks Myriam Miedzian, a philosophy professor and educator. "If so, they are assuming, mistakenly, that a man cannot both be deeply involved in the care of his children and exhibit some of the traits traditionally connected with masculinity."

With all the media attention and all the men's group participants, there are great opportunities to bring active, involved fathering to the forefront. "Surely, the time has come . . . to move beyond soul searching . . . and to lend active support to workable, concrete solutions to the crisis in fathering," writes Miedzian. But Bly and the other leaders have often dropped the ball, and the result for today's fathers is more harmful than helpful.

The Good Fatherhood Movement comes the closest of all the movements to putting together a comprehensive package. Its leaders actually try to provide men with the tools they need to become more involved fathers and educate the public about the importance of fathers. "We believe that every child deserves a loving, committed and responsible father," they write in their "Call to Fatherhood." "Not just the lucky ones, but every child. . . . We come together to call for a fatherhood movement." They've also produced a booklet, *Seven Things States Can Do to Promote Responsible Fatherhood*, which offers state and local governments advice on how they can do exactly that.

Good Fatherhood members acknowledge that one reason men may be psychologically absent from their children is that they lack the skills necessary to be confident, successful fathers. But they don't talk about the media bias against fathers, work-family conflicts, or the ways that feminism stifles involved fatherhood. They don't seem terribly concerned with the rights of never-married fathers, and they have a pie-in-the-sky attitude about divorce: their solution is, just make it harder to get. (They do, however, strongly support legislation that seeks to give fathers more equal time with their children and that enforces their visitation rights.) They also, along with the Christian Men's Movement, approve of traditional gender roles. Finally, they're more concerned with the problem of fatherlessness than with engaging fathers who are not absent. But the Good Fatherhood Movement is clear on the most fundamental point of all: fathers matter. And they're doing everything they can to make sure everyone in this country knows about it.

One of the reasons the men's and fathers' movements have been less than successful in changing attitudes and perceptions about fathers is that they can't seem to agree on a single goal. Until that happens, the movements are doomed to the kind of fragmentation that has thus far kept them powerless.

There is a simple solution: agree to promote the idea that, as the Good Fatherhood people state, fathers matter. Yet even if all the existing men's and fathers' groups got behind this idea, significant change would be unlikely, largely because there aren't enough groups or members to make a real difference.

It's a vicious circle. Men often don't join support groups because there aren't any, and there aren't any because men don't join them. But even if there were more groups, men probably wouldn't join them anyway. There's some truth, it seems, to the old cliché about men not wanting to ask for directions — not just geographical, but also directions on how to change a diaper, soothe a crying baby, or what to do with a rebellious teenage daughter. This is part of an even larger problem: men have been socialized to take care of their problems on their own, and asking someone else for help is considered a sign of weakness. In order to keep their "shortcomings" a secret from those around them — especially the women in their lives — men spend way too much time hoping to stumble upon the perfect solution.

The first step toward creating a powerful, cogent fatherhood movement — even before spreading the word that fathers matter — is for men to disabuse themselves of the notion that they're bullet-proof, that they don't need help from anyone. One of the areas they need the most help in, in fact, is parenting. And men's groups (or, more specifically, fathers' groups) can be just the place to start.

Ronald Levant has developed a comprehensive program, called "The Fatherhood Course," aimed at improving fathers' communication skills, particularly learning to listen and respond to children's feelings and to express their own feelings in a constructive manner. The course also teaches fathers about normal child development and child management. Participating fathers meet one evening a week for eight weeks and use a combination of role-playing and videotape-playback techniques and home exercises for fathers and their children. All kinds of fathers — laborers and lawyers, in their late twenties to mid-fifties, with children from infants to young adults — have participated in this program. And it works. Compared to untrained fathers, the fathers who completed Levant's course showed great improvements, including increased sensitivity and increased acceptance of children's feelings. And the children perceived their relationships with their fathers as more positive after their dads had gone through the training.

Given the important role that fathers play in children's emotional development, the program's focus on communication and sensitivity to feelings may be the key to its effectiveness. And by helping men concentrate on emotions, the course may legitimize the "softer side" of fatherhood and help men become more sensitive fathers and spouses as well.

The next step toward creating a powerful fatherhood movement is to have men get beyond their individual problems. The men who do join support groups tend to stay active only until their particular problems or concerns are ameliorated — then they're on to other things.

Men's support groups provide participants with a "powerful increase of 'ego strength,' of empowered centeredness, arising from a growing sense of affirmed identity within a community," writes John Guarnaschelli. This in turn supports many aspects of personal growth, such as "learning to argue effectively, dealing with money, succeeding at work, loving and communicating more effectively." Groups also help minimize the feelings that so many men have that their fears, worries, joys, sadness, needs, and wants are weird, not masculine, or that experiencing these feelings and emotions makes them somehow defective.

Support groups help men understand and manage a wider spectrum of emotions than they normally do. Despite all the talk about the emergence of sensitive, new-age men, for a man to experience, let alone express, feelings is still considered a highly negative characteristic. "Adult men don't hide their feelings; as an essential requirement for fulfilling their proper role in society — being a man — they are often genuinely oblivious to the fact of having them at all," says Guarnaschelli. Men's groups offer men critical support during very stressful times.

Individual men aren't the only ones who need to learn to work together. Existing groups must also begin cooperating with each other — something that rarely happens today. In many cases, when a man joins a group and for one reason or other it can't help him solve his problem as quickly as he'd like, he goes off and starts another group, either alone or with a few other similarly disgruntled men. And in order to attract new members, the new group's first order of business is often to badmouth the former group. To be successful, men's groups of all kinds are going to have to rally behind the message that fathers matter.

As the women's movement found out long ago, another benefit of working together is that the message is taken far more seriously by the media and the public, a crucial step that results in both increased credibility and increased membership.

*   *   *

While much of the work required to create a fatherhood movement is going to be required from women and men acting together or in groups, state and local governments also have a role to play. Perhaps the best way that government agencies can show their commitment to reinvigorating fatherhood is to take advantage of its bully pulpit to educate the public about the importance of fathers and fatherhood. Wade Horn and Eric Brenner, in *Seven Things States Can Do to Promote Responsible Fatherhood,* suggest that "if the current focus on 'deadbeat dads' is expanded to describe the critical role fathers play as teachers, role models, nurturers, and disciplinarians, the results could generate important public support."

Government-sponsored media campaigns about the importance of recycling and the dangers of drugs, alcohol, and smoking have worked well. And a government-sponsored "Fathers Matter" initiative could have similar benefits for all of society: mothers, children, and, of course, fathers themselves.

10

The Women's Movement

G IVEN WOMEN'S long history of asking men to be more actively involved in childcare, one might expect that women
would be among fathers' most ardent supporters. But the history of the women's movement is filled with contradictory messages
about fathers and their role in the family, especially when it comes to
divorce and custody. Early feminists spoke of equality and sharing, but
in recent years a more radical fringe has dominated the movement
which refuses to allow men an equal role in the family, resulting in the
perpetuation of traditional male and female stereotypes.

In a widely disseminated press release, the National Organization
for Women (NOW) in 1970 challenged the prevailing notion that
childcare was women's work. "The care and welfare of children is in-
cumbent on society and parents. We reject the idea that mothers have
a special child care role that is not to be shared equally by fathers."
Later that same year, NOW passed a resolution declaring that "marriage should be an equal partnership with shared economic and
household responsibility and shared care of the children" and demanding that employers "acknowledge that parenthood is a necessary
social service by granting maternal and paternal leaves of absence
without prejudice and without loss of job security or seniority." And
in 1971, *Ms.* co-founder Gloria Steinem proclaimed, "It's clear that
most American children suffer from too much mother and too little
father."

Over the next decade, fathers became the darlings of the women's movement. In 1979, Betty Friedan addressed a NOW conference on the future of the family. She applauded the "new fatherhood" and argued that "the family, instead of being enemy territory to feminists, is really the underground through which secretly they reach into every man's life." Ellen Goodman, a *Boston Globe* columnist known for her feminist views, declared that 1980 should be the "Year of the Father." And in 1983, Letty Cottin Pogrebin, another co-founder of *Ms.*, delighted in the fact that "all over the country men are materializing in childbirth courses . . . staying home to care for their own children . . . braving the quizzical stares of cops and mothers as they push a baby carriage or watch their children in the playground; asking for joint custody; demanding paternity leave."

Unfortunately, this honeymoon period in male-female relationships was short-lived. Women who had loudly rejected the notion that biology is destiny began insisting that, for men, biology actually *is* destiny. In 1990, Pogrebin made a complete U-turn, declaring that dads were "pathological bullies who abuse their children." And Barbara Jordan, a former congresswoman and adviser to the governor of Texas, insisted that "women have a capacity for understanding and a compassion which a man structurally does not have, does not have it because he cannot have it. He's just incapable of it."

Although dramatic, this shift in the women's movement's take on fathers and fatherhood is little more than a reflection of feminism's changing — and inconsistent — attitudes about men in general. Over the course of a few short decades, feminism's dominant philosophy shifted from egalitarian to victim-based.

Egalitarian feminists (most prominently Betty Friedan, in both *The Feminine Mystique* and *The Second Stage*) demanded that women get equal rights and take on equal responsibilities. They recognized that men, too, are not happy with their lives and that both sexes have been forced by society into the roles they play. In fact, Friedan and others saw that men would play an important role in the success of the then fledgling women's movement.

This open-minded approach has been all but drowned out by a far more vocal and politically savvy group of women with a very different philosophy. Simply put, these radical feminists (also called "gender feminists" and "ideological feminists") are "animated by a spirit of resentment, the tactic of blame, and the desire for vindictive triumph over men that comes out of the dogmatic assumption that women are the innocent victims of a male conspiracy."

"I feel that 'man-hating' is an honorable and viable political act, that the oppressed have a right to class-hatred against the class that is oppressing them," wrote Robin Morgan, a former editor of *Ms.* For the sake of argument, let's concede that a certain amount of women's anger toward men is justified. But can any reasonable person really agree with the radical feminist Andrea Dworkin: "Men are rapists, batterers, plunderers, killers; these same men are religious prophets, poets, heroes, figures of romance, adventure, accomplishment, figures ennobled by tragedy and defeat. Men have claimed the earth, called it Her. Men ruin Her. Men have airplanes, guns, bombs, poisonous gases, weapons so perverse and deadly that they defy any authentically human imagination." Or with feminist legal scholar Catharine MacKinnon, who has said that "in a patriarchal society, all heterosexual intercourse is rape because women, as a group, are not strong enough to give meaningful consent."

Because this kind of rhetoric is so extreme, it's tempting to dismiss it as the rantings of those who claim to — but don't — speak for the majority of women. But such divisive, unsubstantiated remarks are so widely covered (and left unchallenged) in the mainstream media, they're nearly impossible to ignore.

Nevertheless, there's evidence that an increasing number of women are beginning to reject feminism (or at least the word), perhaps in a conscious effort to distance themselves from such outrageous rhetoric. A 1994 *Time/CNN* poll found that while 57 percent of women said they favor a strong women's movement, 63 percent didn't consider themselves feminists.

Of course, feminism's angry rhetoric isn't the only thing keeping women at arm's length. Many women have interpreted feminism's message about female empowerment to mean that a feminist is a woman who puts herself first, before her family. And most women — like most men — put their families first. In addition, there is a large number of women who "are not sure what feminists mean by 'sexual equality' or 'equal rights' but who fear it may mean some form of uni-sexuality or loss of private and traditional distinctions between the sexes," writes political commentator Deirdre English. "If men would drop the door-opening and heavy-lifting parts of masculinity and women would have to give up their nice clothes and makeup, then No Way."

Ironically, at the same time as many women are distancing them-selves from radical feminism's hateful rhetoric, they're wholeheartedly embracing another idea that could be considered just as extreme: equal rights and responsibilities for men and women are out; special preferences for women are in. "The evil that women do — to chil-dren, other women, or men — must be written out of the picture," writes Cathy Young in *Ceasefire: From Gender War to Real Equality*. "The same people who start hyperventilating with indignation if someone suggests that women lack the 'killer instinct' in the market-place or in the military will sneer at the idea that women might be ag-gressors as well as victims."

Although women aren't always sure what they want from men, most of them agree on at least one thing: they want to be supported fi-nancially. "No matter how much they themselves may contribute to the family's resources," David Popenoe says in *Life Without Father*, "[they] still expect the male to be a resource provider." A variety of studies show that, for as long as records have been kept, women have valued the male breadwinner role higher than any other when looking for a mate.

There's a reason that women — especially when they become mothers — value the "good provider": such a man allows his partner to choose between three options: stay at home with the baby, go back to work, or some combination of the two. The good provider gives himself, however, three "slightly different" options, says Warren Far-rell, author of *The Myth of Male Power*: work full time, work full time, or work full time.

Or, as recording artist Paula Cole puts it, "I will do the dishes, you pay all the bills." In the next verse of her wildly successful single "Where Have All the Cowboys Gone?" she adds, "I will raise the chil-dren, you pay all the bills." Cole, who seems to be espousing decidedly

unequal rights and responsibilities for men and women, is nevertheless seen as something of a feminist hero.

So what do feminists want from men? The messages are too conflicting to tell. And when it comes to what feminists want from fathers,
the waters get even murkier.

In one nationwide survey of a thousand mothers from age eighteen to
eighty, only one in ten felt it was sufficient for a father to assume the traditional breadwinner role, and a majority said that fathers should play
an important role. But what kind of role? Well, "not quite as important
as mom's," said the study's participants. In fact, two out of three women
seemed threatened by the idea of equal participation in childcare.

Here's how this contradiction plays out in real life: A father is
cradling his daughter in his arms when she — as babies do — begins
to cry. Suddenly the child's mother comes in and takes the baby away,
saying something like, "Let me take her, honey, I think I know what
she really wants." While a woman's plucking a crying or smelly baby
out of her husband's arms may seem like a minor thing, done for the
sake of expediency, it is an example of how women subtly put "a
damper on men's involvement with their children because they are so
possessive of their role as primary nurturer." Left unchecked, this ordinary dynamic reinforces in everyone's mind — fathers and mothers
alike — old and very damaging stereotypes: that women are naturally
better at parenting, that fathers are irrelevant, and that children essentially belong to women. The next "logical" step is to eliminate fathers
altogether from the parenting picture. And this is precisely what feminists seem to be encouraging women to do.

Attempts to disenfranchise men from being full participants in parenting begin before their babies are born. In fact, the whole process
starts with the decision about whether or not to become a parent. "In
these decisions," writes Susan Faludi, men increasingly don't "have the
final say — or much of a say at all."

The phrase "a woman's right to choose" is usually a euphemism for
a woman's right to have an abortion. And inherent in her right not to
become a parent is the right to become one if she so chooses. That's
what a woman's fundamental right to make her own reproductive

choices is all about. But in our attempts to salvage *Roe v. Wade* and to stave off militant anti-abortion groups like Operation Rescue, we've forgotten (or, worse, maybe never even realized) that men, too, are deeply affected by the reproductive choices women make. The same laws that protect a woman's parental choices also allow her to either deprive a man of his right to become a parent or force him to become one against his will.

Take the hypothetical case of Jane and her live-in boyfriend, Tom. One morning Jane announces that their birth control must have failed and that she's pregnant. If Jane decides she's not financially prepared to become a parent, society will undoubtedly say, "That's okay, you can always get an abortion." But what if Tom wants to keep the child? Under the law, Jane can do what she wants, but when she does, no one will pay any attention to the effect it has on Tom. Women, we're told, grieve — often for years — after an abortion. But is a man's grief somehow not as real or as worthy of compassion as a woman's? There's no evidence that says that it isn't.

Imagine now that Jane decides to keep the child and that Tom says he's not financially prepared to become a parent. Society's reaction? "You should have thought of that sooner, and you'd better keep those child-support checks coming in or we'll throw you in jail."

What if Tom and Jane are about to split up when Jane finds out she's pregnant? Or what if it was just a one-night stand to begin with? Tom, in addition to having to pay eighteen years of support for a child he never wanted, will be forced to have an ongoing relationship with a woman he doesn't love. Again, under the law, Jane can do whatever she wants. Tom has absolutely no rights. As a man, whether or not he becomes a parent is not up to him.

Certainly to most men — or at least the pro-choice ones — it is repugnant to imagine dragging a woman off to get an abortion against her will or forcing her to bear a child just because the baby's father insists. Therefore the final decision should be made by the woman. But the father should have the opportunity to participate in the decision-making process. He should be allowed to express how having — or not having — a child will affect him. He should be encouraged to try to convince his partner that he is right while also allowing her to convince him that she is right.

In some relationships, that's exactly what happens: men are brought into the discussion. But not nearly as often as they should be. In *Back-lash* Susan Faludi cited, rather gleefully, a 1990 Virginia Slims poll in which "nearly 40 percent of the women . . . said that in making a decision about whether to have an abortion, the man involved should not even be consulted." Some feminists go one step further, suggesting that men's propensity for violence and their need to control women's bodies makes telling men about a pregnancy too risky for women to consider.

Men's reproductive rights and their emotional needs in this area have been ignored too long. And for that reason, it's easy to see how some men might feel alienated from the pro-choice movement and how men who have been forced to become parents, or who have been deprived of the opportunity to do so, might feel some hostility toward women and the issues that are important to them.

The rewards of acknowledging men's feelings and needs and encouraging them to get more involved will undoubtedly be significant. Men who feel they have been allowed an active role in planning their own families will be more committed to those families and less likely to abandon them. And men whose needs and feelings are understood and discussed openly will become more involved, passionate defenders of the needs and feelings of others.

When it comes to whether or not to terminate a pregnancy, the final decision should be left to the woman. But excluding men — as we often do in our society — from the debate on abortion and other parenting issues is really just a symptom of a much larger problem: our general disregard for and lack of appreciation of fathers. Denying men a role in their own reproductive choices serves only to reinforce the old stereotypes that men are uninterested in children and that family issues — and fatherhood itself — are women's issues. As Cathy Young asks, "Ethics aside, is that a wise attitude to take if we want men to be more involved in child rearing?"

Just as radical feminists encourage women to make their abortion decisions independent of men, a number of groups also encourage women who chose to become mothers to do so independent of men. "Given time and space, most women discover that the pleasures of being alone are real — and they're not eager to give them up. . . . And without another adult questioning your values, your child-rearing methods, or your wants, you can come to treasure the sense of well-being that you've worked so hard to achieve." Put more succinctly, "Children are a joy; many men are not," writes the poet and journalist Katha Pollitt.

Feminism's support for single motherhood is apparently uncondi-tional and extends to every possible way a woman can become a mother. The actress Michelle Pfeiffer, for example, had this to say about her decision to adopt a child — alone. "Men are like pinch hit-ters. So what's the deal? When it came right down to it, I just couldn't do it [have a child with a man]. I thought, I don't want some guy in my life forever who's going to be driving me nuts."

Every year, more than 30,000 babies in this country are conceived and born through artificial insemination. About 90 percent of the parents are married couples with some kind of fertility problem, but about 3,000 of these births are to "single mothers by choice." In forty-eight states a single woman has the legal right to walk into her neigh-borhood sperm bank and make a withdrawal.

And consider the recent case of Richard Gladu, whose former wife had herself impregnated with a frozen embryo fertilized with Gladu's sperm — but without his knowledge or consent — and then sued him for child support. Gladu responded by suing the fertility clinic, alleging "wrongful birth." "He feels his embryo — his property — was stolen," said Gladu's lawyer, "and his right to be a knowing parent was stolen." Claiming that the embryo in question was "his property" is a bit of a stretch, but there's no question that that particular collection of cells was exactly as much Gladu's as his former wife's, and neither parent had either a superior claim or the right to do anything with it without the other's permission. On the surface these cases may seem small, but they are glaring examples of our institutional disregard of the importance of fathers and of how we've at times eliminated fa-thers from the parenting equation.

For radical feminists, the goal is to live in a society in which "women can shape their reproductive experiences to further ends of their own choosing," writes Anne Donchin. And it seems that a fright-eningly large percentage of women stand firmly behind Donchin and feminist legal scholar Nancy Polikoff, who says, "It is no tragedy, either on a national scale or in an individual family, for children to be raised without fathers." In 1987, for example, "87 percent of single women believed it was perfectly acceptable for women to bear and raise children without getting married — up 14 percent from just 4 years before," Susan Faludi reported. And there's no indication that the blind acceptance of single motherhood is decreasing.

When it comes to the "choice" of raising a child without a father, the consequences are far-reaching — and nasty. Fatherless children are twice as likely to drop out of school as children who live with both parents; children who exhibit violent behavior in school are eleven times as likely not to live with their fathers; overall, fatherless children do far worse in school, are more prone to depression, more likely to abuse drugs, get involved in crime, and commit suicide, and are at much greater risk of becoming teen parents. Seventy-two percent of adolescent murderers and 60 percent of America's rapists grew up in homes without fathers.

As a culture, we're quick to put the blame for all these social ills on the missing fathers. And while some fathers do abandon their families, we would do well to ask, in the words of parenting guru Penelope Leach, why "is it socially reprehensible for a man to leave a baby fatherless, but courageous, even admirable, for a women to have a baby whom she knows will be so?"

"It makes sense to ask women to examine their own attitudes and behaviors that may contribute to the problem," writes Cathy Young. "What doesn't make sense is to chide men for not taking on child-rearing responsibilities . . . and then say that if Mom doesn't want Dad around, he must be a good sport and get out (but keep the checks coming), or gloat over women's ability to exclude fathers from decisions about children. Denying people a say in something is not a good way to get them to take responsibility." Not surprisingly, author Suzanne Fields writes that "a sad corollary of modern feminism is the sharp increase in fatherless families."

Feminists and nonfeminists alike have important allies: the legislatures and the courts, which give custody to mothers well over 80 percent of the time; and the media, who often exclude the male perspective on issues that affect men as well as women, including sex, relationships, children, parenting, and divorce and custody. One of the biggest news-gathering organizations in the country, Gannett, which publishes *USA Today* and other national and regional publications, distributes to its reporters a valuable guide containing six thousand names, phone numbers, and addresses of sources on a variety of subjects. Under "Women's Groups," the guide lists eighteen topic headings, including Battered Women, Magazines, and Political Organizations (which itself contains twenty-three sources). But a reporter looking for a quote from a man on a "men's issue" (divorce and custody, for example) is out of luck. No fathers' rights organizations, male health advocates, or men's groups are listed. The alphabetical index of categories skips directly from Mellon Bank to Mental Health without so much as a single entry for Men. This is not because men's groups don't exist: Rod Van Mechelen, publisher of an on-line men's magazine called *The Backlash!*, has compiled a directory listing more than a hundred.

Even if we assume that leaving out sources on men's issues was merely an oversight, sources listed in the media guide will be the first ones called. Reporters who might otherwise be interested in including a male perspective will have to spend a lot of time and effort tracking one down, something they often won't be able to do on a tight deadline. The result? The male perspective likely gets left out. Perhaps not deliberately, but left out nonetheless.

Legislative bodies and the courts are also reluctant to question any data put out by women's groups. The mission of the U.S. Commission on Child and Family Welfare, for example, was to focus on children's access to the financial and emotional resources of *both* parents. But the majority of the commissioners, more than half of whom were women's activists, refused to endorse any guidelines for a presumption of shared parenting after divorce — "even with strong provisions for exceptions based on spousal violence, substance abuse, or other impediments . . . ," former Commissioner John Guidubaldi wrote in his dissenting report. "The bias against a presumption of joint custody was observable in several Commission actions," he said. "For example, bias was clear in the uncritical acceptance of testimony opposing joint custody, the attempt to limit testimony of those in favor, and the ignoring of substantial supportive documents."

One explanation for this bias is that the commission's male members, several of whom were religious conservatives, sided with their female colleagues out of a sense of chivalry, acting as though women were too dumb to take care of themselves and needed to be protected from the uncertainties of life. Ironically, women are being protected by the very same attitudes they are trying so hard to overcome.

Nowhere are feminism's attitudes about men more apparent than when marriages end. One might think, given feminism's historical insistence that men should share equally in raising their children, that women would support joint physical custody or some other shared parenting arrangement. After all, if a child is living with his father half the time, a divorced mother would have a huge amount of free time on her hands, which she could spend advancing her career or doing all the things she didn't have time for during her marriage. (It's important to understand — and to repeat here — the difference between joint legal custody and joint physical custody. Joint legal custody gives both parents the right to sign their child's report card and make medical, school, and other such decisions; the child still spends almost all her time living with only one parent, usually the mother. Joint physical custody allows the child to spend a more equal amount of time with each parent.) But instead of supporting equal opportunity for divorced parents, feminists like Judith Regan insist that "women are simply better equipped biologically for parenting young children. This absurd notion that men and women are equal in this capacity just isn't true."

"They want to be considered more compassionate than men, though they would be outraged at the suggestion that they are less rational or less ambitious," writes Cathy Young. "They bristle at being told that they should stay home with their children, but they may subtly resist the father's equal involvement in child-rearing and assume, without any subtlety, that they have superior rights to child custody after divorce."

The inconsistencies in the feminist position on fathers and father involvement after divorce appear to be obvious, and the reason behind the inconsistencies is just as obvious: it's all about power. There's little argument that women have had less than their fair share of power outside the home, and there's even less argument that for generations women have reigned supreme inside the home. Like most people who wield great power, they have no real interest in giving it up. And like most people who wield too much power, feminists have too often abused it. According to feminist writer Ann Snitow, when contemplating joint custody (or any other gender-blind arrangement), women "give up something, a special privilege wound up in the culture-laden word 'mother.' . . . Giving up the exclusivity of motherhood is bound to feel to many like a loss. Only a fool gives up something present for something intangible and speculative."

When men resist giving up their dominant spot in the workplace for such "intangible and speculative" things as allowing women to live their lives to their full potential, they're portrayed as insensitive, self-centered, and power-grubbing. But when women resist sharing power in the home and giving up the certainty of exclusive control over their children, for the very same "intangible and speculative" results (and the very concrete result of maintaining the father-child bond), it's supposed to inspire compassion.

Actually, men are supposed to have more than compassion; men are supposed to rally to feminists as they seek to keep their domestic power base strong by rejecting equitable parenting options for fathers and supporting their ongoing quest for sole mother custody. Although joint custody or shared parenting intuitively seems "right" to most people, feminists have contested it, often stretching the truth to support their case.

Joint custody is bad for women

In the minds of some feminists, "forced joint custody, like forced sterilization and forced pregnancy, is a denial of women's right to control their lives," writes Jo Ann Schulman of the National Center on Women and Family Law. The truth, however, is that women are not and have never been in any danger of being "forced" into joint custody. About 90 percent of the time, divorcing parents reach custody agreements without a trial, and nearly all of those cases result in the mother's getting full or primary custody. In a large portion of the cases where both parents agree that they want to share custody equally or give custody to the father, judges refuse, giving custody to the mother anyway.

Had Schulman said that forced sole mother custody is a denial of women's rights to control their lives, she would have been more accurate. "The maternal custody preference . . . can coerce today's 'liberated' women into becoming or remaining fully responsible for raising the children of our society," writes Anne Mitchell in the *American Journal of Family Law.* "To place upon a mother's shoulder the mantle of a unique and inevitable mother-child bond is to also place upon a mother's wrists the shackles of responsibility for that bond, and that child. Where a mother has become so intimately and inextricably bound, she may have little ability to break free to pursue other objectives."

There is, in other words, a powerful argument to be made that joint custody is good for women and that sole mother custody is not.

Joint custody is bad for kids

Saying that kids need "consistency," which most people would agree is extremely important to children in times of stress, opponents of joint custody claim that such custody undermines kids' sense of security and stability. But custody expert Richard Warshak and many others say that it is sole custody that creates inconsistency, "because it disrupts the relationship between child and noncustodial parent."

Academics have conducted numerous studies analyzing the impact of various custody arrangements on children. According to social policy expert Ross Thompson, "At its best joint custody presents the possibility that each family member can 'win' in post-divorce life rather than insisting that a custody decision identify 'winners and losers': mothers and fathers each win a significant role in the lives of offspring and children win as a consequence." And in a hearing before the Commission on Child and Family Welfare, John Guidubaldi asked two officials from the American Psychological Association, one of the nation's largest independent organizations of mental health professionals, to give the commission an objective analysis of the pros and cons of these arrangements. The officials examined nearly two dozen studies according to the following criteria: father involvement, the best interests of the child, financial child support, relitigation and costs to the family, and parental conflict. On each of these criteria, the APA came to the conclusion "that joint custody is associated with favorable outcomes."

Even some fairly high-profile feminist researchers have come to the same conclusions. Jessica Pearson and Nancy Thoennes tracked more than nine hundred divorced parents with a wide variety of custody arrangements and found that conflicts between divorced parents "did not appear to worsen as a result of the increased demand for inter-parental cooperation and communication in joint legal or joint residential custody arrangements. To the contrary, parents with sole maternal custody reported the greatest deterioration in the relationships over time." The bottom line, then, is that joint custody or any other parenting arrangement that gives both parents equal time with their children is good for kids.

There are, of course, some exceptions. Experts have found that the single most accurate predictor of children's long-term adjustment and well-being after divorce is the level of conflict between the parents. Even its supporters agree that joint custody is not a good idea in divorces where the parents are constantly at each other's throats and are verbally, emotionally, or physically abusive to each other in front of the children. Nor is it healthy for children to be caught in the middle of warring ex-spouses by being asked to carry messages between parents and to inform each parent of the other's activities.

Researchers Christy Buchanan, Eleanor Maccoby, and Sanford Dornbusch found that adolescents who often feared "feeling caught" were more likely to experience depression and anxiety and engage in more deviant behavior, such as smoking, taking drugs, fighting, and stealing, than adolescents who experienced more cooperation between their parents. "Court-ordered joint physical custody and frequent visitation arrangements in high-conflict divorce tend to be associated with poorer child outcomes, especially for girls," according to Janet Johnson, whose research is frequently cited by opponents of joint custody. Johnson later reframed this statement, acknowledging that joint physical custody and frequent visitation per se are not detrimental to the majority of children. She noted that "in some cases, especially where parents are cooperative, they are more beneficial."

So how many divorces are high-conflict? Twenty-five percent. But only 10 percent of these — 2.5 percent of all divorces involving children — show any correlation between joint custody or frequent visitation arrangements and poor child adjustment. Clearly, that tiny percentage "should not serve as the basis for policy that affects the welfare of the other 97.5 percent of the population," wrote John Guidubaldi.

The goal of any custody arrangement should be to reduce conflict between the former spouses, thereby reducing the divorce's negative impact on children. Three states, California, Maine, and Delaware, discovered that one of the most effective ways to do this is to mandate mediation of divorce and custody disputes. This means that rather than rev up the expensive adversarial system, and rather than subject the children to a debilitating custody battle, mom and dad are required to sit down with a neutral mediator and try to come up with some reasonable solutions.

Hugh McIsaac, former director of Family Court Services for the Los Angeles Superior Court, reported that mediation offers the following virtues:

- It teaches a conflict-resolution process that most parties can use in future dealings with each other.
- It provides parents with a way to avoid the legal system in resolving disputes about their parental roles.
- It promotes cooperation among attorneys, judges, and mental health professionals, who work together to "find sensible solutions for these families at a very difficult moment in their lives."
- It focuses on the needs of the parties rather than their extreme positions.
- It creates options other than winning and losing and promotes creative compromise.

In 1992, a report by California's Office of Family Court Services found that those who used mediation were very satisfied with it: 90 percent of all clients said that mediation was a good way to draw up a parenting plan; 93 percent reported that mediation procedures had been described to them clearly; 85 percent of parents reported that they did not feel intimidated and freely said what they really felt; and 86 percent said they felt no pressure to go along with something they did not want.

The results weren't limited to California. In one of the few experimental studies of mediation, Robert Emery, author of *Renegotiating Family Relationships,* found in his Virginia project that only 11 percent of families assigned at random to mediation went on to a court custody hearing. In contrast, 72 percent of families in the litigation control group, who didn't go through mediation, proceeded to court. Mediation translated into a dramatic reduction in the number of court hearings, a major financial and emotional savings. In a nationwide study, Jessica Pearson and Nancy Thoennes found that a majority of mediation clients were satisfied with the process, that soon after mediation compliance with agreements was high, that successful mediation improved the relationship between the former spouses, and that mediation resulted in more joint custody arrangements than nonmediated disputes. Moreover, according to Emery, mediated agreements tended to include more specific details about parenting plans, more information about financial arrangements concerning the children, and more balance in the time children spend with mothers and fathers. In short, everybody wins, especially the children, who gain access to both parents and are less likely to get caught in a postdivorce tug of war.

Despite the overwhelming evidence that mediation can truly help high-conflict couples work things out like grown-ups, many feminists are adamantly opposed to the idea. And the reason seems to be plainly stated in the preceding paragraph: mediation resulted in more joint custody arrangements than nonmediated disputes. In other words, they don't like mediation because it just might reduce women's dominance in the parenting sphere.

Men don't get custody because they really don't want it

Since women get sole or primary custody 90 percent of the time, and since 90 percent of those arrangements are entered into voluntarily by the parents, the logical conclusion is that men and women are getting exactly what they want and that the reason men don't have more joint custody is that they simply don't want it.

That would be true if it weren't for what Richard Warshak calls the "motherhood mystique," the prevailing societal wisdom that tells us in no uncertain terms that mothers, by nature, make better parents than men and that mothers are more important to children than fathers. Many feminists have bought into the motherhood mystique completely. And so have a lot of men, who too often conclude that the children belong with the mother. They've "come to believe in the tradition of the sacred mother child bond, and therefore they believe that they are incapable of providing that somehow-unique form of nurturing required by their children," writes Anne Mitchell. "In other words, much as these fathers might genuinely want their children to live with them, they believe they would be hurting their children by removing them from their mother."

The motherhood mystique is more than a theory; it's actually quantifiable. In a recent study of about one thousand divorcing couples in California, Stanford University psychology professor Eleanor Maccoby and law professor Robert Mnookin found that more than two-thirds of the fathers wanted at least some physical custody of their children. It also found that roughly a third asked for less than they really wanted. Men and women were both asked to rate their feelings about custody on a 1 to 10 scale, with 1 indicating apathy about how custody turned out and 10 being a willingness to fight for exactly the "right" custody arrangement. Women averaged 8.8, men 8.4 — a statistically insignificant difference.

What is statistically very significant is the difference between the kinds of custody men and women feel passionate about: women typically want full custody and tend to view joint custody as losing, and men generally want joint custody and tend to view that as a victory. As a result, compromises are skewed. In an "ordinary" disagreement between two parties where each wants 100 percent of something, the parties end up somewhere in the middle, at around 50 percent. But in this case, where women want 100 percent and men want 50, the compromise position ends up being 75 percent in favor of women. Men, it seems, are satisfied to have an equal role in their children's lives, while women are satisfied only if they can be the only parent. Which gender, one might ask, really has the child's best interests at heart? That women view joint custody as losing should be irrelevant to actual custody decisions.

Men always get custody when they fight for it

This completely unfounded hypothesis was put forth by Phyllis Chesler, an ultraradical feminist scholar who insisted that around 70 percent of divorced fathers who fought for custody got it. In recent years, however, even Chesler's political sisters have begun to distance themselves from her. In an article called "Why Are Mothers Losing?" feminist attorney Nancy Polikoff cites several studies that indicate that between 38 and 50 percent of fathers who fight for custody actually win. Assuming that this range is correct, should women be afraid?

First, is there anything wrong with this percentage of fathers having custody of their children? Wouldn't anything less than 50 percent indicate a bias against fathers? Second, the percentage of fathers who fight for custody is extremely small, around 5 percent of all divorce cases. Last, and most important, what fathers are really "winning" is joint custody. In the Stanford child-custody study, Maccoby and Mnookin found that when mothers asked for sole custody and fathers asked for joint custody, the mother got sole custody 68 percent of the time. So mothers still get to see their kids far more than 50 percent of the time. Who could reasonably object to that?

The Stanford study also provided two more telling statistics about men's and women's relative odds of "winning" custody. When both parents asked for full custody, the mother got custody 46 percent of the time, the father less than 10 percent, and joint custody was granted the rest of the time. And in 12.8 percent of the cases where both the mother and the father said they wanted the father to be the primary or sole custodian, the judge still awarded custody to the mother.

The irony here is that under the current system, with regard to the children, the new man in a divorced mother's life has more rights than the former husband. In other words, the new husband or boy-

friend can see his stepchildren anytime he wants, but the biological father can see his children only when a judge says he can.

**Men only want more custody so they can cut their child-support
payments**

It is said that some men fight for custody only as a way to reduce
their child-support payments or to have a bargaining chip to use
against their ex-wives. But overall, it appears that just the opposite is
true: it is women who use custody as a way to exert control over their
ex-husbands.

Since child-support payments are inversely related to the amount of
time a father gets to spend with his kids, the lower that time, the more
money the mother gets. A similar kind of logic was exemplified by
Marcia Clark, the chief prosecutor of the O. J. Simpson case. Early in
the trial, Clark went to court to request an increase in her former husband's child-support payment for the couple's two sons, then aged
three and five. Gordon Clark wasn't delinquent in his support, and he
wasn't paying less than he could afford. And together with Marcia
Clark's salary, the kids were being quite well taken care of. So why did
she demand more child support? "Because of the notoriety of the trial
with press and television coverage, I have purchased five new suits and
shoes at a cost of $1,500," she wrote in court papers. "I am under con-
stant scrutiny and on public display. It has been necessary for me to
have my hair styled . . . and to spend more money on my personal care
and grooming. As I am a county employee, none of these expenses are
reimbursed." As an attorney, Clark — who was making nearly twice as
much as her husband and could certainly have afforded her own
clothes — should have known that child support was intended for the
children, not as an entitlement for her.

Ironically, the nationwide support Marcia Clark received from
women was rivaled only by the support she received when, a few
months into the Simpson trial, Gordon Clark petitioned the court to
make him the children's primary custodian. "I have personal knowledge that on most nights she does not arrive home until 10 P.M. and
even when she is home she is working," Gordon said in his court peti-
tion. Marcia Clark didn't argue the point, acknowledging that she

spent less than an hour a day with her sons, a situation she didn't expect to improve for many months.

Television commentator Barbara Walters publicly expressed outrage that Clark might be found to be an "unfit parent" just because she had a job. And *Washington Post* columnist Judy Mann accused Gordon of trying to steal Marcia's children away when she was most vulnerable. But if Clark had been a man, his long hours would undoubtedly have been used as an excuse to give full custody to his ex-wife and to increase his child-support payments — the bias that millions of divorced fathers before him have faced.

Insisting that men seek joint custody only to reduce their child support, says Lou Ann Bassan, a San Francisco attorney and activist, "neatly avoids the issue that men are human, that they have feelings, that they hurt when their children are taken away from them."

Father custody will harm children

Under 11 percent of fathers are given sole custody of their children after divorce, and there's no real evidence to show that these children are any more maladjusted and troubled than children who live only with their mothers. Psychologist Alison Clarke-Stewart has found that boys are more likely to benefit from father custody than girls. Boys in father custody were less anxious and depressed, had higher self-esteem, and exhibited less difficult behavior than boys in mother custody.

National studies confirm these findings. Sociologists James Peterson and Nicholas Zill found similar benefits for children living with a same-sex parent after divorce: antisocial behavior, depression, and impulsive/hyperactive behavior were all lower for children residing with a same-sex parent following divorce. Others, such as Herb Zimiles, a psychologist and educator, report that high school students living with a same-sex parent are less likely to drop out of school than were students living with an opposite-sex parent — unless the custodial parent remarried.

There are exceptions, of course. In one California study, Christy Buchanan and her colleagues found that adolescents in father custody had poorer adjustment than those in mother custody, especially for the girls. Other studies find few benefits of living with a same-sex parent. But most evidence indicates that custodial fathers, especially the ones living with their sons, are doing a fine job of raising their children. It's not surprising, since divorced fathers often are awarded custody of their sons when they are exceptionally good parents, but fathers are more likely to get custody of their daughters only when the mother is particularly troubled, according to psycho-legal experts Gail Goodman, Robert Emery, and Jeffrey Haugaard.

Joint custody aside, many feminist advocates seem opposed to any efforts to increase the amount of time fathers get to spend with their children. In 1998, for example, the U.S. Department of Health and Human Services announced an experimental program designed to improve the collection of child support by "funding fatherhood involvement projects and encouraging states to incorporate positive messages in their efforts." Instead of welcoming such small steps, Nancy Duff Campbell, co-president of the National Women's Law Center announced, "I'm concerned about diverting too many resources into some untested waters."

For at least the past fifty years, judges heavily favored mothers in awarding child custody in divorce cases. And until the late 1970s, they based their decisions on what used to be called the "tender years doctrine." In a 1978 custody ruling in West Virginia, cited by attorney Ron Henry in his 1994 article "'Primary Caretaker': Is It a Ruse?," Judge Richard Neely expressed the doctrine this way: "Behavioral science is so inexact that we are clearly justified in resolving certain custody questions on the basis of the prevailing cultural attitudes which give preference to the mother as custodian of young children." As a result, Neely rejected a father's argument that he should share custody, because "it violates our rule that a mother is the natural custodian of children of tender years." By 1980, after a number of constitutional challenges, many state legislatures, including West Virginia's, began to eliminate such blatantly discriminatory custody determinations, and judges across the nation were forced to reevaluate some of their previous decisions. "While in [the 1978 case] we expressed ourselves in terms of traditional maternal preference, the legislature has instructed us that such a gender-based standard is unacceptable," wrote Neely.

Not surprisingly, radical feminists feared that this new, supposedly

gender-blind legislation would jeopardize women's 9-to-1 child custody advantage. They fought it hard, lobbying judges to award custody
to children's "primary caretaker." That sounds reasonable, until one
takes a look at how feminists define the term. "Every definition that
has been put forward for this term has systematically counted and
recounted the types of tasks mothers most often perform while systematically excluding the ways that fathers most often nurture their
children. No effort has been made to hide this bias," writes Ron Henry.
In several states, for example, women's groups have suggested — and
judges have agreed — that the primary caretaker is the parent, regardless of gender, "who has devoted significantly greater time and effort
than the other to . . . breast-feeding."

Feminists and others who've bought into the primary-caretaker
theory reward women for spending money on food and clothes for
the kids but punish men for earning the money that paid for those
purchases. They praise mothers for washing the Little League uniform
but ignore the father who developed and nurtured his child's interest
in sports. They view child custody as a prize "for vacuuming the floors
but not for cutting the grass, and for chauffeuring the children but not
for driving to work," writes Henry. The irony here is, as critics have
pointed out, that with more and more two-career couples, a child's
true primary caretaker is more than likely his baby-sitter or daycare
provider.

The primary-caretaker theory, says Cathy Young, is based on the
idea that paid work is fulfilling but childcare is selfless. It is also based
on denying the fact that "for every mother who reduces her hours doing paid work because of 'devotion to a child,' there is a father who
must increase his." Moreover, the primary-caretaker argument makes
no attempt to be proportional. Even the most extreme studies show
that men perform only one-third of all childcare tasks. Obviously, we
have argued that men's participation is far higher, but even if men
really are doing only half of what women do, shouldn't it follow that
men should have custody of their children at least a third of the time?
Not according to radical feminists, who would argue that letting fathers see their children 14 percent of the time (which is what every
other weekend adds up to) is already too much.

In 1996, at a conference of the National Organization for Women,

a resolution called the "NOW Action Alert on 'Fathers' Rights,'"
was adopted. Here are a few excerpts that reflect a jaundiced view of
men and fathers and demonstrate NOW's commitment to keeping
women's grip on children firm and to driving single fathers away from
their children.

> WHEREAS organizations advocating "fathers' rights," whose members
> consist of non-custodial parents, their attorneys and their allies, are a
> growing force in our country; and WHEREAS the objectives of these
> groups are to increase restrictions and limits on custodial parents'
> rights and to decrease child support obligations of non-custodial par-
> ents by using the abuse of power in order to control in the same fashion
> as do batterers;

There is absolutely no evidence to back up any of these claims.
Fathers' rights groups may, in fact, be increasing their strength, but
they are so few in number that "strength" and "growing force" hardly
apply. To the extent that fathers' rights groups have lobbied for limits
on custodial parents' activities, they have done so only to limit custodial parents' "right" to willfully destroy the father-child bond. In California, for example, fathers' rights groups successfully introduced legislation that would have limited mothers with joint custody from
moving a long distance from the children's fathers — fathers who had
the legal right to be with their children half of the time. But under
heavy pressure from feminists, the legislation was defeated, leaving
women free to move anywhere they want, anytime they want, and to
take the children with them.

This raises some interesting problems. Can we limit a mother's, or
anyone else's, right to move? No, we can't: the right to travel freely is
protected by the U.S. Constitution. But when people have children,
they have an obligation to put their children first, not themselves.
Sometimes that means making sacrifices. It would be okay for a
mother to move a child away from the child's father only if the father-
child bond is worthless. And that's exactly what feminists want us to
believe.

Feminists have a demonstrated record of introducing anti-father-
involvement legislation and fighting to defeat legislation proposed by
advocates for fathers. One might reasonably conclude, then, that it is

women's groups, not fathers' rights groups, that are trying to "increase restrictions and limits."

> WHEREAS these groups are . . . working for the adoption of legislation such as presumption of joint custody, penalties for "false reporting" of domestic and child abuse and mediation instead of court hearings;

As Anne Mitchell points out, this may be the most astonishing claim of all: "It seems clear that NOW believes that sole [mother] custody is better than the child having a full relationship with both parents. But do they really hold that falsely accusing someone for such horrible acts as domestic violence and child abuse is OK? And does NOW really believe that litigation is better than mediation and agreement?"

Thousands of divorced men each year are falsely accused by their former wives of having abused their children. And NOW's opposition to mediation — despite its proven benefits to all parties — is unrelenting.

> WHEREAS the success of these groups will be harmful to all women but especially harmful to battered and abused women and children; and WHEREAS the efforts of well-financed "fathers' rights" groups are expanding from a few states into many more, sharing research and tactics state by state;

While it's true that there are around five hundred fathers' rights groups in the United States, says Stuart Miller, a senior legislative analyst for the American Fathers' Coalition, that figure is deceiving. Fewer than ten of these groups have more than a handful of members, fewer still have any luck in collecting dues, and only one or two are able to raise enough money to open a small office. And none of these groups receives any state or federal funding. NOW, on the other hand, has fully staffed offices in many states and, together with other women's groups, receives tens of millions of dollars in government funds each year under the Violence Against Women Act. More telling still, attempts by Miller's organization and others to unite disparate fathers' groups into a cohesive political force have been stunningly unsuccessful.

Despite the true insignificance of the threat that fathers' rights groups pose to women, Phyllis Chesler, who claims to be speaking for the majority of women, says: "The collective message presented by 'fathers' rights' groups is a chilling one: that children belong to men (sperm donors, surrogate contract fathers, live-in boyfriends, legal husbands) when men want them, but not when men don't." A rather startling statement, given that the exact opposite is true: much of modern divorce law is built on the idea that children belong to women.

Chesler ridicules fathers' rights activists for claiming that they are discriminated against by lawyers, judges, and ex-wives in custody matters, that women keep men from seeing their children, and that they, too, can parent. Then she suggests that "there is no comparable movement for mothers' rights — that is, for custody, child support, alimony, marital property, increased levels of welfare, 'free' legal counsel upon divorce, and so forth." Another shocking statement, considering, again, that quite the opposite is true.

So what do other feminists think about the men's and fathers' movements? Well, Gloria Steinem is all for them, in one sense. "Make no mistake about it: women want a men's movement," she writes. "We have to use our instincts in deciding who to trust. We need to ask questions . . . then women can find allies in a shared struggle toward a new future." Basically, Steinem wants the Feminist Men's Movement, the one that has adopted feminism's "bill of indictment" and encourages men to explore their feminine side. In other words, she wants a men's movement just as long as it works to advance women's causes and doesn't advocate for changes that would make men's lives better. Anything less would be considered a threat to women and to humanity.

And many women, such as Robert Bly's former wife, Carol Bly, actually claim to be afraid. "The men's separatist movement is frightening. Separatism breeds feelings of superiority and imbalance — male bonding usually offers permission to regress," she said. Others go so far as to suggest that the men's movement is just a hairsbreadth away from Nazism. "Don't tell me 'it can't happen here,' that no such terrible outcome can arise from something as apparently silly as men in a room with a drum," writes Laura Brown. "As a Jew, I know better; Hitler and his gang began as just a fringe-group joke to the assimilated Jews of Germany. Hitler, too, looked to myth and legend, and to what was 'essentially German' to feed his murderous visions of reality; he, too, relied upon ritual, upon the special bonds between men, to build his movement."

One of the many problems with feminists' approach to men's and fathers' struggle for recognition is that, "not being possessed of a sense of irony, they fail to see how their own metaphorical drumbeat of male-bashing may have called for the real-life drumbeating," explains Ellen Frankel Paul. "It is, apparently, permissible to blame all of women's problems on men, but tit-for-tat is considered iniquitous."

A more serious problem, however, is that by and large women's re-actions to the men's movements (including the fatherhood branches) are based on some fundamental misunderstandings. The first one is that men who get together with other men are sitting around plotting various ways to abuse women. This is absurd and paranoid: these men are talking about themselves and their problems in a safe environ-ment. Having done so, men "return to their relationships with women in a more healthy, generous, and nurturing state," writes John Guar-naschelli. "Adult men will no longer need (however unconsciously) to demand definition, validation, nurturance, or 'basic kindness' from women as surrogate mothers. Their feeling of self-worth will not de-pend, as it so often does now, on 'possessing a woman' in any sense of these words. And they will not need to grow helplessly (and infan-tilely) violent if such validation is not granted."

Could it be that some of the concerns feminists have about the men's movement are the result of their own reluctance to give up the control they have (given to them by men themselves) over men's feel-ings and emotions? Either way, the bottom line is that women have nothing to fear and much to gain from at least some men's groups, es-pecially fathers' groups.

Of course not all women, and not all feminists, are alike in their feelings about men's and fathers' rights. Before she graduated from law school, Anne Mitchell founded the Fathers' Rights Equality Ex-change, which has members in all fifty states and several foreign coun-tries. And Mitchell is not alone. Lou Ann Bassan is first vice president of another fathers' rights group, the Coalition of Parent Support, half of whose members are women. Mary Gorak helped found Men and Women for Gender Justice, a Sonoma County, California, group working to establish the country's first Commission on the Status of Men. Nationwide, fathers' rights organizations report that 30 to 50 percent of the calls they receive are from women.

Many of the women involved in "men's issues" (with the exception of Anne Mitchell) are second wives, girlfriends (who are considering becoming second wives), mothers, and grandmothers, all of whom have seen the men they love suffer. For Lou Ann Bassan, it was seeing her husband's ex-wife refuse to allow him to see his children, and the court's refusal to enforce his visitation rights. "I was shocked," she says. "I couldn't believe this kind of thing was going on in America."

Whatever the personal reasons that brought them there, most of the prominent women in the men's movement share at least one trait: they consider themselves feminists — that is, the way the term was used twenty years ago. "In its early days, feminism was all about equal rights and equal responsibilities," says Mary Gorak, who first became active in the women's movement in the late 1960s. "But most of today's feminists have forgotten all about the responsibility part. It really makes me sad that the very people I had held up as the hope for our society have taken the easy road and found a convenient scapegoat: white men."

Barbara Dority, co-founder of the Northwest Feminist Anti-Censorship Taskforce, agrees. "The system encourages divorcing women to be vindictive," she says. According to Dority and others, the attitude espoused by most radical feminists is "that almost all men are jerks and all divorcing men are jerks and that men don't care about their children."

There are obviously great numbers of women who support men's desires to get and stay involved with their families. But the feminist women's movement continues to be dominated by its most radical and inconsistent element, which seems committed to keeping men and children far, far away from each other. As the social critic Karen Lehrman says, "[Radical] feminists may be the only other group besides creationists who refuse to believe in evolution."

Part 4
The Prospects

11

Where Do We Go from Here?

THE OBSTACLES that keep fathers away from their children are significant, and they extend into nearly every area of our lives. But these obstacles are not insurmountable. There are steps that all of us — men, women, state and local governments, hospitals, industry, and society as a whole — can take to reinvigorate the institution of fatherhood and start us on the path toward making fathers more involved. The process starts with men themselves.

Ten Things Men Can Do to Help Themselves Get More Involved

1. Be more active

If fathers don't start taking the initiative, they'll never be able to assume the child-rearing responsibilities they really want and that they and their children deserve. So instead of letting your partner pluck your crying or smelly baby from your arms, try saying something like, "No, honey, I can take care of this," or "I think I can handle things," or "That's okay, I really need the practice." There's also nothing wrong with asking her for advice: you both have insights that the other could benefit from. But ask her for suggestions instead of allowing her to do it for you.

2. Get more practice

Don't assume that your partner magically knows more than you do. Whatever she knows about raising kids, she learned by doing — just like anything else. And the way you're going to get better is by doing things too. Research has shown that the lack of opportunity may be one of the biggest obstacles to fathers' being more affectionate with their children. Once they get to hold them, fathers are at least as affectionate with their children as their partners are. In addition, fathers seem to respond — in much the same way mothers do — to their children. Fathers are very aware of their infants' visual and behavioral cues. More important, they take appropriate action to respond to those cues. (So much for the old stereotypes about men not having what it takes to care for infants.)

Don't be afraid to get help if you're uncertain or feel ill prepared to be a father. You're not alone. Even among fathers who have taken childbirth classes, many feel totally unprepared for what comes after. Programs are available to help fathers learn the basics of caregiving. And they work. In one study, dads watched a videotape just after their babies were born which provided information about the newborn's perceptual and social competence, about play techniques, and about caretaking skills. After three months, these men were more responsive to their infants during feeding and play, and fed and diapered their babies more often, than fathers who had not seen the videotape.

Learning to be an active and involved father need not be restricted to the period just after the baby is born. Some fathers may be good at the early chores of feeding and diapering but be at a loss when it comes to playing with a rambunctious two-year-old. Others do just fine when their kids are old enough for math problems and football but have difficulty with those middle-of-the-night infant feedings. Adoptive parents may not get their first taste of parenting until their child is months or years old. There is no clear evidence that the period right after birth is in any sense *the* critical time for men to learn fathering skills or to develop emotional ties to their infants and children.

3. Take pride in the special way you are with your kids

Men and women have different ways of interacting with their children. Men tend to stress physical and high-energy activities; women, the social and emotional. But don't let anyone tell you that safely wrestling, bouncing on the bed, or other "guy things" are somehow not as important as the "girl things" your partner may do (or want you to do). Not only do children enjoy the rough-and-tumble of father play, but it also teaches valuable lessons about regulating emotions such as excitement and arousal. Children with physically active dads are more popular and more successful in their relationships with other children. And the effects are not restricted to boys. In fact, there's some evidence that girls who are exposed to higher levels of physical play become more assertive in their peer interactions.

4. Be emotionally available to your children

Physical interaction is undoubtedly an important part of the father-child relationship, but being emotionally available and involved is critical too. As John Gottman, author of *The Heart of Parenting*, suggests, "Men must allow themselves to be aware of their feelings so they can empathize with their children. Then they must take whatever steps necessary to make themselves available to their kids. They must structure their lives so they can give more time and attention to their children."

5. Be a partner, not a helper

Despite the nostalgia of some conservative social critics for the idealized Ozzie-and-Harriet families of the 1950s, the traditional father-as-helper model is outdated, outmoded, and won't work nowadays. As Rosalind Barnett and Caryl Rivers, authors of *She Works/He Works*, observe, "A push for old family values — for more dads who are simply junior partners for their wives — would take us back into a past that was not so wonderful for fathers or their children and one that is out of reach anyway." If men are going to be fully involved, they are going to have to share responsibility for the household and childcare in an active fashion.

6. Be available more than on weekends

To be an effective father, get involved in the day-to-day decisions that affect your kids. Leaving everything to the wife means that the father will miss out on the small pieces that give meaning to a child's

life. Without taking part in the everyday chores, the routines and activities that make up childhood, fathers are not going to know their
children with the kind of intimacy and nuance that is critical to being
a sensitive and involved father. To understand the big picture of your
child's life, you need to focus on the details and not leave them to
some other person or some other time. This means making a special
effort to share with your partner such responsibilities as meal planning, cooking, food and clothes shopping, taking the children to the
library or bookstore, getting to know their friends' parents, and planning play dates. Not doing these things can give the impression that
you don't think they're important or that you're not interested in being an active parent. And by doing them you make it more likely that
your partner will feel comfortable and confident in sharing the nurturing role with you.

7. Show respect for your partner

Being an involved father means recognizing all of the ways in which
your partner keeps the family running and respecting the decisions
she makes when you're unavailable. You can't just announce on a Friday afternoon that you'll be taking the kids canoeing on Sunday;
your partner may have spent the better part of a week arranging the
weekend activities. Try to develop a system with your partner to plan
parent-child and family activities together. As the children mature,
let them take part in the planning process as well. This is a good way
to demonstrate to your children, especially boys, that fathers can be
active and equal participants in planning and implementing family
activities.

8. Be aware of the need to communicate

If you don't like the status quo, let your partner know. But be
gentle — if she at first seems reluctant to share the role of child nurturer with you, don't take it too personally. Many women have been
raised to believe that if they aren't the primary caregivers — even if,
in addition, they work outside the home — they've somehow failed
as mothers. It looks as if men aren't the only ones whom society has
done a bad job of socializing! Give her time to learn that you are serious about wanting to participate more and that you are compe-

tent and sincerely motivated to change your level of involvement in parenting.

9. Know your legal rights

Changes in the law have given fathers more rights in order to help them balance home and work, but you've got to educate yourself about these new rights. And you have to take advantage of them in order to improve your opportunities to become a more involved father. Find out whether you're eligible for a family leave under the Family and Medical Leave Act — if you work full time and your company has fifty or more employees, you probably are. You may be eligible for leave under a state-mandated plan or for a personal leave of absence. Unless you insist on exercising these rights, no one is going to do it for you. Every man we know who has taken family leave says he'd do it again. One even told us he thought that men who didn't take family leave were "nuts." Do yourself and your employer a favor: give everyone at work a few months' notice before you take off. That way, they'll have time to reassign your work to others. But don't be surprised if your boss isn't 100 percent behind you. Many companies that offer family leave feel that no amount of time off is reasonable for a man to take.

10. Stay involved after separation and divorce

Fewer than 15 percent of fathers receive shared or joint custody of their children after divorce, and too many of those who don't get custody end up slowly fading out of their children's lives. But even after divorce, there are lots of ways in which dads can continue to play an active role. The most critical is to stay in touch, by phone, by mail, and in person. And make the time you spend with your kids meaningful. As John Gottman counsels, "When fathers do spend time with their kids, whether as a visitation or as part of a joint custody arrangement, they should make that time as normal as possible." Avoid the "Disneyland dad" syndrome of turning every visit with your kids into an extravagant party.

Avoid, too, trying to settle old marital disputes by using your children as pawns. Parents need to cooperate and support each other for the sake of the children. Men, even if they are no longer members of

the household, are still fathers, and they and their kids need quality —
and quantity — time together. As best they can, dads need to fulfill
their obligations to pay child support. For as Frank Furstenberg and
Andrew Cherlin observe, "Those who don't pay don't visit."

Seven Things Women Can Do to Get Fathers More Involved

1. Look at things from your partner's perspective

"Women usually measure what their husbands do against what
they do," says researcher Jay Belsky. Using this scale, most men fail
miserably. But men tend to "measure their domestic contributions
against what their fathers did," adds Belsky, "and sometimes even
against what their male friends and coworkers are doing." By this standard, many husbands feel pretty satisfied with themselves and their
contributions around the house.

2. Adjust your standards

Let's face it, men and women often have very different standards.
"When my husband says the kitchen is clean, he means that the dishes
are in the dishwasher," says one mother. "The counter might still be
filthy and the floor might be covered with crumbs." Adjusting your
standards to his level doesn't mean that the kids will be wearing the
same clothes every day. Also, there are many different ways to change
diapers, play, teach, and entertain the children. Yours isn't always
right. And when wives adjust their standards, husbands are more involved in the household and with the kids. No child ever suffered
long-term trauma by having her diaper put on a bit looser than
mother would like. It's hard to shift standards, because for many
women attention to domestic details is part of their upbringing and
part of how they define themselves.

3. Treat men as partners, not as helpers

Just as men need to rethink their family roles as "assistants" to
mothers, women need to change their ideas about what's reasonable to expect from their partners. Asking your partner for help only

reinforces the view that men have little direct responsibility for the care and management of children. Instead, ask him to do his share. "Every woman who asks her husband to help with the dishes or change a diaper immediately puts herself at a disadvantage," says Rikki Robbins Jones, author of *Negotiating Love: How Women and Men Can Resolve Their Differences.* Asking for help makes it seem as if whatever he's helping with is really the woman's job and that she should be grateful.

4. Praise your partner

As a group, men generally dislike doing things that make them feel incompetent. At the same time, most men love compliments. The television characters Lucy Ricardo and Roseanne Conner figured this out long ago, and the same applies in real life: sweet talk soothes; nagging only irritates. Tell him what a great job he's doing, and ask him to do the same thing again — even if it's not exactly the way that you would have done it.

5. Don't be a gatekeeper

Many women tend to take charge of the household and childcare domains because this is the one arena that they can still control. But far too many women are so intent on keeping control of the household that they don't leave enough space for their partners to participate. For other women, control is not the issue; they assume that men are either uninterested or incompetent. And men get the message: many find it easier just to back off. This is the first generation of fathers to be seriously expected to take an active role in the home. By the time women become mothers, most have had years of training. Female role models are plentiful, as are resources, from women's magazines to breast-feeding guides. But good male role models are rare, as is information specifically designed to help men prepare for fatherhood. The moral? Even if you know how to stop the baby from crying, let your partner try to figure it out for himself before jumping in. Men and women have different approaches to the same task, and fathers need the confidence that only comes with practice.

Especially after divorce, mothers need to open the gates and encourage their children's relationships with their fathers. It is important to remember that they may be ex-husbands, but they'll never be ex-fathers.

6. Recognize that you can't do it all

The days of the "second shift," when women tried to do it all — work at the office all day and do all the work at home too — are over. Let your spouse or partner know that you have limits. Increasing his awareness that you simply can't do everything will go a long way to bringing men into action on the home front. A well-timed "your arm's not broken, do it yourself" may occasionally be a helpful reminder that men and women are partners in parenting.

7. Redefine work

When dividing up responsibilities, many couples have trouble defining what exactly the term "work" means. In many families, for example, couples err by neglecting to give parenting the same weight as other domestic chores. So when your partner is wrestling with the baby while you're making dinner, things might not seem equal. True, he may be having more fun, but play is still a very important contribution to the household. Still, just to make sure that everyone gets to have fun, switch responsibilities once in a while — let him make dinner while you do some wrestling. This kind of trading can change your understanding of what both of you contribute.

Of course, some couples with strong preferences for one sort of job over another may divide household tasks unequally but still end up satisfied. The point is that as a team, you and your partner can devise your own ways of assigning responsibilities. Then you can change them as preferences or schedules change and as the needs of your growing children change over time.

Twelve Things That Government and the Private Sector Can Do

1. Reduce gender stereotyping in schools

There's no reason to emphasize gender in schools — boys and girls can line up together rather than in separate lines. Some parents and schools today are working toward reducing the degree of gender typing. In open preschools, where the staff consciously attempts to minimize gender stereotyping, children spend more time in mixed-sex groups and less time in conventional gender-typed activities than children in traditional schools. In these open schools, children of both sexes are likely to be playing house and gassing up their toy trucks.

2. Encourage schools to provide parenting education earlier in life

As one noted researcher said, "Almost nothing in the prefatherhood learning of most males is oriented in any way to training them for this role. Males are actively discouraged as children from play activities involving baby surrogates, and, except in rare instances of large families with few or no older sisters, they are not usually required to help much in the daily care of young siblings. In short, a new father has only the vaguest idea of what he is expected to do and how he ought to do it."

As early as 1925, the national PTA recommended that parenthood education begin during adolescence. Today there are many courses aimed at preparing girls and boys for the day when they will become parents. For the adolescent boys who take them, such courses provide an opportunity to acquire caretaking skills and realistic expectations about fatherhood.

The problem is, we need to provide formal parenting education earlier — a lot earlier. By about age six, most boys have already learned that anything to do with babies and childcare is "girls' stuff," says educator Myriam Miedzian. If we taught kids — especially boys — parenting skills while they were still in elementary school, and again at a more sophisticated level in high school, we would have far fewer fatherless boys and far more nonviolent, responsible, involved fathers.

Parenting classes have been proven to sensitize boys and girls to the needs of young children, deter them from child battering, and encourage young boys to view themselves as future involved, caring, responsible fathers. They also serve as a deterrent to teen pregnancy. "Once children learn how demanding and important it is to be a good parent, they become far more interested in putting it off until they are psychologically and financially ready," says Miedzian. The start-up costs for these early parenting education programs would be relatively modest — especially when compared to what it costs to give government benefits to pregnant teens and their kids, put neglected kids in foster care, and run thousands through the criminal justice system.

3. Provide government funds and other support for fatherhood projects on the local level

Communities need to develop fatherhood policies aimed at increasing and encouraging father involvement in the lives of their children. As James Levine and Edward Pitt document in *New Expectations: Community Strategies for Responsible Fatherhood,* a host of programs in operation across the United States are aimed at teaching fathers about the joys and responsibilities of fatherhood. And these programs work.

To be successful, they need to be tailored to the age, ethnic background, and social class of the fathers. A variety of programs are currently available that are specially organized for fathers of different ethnic backgrounds. This kind of cultural sensitivity is crucial to attracting and retaining men in these programs.

The programs also need to accommodate men's schedules. Most men can't show up at a parenting class in the middle of the day. Nor can many fathers travel long distances to attend these groups. By scheduling classes in the evenings and on weekends and in convenient locations in local communities, more men will participate and reap the benefits of these efforts.

4. Make fathers welcome in doctors' offices

Too often hospitals and doctors treat fathers and expectant fathers as second-class citizens whose primary usefulness is to pay the bills. Fathers — perhaps even more than mothers — need opportunities to learn about the care and feeding of new babies in the hospital and to have programs available that are sensitive to their needs and roles. If dads are encouraged and included in sessions about how to care for babies during the postpartum period, they will be more involved later in infant care and housework. But too often the medical environment is indifferent to new fathers' needs for instruction and support and even to the important role fathers play in raising their children. Pediatricians can play a more active role too by encouraging dads to be present at well-child checkups. Providing fathers with accurate information about their child's expected developmental milestones is an important way to increase fathers' sensitivity to children of different ages and stages of development.

5. Fund more public-awareness campaigns by federal, state, and local governments about the importance of fathers

At present, there are more public-awareness campaigns devoted to the advantages of recycling, the benefits of exercise, the evils of smoking, and the risks of unsafe sex than there are to the importance of fathers. Existing campaigns have achieved much, and there's no reason to believe that programs aimed at educating men and women about the importance of fathers in the lives of families would be any less successful.

People need to know about the connection between fathers' absence and such negative social consequences as increased school dropout and teen pregnancy rates, more juvenile delinquency, and increased risk of psychiatric illness. The state of Virginia recently began a public-awareness campaign to increase fathers' involvement and responsibility. Other states must follow its lead.

6. Overhaul welfare practices to encourage fathers' involvement

When it comes to fathers, current welfare regulations are punitive and ultimately anti-family. Most states continue to require that fathers abandon their families before their wives or girlfriends can get government benefits. In short, writes Wade Horn, director of the National Fatherhood Initiative, "welfare rules continue to discourage, rather than encourage, family formation and the presence of a father in the home." Several states have made moves in this direction, but they've been small and have yet to be imitated on a wider scale.

7. Encourage joint custody

Encouraging joint custody is the surest way to accomplish the goals of keeping more fathers involved in their children's lives and reducing the ravages of divorce on children. Men with joint custody are far more likely to pay their child support on time and in full; they're also a lot more likely to be involved with their kids after the divorce. Making joint custody a rebuttable presumption in divorce cases will ensure that every parent is at least given the opportunity to spend as much time as possible with his or her children. The individual wishes of the parties should, of course, be taken into consideration. And if there is documented proof of abuse or irresponsible behavior, the courts should be free to make their decisions accordingly.

8. Uphold divorced fathers' visitation rights

One of the ways to keep fathers involved after divorce is to provide stronger enforcement of child visitation rights for noncustodial parents — which generally means fathers. Efforts should be made to educate judges, social workers, and other decision-makers about the important roles that a father plays in the lives of his children, even if he's not living in the same household. It will probably be a long time and a slow process of education before we are able to overcome the judicial bias against giving fathers access to their children. In the meantime, stronger enforcement of child visitation agreements will at least ensure that men have more contact with their children.

9. Implement father-friendly employment practices

The Family and Medical Leave Act gives fathers the same right as mothers to take time off after the birth of their children. But most fathers don't. Men need to be made aware of the importance of taking time off and be assured that it won't kill their careers. This awareness will have a snowball effect, as more men see that their peers are allowed and encouraged to take a leave or enjoy other family-friendly benefits such as job sharing, flextime, part-time employment, and telecommuting. There's proof that they work too. Los Angeles Water and Power, for example, found that the costs of more father-friendly policies were greatly offset by increased morale and lower turnover.

10. Insist on more accurate portrayals of fathers in the media

Fathers are still portrayed in a majority of television programs and movies as inept, uninvolved, or unimportant. The longer the media continue to promote outdated or inappropriate images of fatherhood, the harder it will be to change the attitudes boys and girls have about the importance of fathers, and the harder it will be to get men to change the way they view themselves as fathers or future fathers. Progress has been made in persuading TV producers to voluntarily reduce graphic violence and increase the positive portrayals of women and minorities. Now it's time to apply the same logic to fathers — not only to portray fathers realistically, but to use television to help shape our visions of men as partners for their wives and as involved and equal contributors to the care and upbringing of their kids. One good place to start might be with soap operas, in which a shockingly large portion of fathers seem to lie, cheat, and have weekly affairs. Changing television commercials wouldn't be hard, either. Can't devoted and attentive dads sell products just as well as outlandish caricatures?

11. Encourage better books for better fathers

Book publishers should be encouraged to publish more books that provide advice for fathers. While there are a multitude of books aimed at new mothers, divorced mothers, and breast-feeding mothers, there are only a handful targeted to dads. The shortage of such books itself sends a strong message to men every time they visit a bookstore: women as mothers are of crucial importance, and men as fathers are peripheral players on the parenting stage.

Young adult novels often focus on boys and men in action and on adventures. Rarely do they feature plots that highlight the impact of involved fathering on the story's characters. Instead, you have to turn to historical or political books or memoirs to read about fathers. Publishers, in response to feminist critics, have begun to publish novels about powerful women and effective minorities, with the goal of empowering girls and minorities to be more assertive and self-confident. We need to empower boys and young men as well, by letting them know that being an active and involved father is a viable and important choice for a man to make. We need to tell stories that inspire boys to want to be involved and responsible fathers and to show them that fatherhood is not incompatible with being successful, exciting, and adventurous.

12. There is no single solution, only multiple ones

Promoting a cultural change in the ways that society views fathers and the ways that men view themselves in this role is no easy task. No single program, book, or corporate policy alone is going to change fathering in our time. Just as there are myriad barriers that converge and conspire to limit fathers' involvement, it will take a coordinated effort by men, women, the media, government, and the private sector to bring about a new and more involved era of fatherhood. It's no easy task, but children, women, and men themselves will all benefit if we can increase fathers' involvement as we enter the twenty-first century.

Notes

Index

Notes

Chapter 1: Do Fathers Really Matter?

page

3   "For 19 Million There's No Father Home": Barbara Vobejda, "For 19 Million There's No Father Home," *Washington Post*, April 24, 1995, p. A5; Elaine Ciulla Kamarck, "Fatherless Families: A Violent Link," *Los Angeles Times*, May 7, 1992, p. B7; Steven Waldman, "Deadbeat Dads," in *Newsweek*, May 4, 1992, p. 46; Marcus Mabry, "No Father, No Answers," *Newsweek*, May 4, 1992, p. 50.

3   Some are scholarly, such as: Robert I. Lerman and Theodora J. Ooms, eds., *Young Unwed Fathers* (Philadelphia: Temple University Press, 1993); Sara McLanahan and Gary Sandefur, *Growing Up with a Single Parent* (Cambridge, Mass.: Harvard University Press, 1994).

3   Others are more political and ideological: David Blankenhorn, *Fatherless America: Confronting Our Most Urgent Social Problem* (New York: Basic Books, 1995); David Popenoe, *Life Without Father* (New York: Free Press, 1996).

3   Newspapers occasionally run feature articles: See, for example, Michele Ingrassia and Pat Wingert, "The New Providers," *Newsweek*, May 22, 1995, p. 3; Sheryl Stolberg, "No Longer Missing in Action," *Los Angeles Times*, June 16, 1996; Barbara Meltz, "Nurturing Nature: Stay-at-Home Dads Ease Stereotypes," *Boston Globe*, June 13, 1996, p. 85.

3   One of us (Brott) has published: Armin Brott, *The Expectant Father: Facts, Tips, and Advice for Dads-to-Be* (New York: Abbeville, 1995); *The New Father: A Dad's Guide to the First Year* (New York: Abbeville, 1997); *A Dad's Guide to the Toddler Years* (New York: Abbeville, 1998).

4   Other recent titles: Richard Louv, *Father Love: What We Need, What We Seek, What We Must Create* (New York: Pocket Books, 1993); Richard A. Warshak, *The Custody Revolution: The Father Factor and the Motherhood Mystique* (New York: Poseidon Press, 1992).

4   "Fatherlessness is the most harmful": Blankenhorn, *Fatherless America*, p. 1.

5   So what exactly do fathers do?: See Ross D. Parke, *Fatherhood* (Cambridge, Mass.: Harvard University Press, 1996), for a comprehensive summary of fathers' contributions.

5 Pediatricians Michael Yogman: Michael W. Yogman et al., "The Goals and Structure of Face-to-Face Interaction Between Infants and Fathers," paper presented at the biennial meeting of the Society for Research in Child Development, New Orleans, March 1977.

5 "Most fathers seem to present": T. Berry Brazelton, "Behavioral Competence of the Newborn Infant," *Seminars in Perinatology* 3 (1979), 42.

6 In fact, when given a choice of play partners: K. Alison Clarke-Stewart, "The Father's Contribution to Children's Cognitive and Social Development in Early Childhood," in Frank A. Pederson, ed., *The Father-Infant Relationship: Observational Studies in the Family Setting* (New York: Praeger, 1980), pp. 111–146; K. Alison Clarke-Stewart, "And Daddy Makes Three: The Father's Impact on Mother and Young Child," *Child Development* 49 (1978), 466–478.

6 Boys reacted more positively to both their parents: Hildy Ross and Heather Taylor, "Do Boys Prefer Daddy or His Physical Style of Play?" *Sex Roles* 20 (1989), 23–33.

6 Children who get along best with other children: Kevin MacDonald and Ross D. Parke, "Bridging the Gap: Parent-Child Play Interaction and Peer Interactive Competence," *Child Development* 55 (1985), 1265–1277.

6 In addition, three-year-olds who had good relationships: Lise M. Youngblade and Jay Belsky, "Parent-Child Antecedents of 5-Year-Olds' Close Friendships: A Longitudinal Analysis," *Developmental Psychology* 28 (1992), 700–713.

6 "while they're roughhousing with their fathers": John Snarey, *How Fathers Care for the Next Generation* (Cambridge, Mass.: Harvard University Press, 1993), pp. 35–36.

6 "The kids who did best in terms of peer relationships": John M. Gottman, *The Heart of Parenting* (New York: Simon & Schuster, 1997), p. 171.

7 Specifically, Gottman found that fathers' acceptance: John M. Gottman, Lynn Fainsilber Katz, and Carol Hooven, *Meta-Emotion: How Families Communicate Emotionally* (Mahwah, N.J.: Erlbaum, 1996).

7 Twenty-six years later, another group of researchers: Richard S. Koestner, Carol E. Franz, and Joel Weinberger, "The Family Origins of Empathic Concern: A 26-Year Longitudinal Study," *Journal of Personality and Social Psychology* 61 (1990), 586–595.

7 In yet another follow-up: Carol E. Franz, David C. McClelland, and Joel Weinberger, "Childhood Antecedents of Conventional Social Accomplishment in Midlife Adults: A 36-Year Prospective Study," *Journal of Personality and Social Psychology* 60 (1991), 586–595.

8 "The evidence is quite robust that kids": Norma Radin, Testimony before the Select Committee on Children, Youth, and Families of the U.S. House of Representatives, June 1991, p. 6.

8 In one study, Radin found that children: Norma Radin, "The Influence of Fathers upon Sons and Daughters and Implications for School Social Work," *Social Work in Education* 8 (1986), 77–91.

8 In another study, toddlers whose fathers: Norma Radin, "Primary Caregiving Fathers in Intact Families," in Adele Eskeles Gottfried and Allen W. Gottfried, eds., *Redefining Families* (New York: Plenum Press, 1994), pp. 11–54.

8 "there's a strong connection between kids' math skills": Radin, Testimony before the Select Committee on Children, Youth, and Families, p. 6.

8 In a study of working-class Irish fathers: J. Kevin Nugent, "Cultural and Psychological Influences on the Father's Role in Infant Development," *Journal of Marriage and the Family* 53 (1991), 475–485.

8 the earlier (within reason) the father expected: See Clarke-Stewart, "And Daddy Makes Three"; Clarke-Stewart, "The Father's Contribution to Children's Cognitive and Social Development in Early Childhood."

8 The evidence is both striking and clear: McLanahan and Sandefur, *Growing Up with a Single Parent,* pp. 39–66.

9 In a classic study: Robert W. Blanchard and Henry B. Biller, "Father Availability and Academic Performance among Third Grade Boys," *Developmental Psychology* 4 (1971), 301–305.

9 "Highly available fathers can be models of perseverance": Henry B. Biller, *Father Child, and Sex Roles* (Lexington, Mass.: D. C. Heath, 1971), p. 59.

10 They were the ones who displayed aggressive behavior: John M. Gottman, *The Heart of Parenting* (New York: Simon & Schuster, 1997), p. 172.

10 "boys' greater experience": Lois W. Hoffman, "Changes in Family Roles, Socialization, and Sex Differences," *American Psychologist* 32 (1977), 644–658.

10 Girls whose fathers play with them a lot: Ross D. Parke et al., "Family-Peer Systems: In Search of the Linkages," in Kurt Kreppner and Richard M. Lerner, eds., *Family Systems and Life Span Development* (Hillsdale, N.J.: Erlbaum, 1989), pp. 65–92.

10 "He taught me the importance of thinking clearly": Margaret Mead, *Blackberry Winter: My Earlier Years* (New York: Morrow, 1972), p. 40.

11 "Perhaps both monkey and human males are more susceptible": Eleanor Maccoby, *The Development of Sex Differences* (Stanford, Cal.: Stanford University Press, 1966), p. 761.

11 And there's little doubt that cultural: See J. T. Gibbs, "Black Adolescents," in J. T. Gibbs and L. N. Huang, eds., *Children of Color* (San Francisco: Jossey Bass, 1989).

11 "One of the most surprising findings": Rosalind C. Barnett and Caryl Rivers, *She Works/He Works: How Two-Income Families Are Happier, Healthier, and Better-Off* (San Francisco: Harper San Francisco, 1996), p. 59.

12 "One of the first things a father learns": Maureen Green, *Fathering* (New York: McGraw Hill, 1976), p. 102.

12 Fathers who provided high levels of socioemotional support: See John Snarey, *How Fathers Care for the Next Generation* (Cambridge, Mass.: Harvard University Press, 1993).

Chapter 2: The Biologically Unfit Father

17 "The conventional wisdom was that infants": Interview with John Bowlby, conducted by Barbara Smuts, July 23, 1977. Cited in Robert Karen, *Becoming Attached* (New York: Warner Books, 1994), p. 93.

18 Regardless of which inanimate mother provided the food: Harry J. Harlow and

Robert R. Zimmerman, "Affectional Responses in the Infant Monkey," *Science* 130 (August 1959), 421–432.

18 Fathers in a number of other cultures share: They include the Taira of Okinawa, the Aka Pygmies of Africa, and the Ilocos of the Philippines. See also Barry Hewlett, *Intimate Fathers: The Nature and Context of Aka Pygmy Paternal Infant Care* (Ann Arbor, Mich.: University of Michigan Press, 1991), p. 173.

18 Pruett . . . has documented: Kyle D. Pruett, *The Nurturing Father* (New York: Warner Books, 1987).

19 Instead, they vary with prevailing: Ross D. Parke, *Fatherhood* (Cambridge, Mass.: Harvard University Press, 1996), p. 72.

19 One study by Harry Harlow: Arnold S. Chamove, Harry F. Harlow, and Gary D. Mitchell, "Sex Differences in the Infant-Directed Behavior of Preadolescent Rhesus Monkeys," *Child Development* 38 (1967), 329–335.

19 The males of dozens of species: Marmosets and tamarins (monkeys who live in Central and South America) not only carry infants during the day for the first few months of life, but may chew food for their babies. They sometimes even assist during birth. See the following for many more examples: Gary D. Mitchell, "Paternalistic Behavior in Primates," *Psychological Bulletin* 71 (1969), 399–417; Gary D. Mitchell, William K. Redican, and Jody Gomber, "Males Can Raise Babies," *Psychology Today* 7 (1974), 63–68; William K. Redican and D. M. Taug, "Male Parental Care in Monkeys and Apes," in Michael E. Lamb, ed., *The Role of the Father in Child Development*, 3rd ed. (New York: Wiley, 1997); James J. McKenna, "Parental Supplements and Surrogates among Primates: Cross-Species and Cross-Cultural Comparisons," in Jane B. Lancaster et al., eds., *Parenting Across the Life Span: Biosocial Dimensions* (New York: Aldine DeGruyter, 1987).

19 And, as with humans, a male animal's presence: Debora Cantoni and Richard E. Brown, "Paternal Investment and Reproductive Success in the California Mouse, *Peronyscus californicus,*" *Animal Behavior* 54 (August 1987), 377–386.

19 "Such arguments involved using what look like": Daniel Lehrman, Robert A. Hinde, and Evelyn Shaw, eds., *Advances in the Study of Behavior* (New York: Academic Press, 1972), p. 174.

19 "The variability among rodent species": Michael E. Lamb, ed., *The Role of the Father in Child Development* (New York: Wiley, 1981), p. 3.

19 the role that hormones play in determining sexual behaviors: Clellan S. Ford and Frank A. Beach, *Patterns of Sexual Behavior* (New York: Harper and Paul B. Hoeber, 1951), p. 173.

20 "There is every reason to believe that among humans": Lamb, *The Role of the Father in Child Development*, pp. 3–14.

20 Fathers experience a drop in testosterone: See D. Gubenick, C. Worthman, and J. Stallings, "Hormonal Correlates of Fatherhood in Men: A Preliminary Study," unpublished paper, Emory University, 1994.

20 Even in animal species: Jay S. Rosenblatt, "The Development of Maternal Responsiveness in the Rat," *American Journal of Orthopsychiatry* 39 (1969), 36–56; Jay S. Rosenblatt, "Hormonal Basis of Parenting in Mammals," in Marc H. Bornstein, ed., *Handbook of Parenting*, vol. 2 (Mahwah, N.J.: Erlbaum, 1995), pp. 3–25;

Alison S. Fleming and Carl M. Corter, "Psychobiology of Maternal Behavior in Nonhuman Mammals," in ibid., pp. 59–85.

20 In one recent study, adoptive mothers: Rachel Levy-Shiff, Ilana Goldschmidt, and Dov Har-Even, "Transition to Parenthood in Adoptive Families," *Developmental Psychology* 27 (January 1991), 131–140.

20 "Pregnancy may set the stage for parenthood": David Brodzinsky and Marshall D. Schechter, eds., *The Psychology of Adoption* (New York: Oxford University Press, 1990), p. 213.

21 Wainwright article: *American Journal of Psychiatry* 123 (July 1966), 40–44.

21 Although most of what expectant fathers go through: J. Cain, "The Couvade or 'Hatching,' " *Indian Antiquary* 3 (1874), 151. Cited in J. H. Wapner, "An Empirical Approach to the Attitudes, Feelings, and Behaviors of Expectant Fathers," Ph.D. diss., Northwestern University, 1975.

22 One recent study found that men were more anxious: Howard Osofsky and Rex Culp, "Risk Factors in the Transition to Fatherhood," in Stanley H. Cath, Alan Gurwitt, and Linda Gunsberg, eds., *Fathers and Their Families* (Hillsdale, N.J.: Analytic Press, 1989), pp. 145–165.

22 For some expectant fathers these worries: ibid.

22 A small percentage experience severe depression: ibid.

22 Whether the cause is jealousy: Donald G. Dutton, *The Domestic Assault of Women: Psychological and Criminal Justice Perspectives*, rev. and exp. ed. (Vancouver: University of British Columbia Press, 1995).

22 Most men, though, no matter how prepared: Katharyn May, "Factors Contributing to First-Time Fathers' Readiness for Fatherhood: An Explanatory Study," *Family Relations* 32 (1982), 353–361.

22 The concept of parent-infant bonding: See Marshall H. Klaus and John H. Kennell, *Maternal-Infant Bonding* (St. Louis: Mosby, 1976); Marshall H. Klaus and John H. Kennell, *Parent-Infant Bonding* (St. Louis: Mosby, 1981).

23 "This bonding business is nonsense": Cited in Mosedale, "Fathers in the Delivery Room," *Self*, April 1991, pp. 104–108.

23 "fathers begin developing a bond": Martin Greenberg and Norman Morris, "Engrossment: The Newborn's Impact upon the Father," *American Journal of Orthopsychiatry* 44 (1974), 526.

23 To find out whether men walk the walk: Ross D. Parke and Sandra E. O'Leary, "Father-Mother-Infant Interaction in the Newborn Period: Some Findings, Some Observations, and Some Unresolved Issues," in Klaus F. Riegel and John A. Meacham, eds., *The Developing Individual in a Changing World*, vol. 2, *Social and Environmental Issues* (The Hague: Mouton, 1976), pp. 653–663.

24 To control for these flaws, researchers observed men: ibid.

24 The truth is that fathers and mothers react: Ann M. Frodi et al., "Fathers' and Mothers' Responses to Infant Smiles and Cries," *Infant Behavior and Development* 1 (1978), 197.

24 Fathers, like mothers, are also capable of discriminating: Ann M. Frodi et al., "Fathers' and Mothers' Responses to the Faces and Cries of Normal and Premature Infants," *Developmental Psychology* 14 (1978), 490–498.

25 Mothers can differentiate between types of cries: Peter H. Wolff, "The Natural History of Crying and Other Vocalizations in Early Infancy," in Brian M. Foss, ed., *Determinants of Infant Behavior*, vol. 4 (London: Methuen, 1969), pp. 81–115; Ole Wasz-Hockert et al., *The Infant Cry: A Spectrographic and Auditory Analysis* (Suffolk, England: Lavenham Press, 1968); Alan Wiesenfeld, Carol Z. Malatesta, and Linda L. DeLoach, "Differential Parental Response to Familiar and Unfamiliar Infant Distress Signals," *Infant Behavior and Development* 4 (1981), 281–295.

25 Fathers . . . aren't as capable as mothers: George W. Holden, "Adults' Thinking about a Child-Rearing Problem: Effects of Experience, Parental Status, and Gender," *Child Development* 59 (1988), 1623–1632.

25 After an infant vocalizes: Ross D. Parke and Douglas B. Sawin, "Infant Characteristics and Behavior as Elicitors of Maternal and Paternal Responsiveness in the Newborn Period," paper presented at the biennial meeting of the Society for Research in Child Development, Denver, 1975; Ross D. Parke and Douglas B. Sawin, "The Father's Role in Infancy: A Reevaluation," *The Family Coordinator* 25 (1976), 365–371.

25 The baby's mouth movements: Ross D. Parke and Douglas B. Sawin, "The Family in Early Infancy: Social Interactional and Attitudinal Analyses," in Frank A. Pedersen, ed., *The Father-Infant Relationship: Observational Studies in the Family Setting* (New York: Praeger, 1980), pp. 44–70.

25 When Parke and his co-workers watched mothers and fathers feeding their babies: ibid.

25 Fathers, like mothers, respond to these infant cues: ibid.

26 most men feel that their presence at the prenatal visits: Pamela L. Jordan, "The Mother's Role in Promoting Fathering," in Jerrold Lee Shapiro, Michael J. Diamond, and Martin Greenberg, eds., *Becoming a Father: Contemporary Sociall Developmental, and Clinical Perspectives* (New York: Springer, 1995), pp. 61–71.

27 But researcher Katharyn May has found: May, "Factors Contributing to First-Time Fathers' Readiness for Fatherhood," 353–361.

27 encourage fathers to "play doctor": Myron Levine and Robert Block, unpublished study cited in James G. McCullagh, "June 15—Father's Day," *Baby Talk* 45, no. 6 (1980), 3.

28 about 90 percent of all American males: Jerrold Lee Shapiro, *When Men Are Pregnant: Needs and Concerns of Expectant Fathers* (New York: Delta, 1993), p. 98.

28 "I felt tremendous": Doris R. Entwisle and Susan G. Doering, *The First Birth* (Baltimore: Johns Hopkins University Press, 1981), p. 98.

28 "The father, of course, is not lying down": ibid., p. 101.

29 While some critics claim . . . fathers aren't as interested: William T. Bailey, "Fathers' Involvement in Their Children's Healthcare," *Journal of Genetic Psychology* 152 (September 1991), 289–293.

29 Fathers were more than twice as likely to bring their children: E. Baihireyo Turya and Jane N. Webster, "Acceptability of and Need for Evening Community Child Health Clinics," *Child Care, Health and Development* 12 (March–April 1986), 93–98.

29 As pediatrician and fatherhood expert Michael Yogman: Michael W. Yogman

and Daniel Kindlon, "Pediatric Opportunities with Fathers and Children," *Pediatric Annals* 27 (1998), 6.

Chapter 3: The Dangerous Father

30   "We don't have a clue what happens": Cited in Sharon Churcher, "America's Most Exploited," *Penthouse,* January 1996, p. 47. See also Tom Riley, *Where Are All the Missing Children?* (Washington, D.C.: Statistical Assessment Service, May 1995), p. 1. See also Michael Zeigler, "Missing the Real Story," *Rochester* (N.Y.) *Democrat and Chronicle,* April 6, 1986, p. 1.

31   Thousands of parents had . . . implanted: Tom Riley, *Where Are All the Missing Children?,* pp. 1–5.

31   "another Adam": A television dramatization of John Walsh's story, which has aired numerous times on network television.

31   The actual number of children: Editorial in the *Denver Post,* cited in Joel Best, "Dark Figures and Child Victims: Statistical Claims about Missing Children," in Joel Best, ed., *Images of Issues: Typifying Contemporary Social Problems* (New York: Aldine de Gruyter, 1989), p. 24. See also U.S. Department of Justice, Office of Juvenile Justice and Delinquency Prevention, *Stranger Abduction Homicides of Children,* January 1989, p. 1.

31   According to their most recent figures: U.S. Department of Justice, *Fact Sheet on Missing Children,* National Incidence Studies of Missing, Abducted, Runaway, and Thrownaway Children, May 1990, pp. 1–2.

31   In some states . . . the law defines "abduction": Cited in David Finkelhor et al., *Missing, Abducted, Runaway, and Thrownaway Children in America. First Report: Executive Summary,* U.S. Department of Justice, Office of Juvenile Justice and Delinquency Prevention, May 1990, p. viii.

32   "both serious and minor episodes": *Fact Sheet on Missing Children,* pp. 1–3.

32   "of a more serious nature": ibid.

33   "It is possible . . . take matters into their own hands": ibid.

33   Around three thousand per year: Cited in Churcher, "America's Most Exploited."

33   six million incidents each year: Interview with David Levy, president of the Children's Rights Council, Washington, D.C. See Chapter 4 for more detailed analysis of the number of men whose court-ordered access to their children is interfered with or denied by the children's mothers.

34   "A few years ago the police came": Personal correspondence with Mark Warr, 1997.

35   55 percent of whom are women: U.S. Department of Justice, Bureau of Justice Statistics, *Murder in Families,* July 1994, pp. 5–6.

35   doesn't . . . bring in federal funding: The National Center for Missing and Exploited Children, for example, receives $3 million a year in federal funds, nearly half of its $6 million revenues. The rest comes from private sources; wages and benefits for its staff of eighty consume $3.2 million. Source: Churcher, "America's Most Exploited."

36   "while the proverbial stranger . . . pose a threat": Kenneth Wooden, *Child Lures:*

What Every Parent and Child Should Know about Preventing Sexual Abuse and Abduction (Arlington, Tex.: Summit, 1995), p. 5.

36 "She had a new teacher": Lawrence Wright, "Are Men Necessary?" *Texas Monthly,* February 1992, p. 82.

37 more than half involve "neglect": Department of Health and Human Services, National Center on Child Abuse and Neglect, *Child Maltreatment 1995: Reports from the States to the National Child Abuse and Neglect Data System* (Washington, D.C.: U.S. Government Printing Office, 1997), p. 2–7.

37 "a huge majority of parents . . . believe": Neil Gilbert, *Welfare Justice: Restoring Social Equity* (New York: Yale University Press, 1995), p. 90.

38 "Contrary to popular belief ": Richard Wexler, *Wounded Innocents: The Real Victims of the War Against Child Abuse* (Amherst, N.Y.: Prometheus Books, 1995), p. 25.

38 The problem of relying on advocacy research: Peter Rossi, "No Good Applied Social Research Goes Unpunished," *Society* 25, no. 1, 73–79. Cited in Gilbert, *Welfare Justice.*

38 distorting the facts and statistics is justifiable: Gilbert, *Welfare Justice,* p. 118.

38 The questions included: Diana Russell, *Sexual Exploitation: Rape, Child Sexual Abuse, and Workplace Harassment* (Beverly Hills, Cal.: Sage, 1984), p. 182.

38 "by designing research that lumps together": Gilbert, *Welfare Justice,* p. 94.

39 clinically recognized syndrome: SAID: Gordon J. Blush and Karol L. Ross, "Sexual Allegations in Divorce: The SAID Syndrome," *Conciliation Courts Review* 25 (June 1987), 1–11.

39 75 to 80 percent of these divorce-related: Interview with Dr. Melvin Guyer, a lawyer and psychologist who has done extensive research in this area, 1996. See also Holida Wakefield and Ralph Underwager, "Sexual Abuse Allegations in Divorce and Custody Disputes," *Behavioral Sciences and the Law* 9 (1991), 451–468.

39 nearly 95 percent of the accusers are women: H. Wakefield and R. Underwager, "Personality Characteristics of Parents Making False Accusations of Sexual Abuse in Custody Cases," *Issues in Child Abuse Accusations* 2 (1990), 121–136.

39 Richard Gardner: Interviews with Lee Coleman, Richard Gardner, and Melvin Guyer. See also Wakefield and Underwager, "Personality Characteristics," pp. 121–136.

39 "They'll frequently coach their children": Interview with Richard Gardner. See also Wakefield and Underwager, "Personality Characteristics."

40 "It's a way of getting this guy you hate": Cited in Wright, "Are Men Necessary?"

40 "It's a simple, fast": Interview with Anne Mitchell, a San Jose, California, attorney, 1997.

40 "With child abuse and spouse abuse": Eric Zorn, "A Seminar in Divorce, Down-and-Dirty Style," *Chicago Tribune,* November 4, 1988, sec. 2, p. 1.

40 "And that's not easy": Interview with Peter Firpo, Walnut Creek, Cal.

40 "They're advocates who seek to promote": Interview with Lee Coleman, 1996. See also Lee Coleman, "False Allegations of Child Sexual Abuse: Have the Experts Been Caught with Their Pants Down?," *The Law Forum,* January–February 1986, p. 16.

41 "They . . . hold that 'children never lie' ": Richard Gardner, *True and False Allegations of Child Sexual Abuse* (Creeskill, N.J.: Creative Therapeutics, 1992), p. 264.

41 "children never fabricate": Roland Summit, "The Child Sexual Abuse Accommodation Syndrome," *Child Abuse and Neglect* 7 (1983), 177–193.

41 "If a child suspected of being abused": Roland Summit, "No One Invented McMartin 'Secret,' " *Los Angeles Times*, February 5, 1986, p. 5.

41 Children are more likely to make untrue statements: S. J. Ceci and M. Bruck, "Children's Testimony: Applied and Basic Issues," in W. Damon, gen. ed., *Handbook of Child Psychology*, 5th ed., and I. E. Sigel and K. A. Renninger, vol. eds., *Child Psychology in Practice*, vol. 4 (New York: Wiley, 1998), p. 52.

42 "When children's responses": Ceci and Bruck, "Children's Testimony."

42 "Unless there is a special support": Summit, "The Child Sexual Abuse Accommodation Syndrome," p. 188.

42 detectives "will integrate elements": San Diego County Grand Jury, "Analysis of Child Molestation Issues," Report No. 7, June 1994, p. 36.

42 In 97 percent of the cases: ibid , p 28 Only 276 criminal charges filed out of 54,000 investigations.

43 "These are people who . . . are given an enormous": Interview with Melvin Guyer, Ann Arbor, Mich.

43 selected from a court-approved list: San Diego County Grand Jury Report No. 7, p. 36.

43 the Mondale Act: The act, passed in 1974, provided federal matching funds to states that set up child abuse detection, prosecution, and prevention programs.

43 "As a result, everyone's on the defensive": Interview with Richard Gardner.

43 The following facts: Thomas M. Horner, Melvin Guyer, and Neil Kalter, "Clinical Expertise and the Assessment of Child Sexual Abuse," *Journal of the American Academy of Child and Adolescent Psychiatry* 32 (September 1993), 929.

43 76 percent of the professionals: Thomas Horner, Melvin Guyer, and Neil Kalter, "Prediction, Prevention, and Clinical Expertise In Child Custody Cases in Which Allegations of Child Sexual Abuse Have Been Made. III: Studies of Expert Opinion Formation," *Family Law Quarterly* 26 (Summer 1992), 141–170.

43 sodomized as well as subjected to: Horner et al., "Clinical Expertise and the Assessment of Child Sexual Abuse," p. 929.

44 "My job is not to do an investigation": Gardner, *True and False Allegations*, p. 268.

44 "Any normal child might at some point": R. Legrand et al., "Alleged Behavioral Indicators of Sexual Abuse," *Issues in Child Abuse Accusations* 1, no. 2 (1989), 1–5.

44 Therapists who do dare to disagree: San Diego County Grand Jury Report No. 7, p. 36.

44 An additional $10,000 is available: Government Code sec. 13964, provided by Victim/Witness Assistance Division of the Alameda County District Attorney's Office.

45 "Just because there wasn't a conviction": Interview with Curt Soderlund, administrator of the California Board of Control.

45   "There's no question in my mind": Interview with Nick O.

45   "in medicine, statements made": Interview with Lee Coleman.

46   "there is nothing that looks suspicious": Transcript of Ohio Common Pleas Court, case no. 92-CR-375, pp. 42, 45.

46   she believed she had this scar: ibid., p. 45.

46   recurring urinary tract infections: ibid., pp. 48, 50.

46   "Nevertheless, there are doctors": Interview with Peter Firpo.

46   "CPS workers very selectively look": Interview with Melvin Guyer.

46   "frequently distort reports": San Diego County Grand Jury Report No. 7.

47   "may have been falsely accused": Psychological evaluation (pp. 7–8), conducted after subject had been accused of sexually abusing his five-year-old daughter, provided by Rob W.

47   In a report to the court: Letter from a CPS worker at the area Department of Human Services, provided by Rob W.

47   She also ignored: Progress notes from Rob's daughter's therapists, provided by Rob W.

47   "The best that can be said": San Diego County Grand Jury, "The Case of Alicia W.," Report No. 6, June 1992, p. 12.

48   "there is a strong perception": San Diego County Grand Jury Report No. 7, pp. 32–33.

48   "There's this feeling out there": Interview with Melvin Guyer.

48   To be eligible for federal funding: Child Abuse Prevention and Treatment Act (Mondale Act), sec. 5106a–c.

48   "This was a pretty well-meaning provision": Interview with Richard Gardner.

48   suffering from injuries": California Court of Appeals, 224 Cal. App. 3d 813 (1990).

49   "reckless, or intentionally false reports": ibid.

49   "You have to prove malice": Interview with Kim Hart.

49   has spent more than $150,000: Interview with Nick O.

49   Bankruptcy . . . health problems, alcoholism: Interview with Melvin Guyer.

50   "Unless a man is found not guilty": Interview with Kim Hart.

50   However, this shotgun approach: T. M. Horner and M. J. Guyer, "Prediction, Prevention, and Clinical Expertise in Child Custody Cases in Which Allegations of Child Sexual Abuse Have Been Made. I: Predictable Rates of Diagnostic Error in Relation to Various Clinical Decision-Making Strategies," *Family Law Quarterly* 25 (1991), 217–252; and "II: Prevalence Rates of Child Sexual Abuse and the Precision of 'Tests' Constructed to Diagnose It," *Family Law Quarterly* 25 (1991), 381–409.

50   "Often the therapist actively fosters": Gardner, *True and False Allegations,* p. 496.

50   mothers abuse their children twice as often as fathers do: The Children's Rights Coalition in Texas compiled data from child protective services agencies in all fifty states and examined the relationship (where available) between confirmed child abusers and the children they abused. In the fourteen states that broke down the data along mother-father lines, the ratio was consistently 2 to 1. Interestingly, some critics say that this is due to the fact that mothers spend more

time with children than fathers do. But the evidence doesn't support this. In 1989 the state of Texas passed minimum visitation standards that allowed noncustodial fathers a minimum of 34 percent time with their children (that percentage has been gradually raised, to roughly 42 percent in 1998). The percentage of abuse committed by mothers has increased since the minimum visitation standards were imposed. Of the abuse committed by mothers and fathers, 66 percent was by mothers in 1989, 68 percent in 1991.

50 55 percent of people who kill their own children: U.S. Department of Justice, Bureau of Justice Statistics, *Murder in Families,* July 1994, pp. 5–6.

51 the problem of female abusers: Many social scientists believe that all child abuse is underreported. While this may be true, the discussion here concerns the percentage of all abusers who are women.

51 might occur more often as incest: Craig M. Allen, " 'Women Don't Do These Kinds of Things': Biases among Professionals about Women Who Sexually Abuse Children," unpublished ms., 1994, pp. 7–8. For a more thorough discussion, see Anne Horton et al., *The Incest Perpetrator: A Family Member No One Wants to Treat* (Beverly Hills, Cal.: Sage, 1990), and Craig Allen, *Women and Men Who Sexually Abuse Children: A Comparative Study* (Orwell, Vt.: Safer Society Press, 1985).

51 "Society tends to be more concerned": C. K. Kempe and R. E. Helfer, *The Battered Child,* 3rd ed. (Chicago: University of Chicago Press, 1980). Cited in ibid., p. 207.

51 That she might seduce a helpless child": J. L. Mathis, *Clear Thinking about Sexual Deviation* (Chicago: Nelson-Hall, 1972), p. 54.

51 "The explanation of male preponderance": D. Russell with D. Finkelhor, "The Gender Gap among Perpetrators of Child Sexual Abuse," in D. Russell, *Sexual Exploitation: Rape, Child Sexual Abuse, and Workplace Harassment* (Beverly Hills, Cal.: Sage, 1984), p. 228.

52 between 25 and 40 percent of sexual abuse victims are boys: Anne Banning, "Mother-Son Incest: Confronting a Prejudice," *Child Abuse and Neglect* 13 (1989), 563–570.

52 when boys do acknowledge their own abuse: See, for example, C. M. Allen, *Women and Men Who Sexually Abuse Children* (Orwell, Vt: Safer Society Press, 1991).

52 "women ... can be brutal too": Cited in Katherine Dunn, "Just as Fierce," *Mother Jones,* November–December 1994, p. 39.

52 "I was pushing my daughter": Armin Brott, "Taken for a Stranger," *New York Times Magazine,* November 21, 1994, p. 44.

53 "by focusing solely on male abuse": Andrew Kimbrell, *The Masculine Mystique: The Politics of Masculinity* (New York: Ballantine, 1995), p. 162.

Chapter 4: The Lazy Dad and the Deadbeat Dad

55 Hochschild: Arlie Hochschild, *The Second Shift: Working Parents and the Revolution at Home* (New York: Viking, 1989), p. 3.

56 "In navigating through the territory": James Levine and Todd Pittinsky, *Working Fathers: New Strategies for Balancing Work and Family* (Reading, Mass.: Addison-Wesley, 1997), p. 23.

56 "employed fathers actually spent": Joseph Pleck, "Are Family-Supportive Employer Policies Relevant to Men?," in Jane C. Hood, ed., *Men, Work, and Family* (Newbury Park, Cal.: Sage, 1993), p. 219. See also Joseph Pleck, "Families and Work: Small Changes with Big Implications," *Qualitative Sociology* 15, no. 4 (1992), 427–432.

56 Remember, this was in 1965: Pleck, "Are Family-Supportive Employer Policies Relevant to Men?" Pleck says that men's time devoted to housework and child-care activities "increased between the mid-1960s and the early 1980s, with men's share of the total performed by both sexes rising from 20% in 1965 to 30% in 1981" (p. 219). Robinson and Godbey say that in 1965, employed men spent 4.4 hours per week on housework. By 1985 that number had nearly doubled, to 8.4 hours per week. Source: John P. Robinson and Geoffrey Godbey, *Time for Life: The Surprising Ways Americans Use Their Time* (University Park: Pennsylvania State University Press, 1997), p. 105.

56 fathers . . . engaged with their children: B. A. McBride, and G. Mills, "A Comparison of Mother and Father Involvement with Their Preschool-Age Children," *Early Childhood Research Quarterly* 8 (1993), 457–477.

57 When employed parents' paid and unpaid: Robinson and Godbey, *Time for Life*, pp. 95, 105. See also Thomas Juster and Frank Stafford, "The Allocation of Time: Empirical Findings, Behavioral Models, and Problems of Measurement," *Journal of Economic Literature* 29 (June 1991), 477.

57 Including commute time, women: Robinson and Godbey, *Time for Life*, p. 109.

57 One recent article, entitled: Cited in Peter Vogel, "When It Comes to Men, No News Is Good News," *Certified Male*, Spring 1995, p. 1.

57 "Women continue to bear a larger part": ibid.

57 "Had the reporter not been so interested": ibid.

58 In 1997, 94.6 percent: "Employment Characteristics of Families in 1997" (USDL 98-217), U.S. Department of Labor, Bureau of Labor Statistics, May 1998, Table 5.

58 96.8 percent of those: ibid. See also Ellen Galinsky and James T. Bond, "Work and Family: The Experiences of Mothers and Fathers in the U.S. Labor Force," in D. Costello and B. K. Krimgold, eds., *The American Woman 1996–1997* (New York: W. W. Norton, 1996), p. 83.

58 Families and Work Institute study: Families and Work Institute, National Study of the Changing Workforce, 1993, cited in Levine and Pittinsky, *Working Fathers*.

58 "the average working father is": Levine and Pittinsky, *Working Fathers*, p. 25.

58 "The good news is": Rosalind C. Barnett and Caryl Rivers, *She Works/He Works* (San Francisco: Harper San Francisco, 1996), p. 178.

58 Neither fathers nor mothers in today's: J. P. Robinson, "The Time Squeeze," *American Demographics* 12, no. 2 (1990), 30–33.

59 "The linkage between fatherhood and breadwinning": Robert Griswold, *Fatherhood in America: A History* (New York: Basic Books, 1993), p. 3.

59 Because he "had been battering her": Lenore Walker, *The Battered Woman Syn-*

drome (New York: Springer, 1984). Cited in Cathy Young, *Ceasefire: From Gender War to Real Equality* (New York: Free Press, in press).

59 One recent study in *Behavior and Brain Sciences*: Cited in David Thomas, *Not Guilty: The Case in Defense of Men* (New York: William Morrow, 1993), p. 67.

59 "The evolution of the female preference": David M. Buss, *The Evolution of Desire: Strategies of Human Mating* (New York: Basic Books, 1994), p. 22. Cited in David Popenoe, *Life Without Father* (New York: Free Press, 1996), p. 141.

59 Nearly 60 percent of men: Gregory E. Kennedy, "Involving Students in Participatory Research on Fatherhood: A Case Study," *Family Relations* 38 (October 1989), 363–370.

59 "no matter how much they themselves": Popenoe, *Life Without Father,* p. 141.

60 And for twenty years men have consistently rated: Yankelovich Monitor Survey, cited in Susan Faludi, *Backlash: The Undeclared War Against American Women* (New York: Doubleday, 1991), p. 65. "For twenty years the Monitor's pollsters have asked its [male] subjects to define masculinity. And for twenty years, the leading definition, ahead by a huge margin, has never changed. It isn't being a leader, athlete, Lothario, decision-maker, or even being 'born male.' It is simply this: being a 'good provider for his family.' "

60 "Emphasizing fatherhood in largely economic terms": Wade Horn, *Father Facts* 2, rev. ed. (National Fatherhood Initiative, 1996), pp. I–VI.

60 With the focus on the man-as-breadwinner: Ralph Larossa, "Fatherhood and Social Change," *Family Relations* 37 (October 1988), 457. Larossa says that "the man-as-breadwinner model of fatherhood" erects harmful "structural barriers to men's involvement with their children."

60 "African Americans are still living": Sylvia Ann Hewlett and Cornel West, *The War Against Parents* (Boston: Houghton Mifflin, 1998), p. 181.

61 Young fathers who felt they weren't earning: Sandra K. Danziger and Norma Radin, "Absent Does Not Equal Uninvolved: Predictors of Fathering in Teen Mother Families," *Journal of Marriage and the Family* 52 (August 1990), 636–642.

61 They see themselves as a burden: Harvey Deutschendorf, *Of Work and Men: How Men Can Become More Than Their Careers* (Minneapolis: Fairview Press, 1996), p. 49.

61 The difference was they did not see": Gloria Emerson, *Some American Men* (New York: Simon & Schuster, 1985), p. 157.

61 For women, there's no difference: Deutschendorf, *Of Work and Men,* p. 49.

61 the link between masculinity: Faludi, *Backlash,* p. 65.

61 "Men are being doubly emasculated": Thomas, *Not Guilty,* p. 66.

61 "I think men increasingly feel": Quoted in Jack Kammer, *Good Will Toward Men* (New York: St. Martin's Press, 1994), p. 145.

62 In Canada: These three examples were cited by Faludi in *Backlash,* pp. 66–67.

62 men like Michael Kojima: " 'Deadbeat Dad' Avoids Jail in Plea Agreement," Reuters news wire article, appeared in *New York Times,* October 17, 1992, p. A6.

62 Or of Jeffrey Nichols: Karen S. Schneider, "Daddy Meanest: After a Six-Year Pursuit, an Angry Mother Sees Her Elusive Ex-Husband Jailed for Dodging $589,000 in Child Support," *People,* September 4, 1995, p. 40.

62 Sixty-six percent of mothers: General Accounting Office, *Interstate Child Support: Mothers Report Receiving Less Support from Out-of-State Fathers,* January 1992, p. 19.

63 In fact, the unemployment rate: See, for example, Sanford Brauer et al., "Noncustodial Parents' Report of Child Support Payments," *Family Relations* 40 (April 1991), 180–185; Freya Sonenstein and Charles Calhoun, *The Survey of Absent Parents: Pilot Results,* U.S. Department of Health and Human Services, Office of the Secretary for Planning and Evaluation, July 1988; Sumati N. Dubey, "A Study of Reasons for Nonpayment of Child Support by Noncustodial Parents," *The Children's Advocate,* July–August 1996, p. 10–17; Judi Bartfeld and Daniel Meyer, "Are There Really Deadbeat Dads? The Relationship Between Ability to Pay, Enforcement, and Compliance in Nonmarital Child Support Cases," Institute for Research on Poverty, discussion paper 994–93, February 1993.

63 One large study found that 81 percent of men: Jessica Pearson and Nancy Thoennes, "Supporting Children after Divorce: The Influence of Custody on Support Levels and Payments," *Family Law Quarterly* 22 (Fall 1988), 319–339.

63 Lloyd R., a divorced father: Interview with Lloyd R.

63 Brian G., a former logger: Interview with Brian and Linda G.

63 A recent list of the top ten: Virginia Department of Social Services, Division of Child Support Enforcement, *The Support Report* 6 (January 1993).

64 A recent study conducted by: Bartfeld and Daniel, "Are There Really Deadbeat Dads?"

64 "Sometimes a guy got a nice job": Cited in M. L. Sullivan, "Young Fathers and Parenting in Two Inner-City Neighborhoods," in R. I. Lerman and J. J. Ooms, eds., *Young Unwed Fathers* (Philadelphia: Temple University Press, 1993), p. 62.

64 "Men can be brought back": F. F. Furstenberg, "Fathering in the Inner City: Paternal Participation and Public Policy," in W. Marsiglio, ed., *Fatherhood: Contemporary Theory, Research, and Social Policy* (Thousand Oaks, Cal.: Sage, 1995), p. 146.

64 "Even if I would have known": Interview with Lloyd R.

64 "a reluctance to reduce": Elaine Sorensen, "A Little Help for Some 'Deadbeat' Dads," *Washington Post,* November 15, 1995, p. A25.

65 Only 4 percent of noncustodial fathers: ibid.

65 One federal law, for example: Child Support Recovery Act of 1992, Public Law 102–521, 18 USC sec. 228.

65 The intent of this law has been so twisted: Monica Allen, "Child State Jurisdiction," *Family Law Quarterly* 26, no. 3 (Fall 1992), 293–318 (discussing the case of *Kulko v. Kulko*).

65 Other enforcement efforts are just as bizarre: Kathleen Ostrander, "40-cent Child Support Bill Lands Father in Court," *Milwaukee Journal Sentinel,* April 10, 1998, p. A9.

66 "It seemed pretty idiotic": Interview with Brian G.

66 But Texas's attorney general still: Gary Taylor, "Death Sentence Is No Excuse to Avoid Child Support," *National Law Journal,* March 1, 1993.

66 Forty percent were receiving: Sorensen, "A Little Help for Some 'Deadbeat' Dads," p. A25.

66 "The perverse effect would be": ibid.

67 In 1993 the Urban Institute: Elaine Sorensen, *Noncustodial Fathers: Can They Afford to Pay More Child Support?*, The Urban Institute, September 1993, rev. ed. January 1994.

67 First, more than 42 percent: Gordon Lester, *Child Support and Alimony: 1989*, U.S. Department of Commerce, Bureau of the Census, Current Population Reports, Consumer Income, Series P60–173, September 1991, p. 6.

67 as many as 14 percent: General Accounting Office, *Mothers Report Receiving Less Support from Out-of-State Fathers*, HRD-92-39FS, January 1992, p. 19.

68 The Office of Child Support Enforcement: Interview with Stuart Miller, senior legislative analyst of the American Fathers' Coalition, a Washington, D.C., lobbying group, 1998.

68 Lockheed-Martin: *The Statewide Automated Child Support System (SACSS)*, report published by the State of California, Legislative Analyst's Office, October 20, 1997; Robert E. Pierre, "Registry Targets Child Support; State's New-Employee List Traces Parents Who Owe," *Washington Post*, January 22, 1998, p. M1; Margaret Kane, "Lockheed System Transfers Child-Support Payments," *PC Week* on-line edition, July 12, 1996 (http://www8.zdnet.com/pcweek/news/0708/12echild.html).

68 "Her first day at school": National advertisement run by Find Dad America, 1997.

69 "the incentive program from hell": Robert Rector, cited in "On Need for Two Parents: Conservative and Liberal Groups Agree," in *Speak Out for Children* (quarterly newsletter of the Children's Rights Council) 7 (Spring 1992), p. 6.

69 In fact, perfect compliance: Lydia Scoon-Rogers and Gordon Lester, *Child Support for Custodial Mothers and Fathers*, U.S. Department of Commerce, Bureau of the Census, Current Population Reports, Consumer Income, Series P60–187, August 1995.

69 "Since the mid-1960s": Sylvia Ann Hewlett and Cornel West, "Give Dads Their Parental Due," *San Francisco Chronicle*, June 19, 1998, p. A23.

69 The U.S. Census Bureau found: Lester, *Child Support and Alimony*, p. 7.

70 It is only when custody and visitation: ibid.

70 One of the few national studies: Freya L. Sonenstein and Charles Calhoun, *The Survey of Absent Parents Pilot Result*, U.S. Department of Health and Human Services, July 1988. See also Sanford L. Braver, Pamela J. Fitzpatrick, and R. Curtis Bay, "Noncustodial Parents' Report of Child Support Payments," *Family Relations* 4 (1991), 180–185.

70 "Simply making child-support payments": J. D. Teachman, "Intergenerational Resources Transfers Across Disrupted Households: Absent Fathers' Contribution to the Well-Being of Their Children," in S. J. South and S. E. Tolnay, eds., *The Changing American Family: Sociological and Demographic Perspectives* (Boulder, Colo.: Westview Press, 1992), p. 226.

70 Eighty-seven percent of women on AFDC: Pearson and Thoennes, "Supporting Children after Divorce," pp. 319–339.

70 To take things a step further: Scoon-Rogers and Lester, *Child Support for Custodial Mothers and Fathers*, p. 6.

71 "Almost nothing is known": Teachman, "Intergenerational Resources Transfers Across Disrupted Households," p. 225.

71 "Assistance is more likely to be": ibid.

71 Recent Census Bureau data revealed: Figures in this and the following paragraph are from Scoon-Rogers and Lester, *Child Support for Custodial Mothers and Fathers*, pp. 5–6.

72 Custodial mothers' support awards: ibid., pp. 1–2. The actual amounts are $3,011 for mothers, $2,292 for fathers.

72 The mother is the sole custodian: Lester, *Child Support and Alimony*, p. 7.

72 Nearly 40 percent: ibid. Exactly 37.9 percent have neither visitation nor custody.

73 "actively tried to sabotage the meetings": Judith S. Wallerstein and Joan Berlin Kelly, *Surviving the Breakup* (New York: Basic Books, 1980), pp. 125–126.

73 Other studies, such as those: Joyce A. Arditti, "Factors Related to Custody, Visitation, and Child Support for Divorced Fathers: An Exploratory Analysis," *Journal of Divorce and Remarriage* 17 (1992), 34, 39.

73 Translated, this means: Interview with David Levy, president of the Children's Rights Council, Washington, D.C.

73 "Many times, mothers will disrupt": Interview with Richard Warshak, 1997.

73 "My daughter was supposedly": Interview with Larry K.

73 A recent survey in Indiana: Interview with David Dinn, state coordinator of the Children's Rights Council in Indiana, January 1998. Dinn supervised the study, conducted in the late 1980s.

73 In 1998 Lisa Barbosa, a divorced: Patricia Orwen, "Mom in Jail as Daughter Turns 5: Prison Term for Denying Access Is Denounced," *Toronto Star*, March 4, 1998, p. A3.

74 Far more typical . . . Cyndy Garvey: "Cyndy Garvey Gets Suspended Sentence," Associated Press news wire, November 3, 1989.

74 In 1997 Virgil Chase's former wife: Ronald J. Hansen, "Divorced Man Wants Visitation Enforced," *Washington Times*, June 21, 1998, p. A1.

74 But in cases where a custodial parent: E. Nichols and Annette Vanini, *Visitation Interference: A National Study* (FAIR, the National Fathers' Organization, undated). Survey of 2,228 noncustodial parents conducted by Annette Vanini, MSW.

74 According to researcher Sanford Braver: Sanford L. Braver et al., "A Longitudinal Study of Noncustodial Parents: Parents Without Children," *Journal of Family Psychology* 7 (1993), 9–23.

75 In Michigan, for example: This program is described in detail in Jessica Pearson and Jean Anhalt, *The Visitation Enforcement Program: Impact on Child Access and Child Support: Final Report* (grant no. 89M-E-021), September 30, 1992.

75 "More parents are willing to pay": Cited in "On Need for Two Parents," p. 6.

75 "I felt that if we were going to make": Interview with Don Chavez.

76 Single fathers, whether they're divorced: Summarized in Geoffrey L. Grief, *Single Fathers* (Lexington, Mass.: Lexington Books, 1985).

Chapter 5: The Bumbling Father and the Useless Father

78 In many homes, especially those in which girls live: See, for example, Jack Zipes, *Don't Bet on the Prince: Contemporary Feminist Fairy Tales in North America and England* (Routledge Kegan & Paul, 1989); *Richard Scarry's Best Little Word Book Ever* (Golden Books, 1997); and many others.

78 Take, for example, a recent retelling: Chris Connover, *Mother Goose and the Sly Fox* (Sunburst, 1991).

79 In *Toes Are to Tickle*: by Shen Roddie, illustrated by Kady MacDonald Denton (Berkeley, Cal.: Tricycle Press, 1997).

79 A recent exhaustive review: The head children's librarian at the Berkeley Public Library was kind enough to assemble a list of two hundred of the library's most popular picture books, with particular emphasis on books published in the last ten years or so. Each was carefully examined. About a quarter of them don't include a parent at all — and that seems reasonable. But of those that remain, about 30 percent portray fathers as much less loving and caring than mothers. And fewer than 20 percent contained what could be considered "equal" treatment of mothers and fathers.

79 If a dad is there at all: The same negative stereotype of the father who doesn't care is also perpetuated in reading material aimed at the parents of small children. In the enormously successful *What to Expect the First Year* (as well as its predecessor, *What to Expect When You're Expecting*), the authors answer almost every conceivable question the parents of a newborn or toddler could have. The authors are meticulous in alternating between boys and girls in their examples. At the same time, however, they refer almost exclusively to "mother" taking the child's temperature or "mommy" changing diapers — or doing anything, for that matter, with the kids. Men and their feelings about parenting are relegated to a nine-page chapter preceding the recipe section of this 671-page tome.

79 In an even larger study: Michele Otstott, "The Role of the American Father as Revealed in Selected Fiction Books for Children in the Elementary Grades: An Historical Overview and Content Analysis," unpublished diss., September 1985. In *Dissertation Abstracts International* 46, no. 3A, 541.

80 "the position of fathers in society": Lesley Boyd, "The Portrayal of Fathers in Adolescent Fiction," master's thesis, Loughborough University, 1996.

80 The truth is that in the real world: Phone conversations with Kathy Gerstner, spokesperson for the U.S. Fire Administration, a U.S. government agency, and with Theresa Florin, spokesperson for Women in the Fire Service, Wisconsin, 1997.

82 Take ... Little Nutbrown Hare: Sam McBratney, *Guess How Much I Love You* (Cambridge, Mass.: Candlewick Press, 1996).

82 "Nothing is more important": Bruno Bettelheim, *The Uses of Enchantment* (New York: Vintage, 1989), p. 4.

84 What's more, the average American watches: S. Coltrane, "New Fathers and Old Stereotypes: Representations of Masculinity in 1980s Television Advertising," *Masculinities* 2 (1994), 43–66. See also *Statistical Abstract of the United States*

1997: The National Data Book, U.S. Department of Commerce, October 1997, tables 3 and 409.

84 But by the 1980s, this situation: ibid.

84 "Images of autonomous and controlling men": ibid.

85 "orchestrate everyday consciousness": Todd Gittlin, *The Whole World Is Watching: The Mass Media in the Making and Unmaking of the New Left* (Berkeley: University of California Press, 1980) pp. 1–2. For other interesting examples of the media's impact, see Gaye Tuchman, *Making News: A Study in the Construction of Reality* (New York: Free Press, 1978); and Gaye Tuchman, Arlene Kaplan Daniels, and James Benet, *Hearth and Home: Images of Women in the Mass Media* (New York: Oxford University Press, 1978).

85 Because they're "focusing on mothers' desires": Unpublished correspondence with Scott Coltrane relating to his preparation for a segment on *Good Morning America*, June 5, 1996.

86 "in touch with the shifting realities": Caryn James, "A Baby Boom on TV as Biological Clocks Cruelly Tick Away," *New York Times*, October 16, 1991, p. B1.

87 In the 1950s, when 1 percent: Thomas Skill and James Robinson, "Four Decades of Families on Television: A Demographic Profile, 1950–1989," *Journal of Broadcasting and Electronic Media* 38 (Fall 1994), 449–464, table 5.

87 "More and more real-life mothers": ibid.

87 Women are over 50 percent more likely than men: Coltrane, "New Fathers and Old Stereotypes."

88 Fathers who do take some parenting initiative: ibid.

88 "This corresponds . . . to the phenomenon": ibid.

89 "real-life action heroes": These commercials were aired starting in the spring of 1997.

89 "For years, women got the short end": Quoted in Bruce Horovitz, "Some Fuming, Few Surprised by Madison Avenue's 'Male Bashing' Ads," *Los Angeles Times*, August 8, 1989, p. 6.

89 "Now there are so many women's advocacy groups": ibid.

90 "100 percent of the jerks": Fred Hayward, "Media Watch Best and Worst in Advertising Awards," MR, Inc., 1987. Hayward's findings may be extreme, but the point is well taken. Women are almost never portrayed as jerks or idiots or incompetents; men are.

91 In fact, consumers remembered: Interview with Donald F. Bruzzone, 1996.

91 "Advertisers are trying to make women": Leonard Perlstein, president of the Los Angeles advertising agency Keys/Donna/Perlstein, quoted in Horowitz's Marketing column.

91 "The naked father is seen most often": Anita Diamant, "Peeling Off a Father Image," *Boston Globe Magazine*, January 31, 1993, p. 9.

92 "The kinder, gentler image of men": Cited in Bernice Kanner, "Big Boys Don't Cry: Returning the Macho Message," *New York*, May 21, 1990, p. 20.

93 "*Falling Down* is about": David Blankenhorn, *Fatherless America* (New York: Basic Books, 1995), p. 142.

93 "I thought about hanging around": Cited in Richard Warshak, *The Custody*

Revolution: The Father Factor and the Motherhood Mystique (New York: Poseidon Press, 1992), p. 18.

95 "If you were an alien": Blankenhorn, *Fatherless America*, p. 67.

95 "that fatherhood is superfluous": ibid.

96 From 1990 to 1995, when: David Brenner, *Changes in Newspaper Coverage of Fatherhood on Father's Day from 1990 to 1995*, Institute for American Values, Working Paper No. 51, June 1996. Articles about the changing role of fathers more than doubled, from 6 to 14 percent, but the total number remained low.

96 "Media attention to this topic": ibid.

96 On Father's Day in 1997, a front-page article: "Why Do Parents Murder Kids?" *Toronto Sun*, June 15, 1997, p. A1.

97 To its credit, the *New York Times*: Gail Sheehy, "The Divorced Dad's Burden," June 21, 1998. See also Heather Mills, "You Can Always Count on Children to Be Honest," London *Observer*, June 21, 1998, p. 1.

97 "The seductively realistic portrayals": G. Gerbner et al., *Media and the Family: Images and Impact*, White House Conference on the Family, National Research Forum on Family Issues, Document Reproduction Service No. ED 198–919.

97 And our children are buying into those beliefs: "Sending Signals: Kids Speak Out about Values in the Media" ("Children Now" poll conducted by Fairbank, Maslin, Maullin, and Assoc., Los Angeles, 1995), p. 5. Interestingly, for boys the percentage is even higher: 76 percent.

98 "with predictable regularity": Coltrane, "New Fathers and Old Stereotypes."

98 "Men are being almost constantly told": Ralph Larossa, "Fatherhood and Social Change," *Family Relations* 37 (1988), pp. 451–457.

98 "Stereotyped and conventional portrayals of gender: Kenneth Allan and Scott Coltrane, "Gender-Displaying Television Commercials: A Comparative Study of Television Commercials in the 1950s and the 1980s," *Sex Roles* 35, no. 3/4 (1996), 185–203.

98 When media researcher Michael Morgan: Michael Morgan, "Television, Sex-Role Attitudes, and Sex-Role Behavior," *Journal of Early Adolescence* 6 (1987), 269–282.

99 "Research on shame and guilt": Nancy Heleno Obotz, "Father Absence. Shame and the Noncustodial Father," unpublished paper, presented at the 104th annual convention of the American Psychological Association, Toronto, August 1996.

99 "The stereotype of young, unwed fathers": Institute for Mental Health Initiatives, *Dialogue* 4 (Spring 1996).

100 "personally didn't create the system": Betty Friedan, *The Second Stage*, rev. ed. (New York: Summit Books, 1986), p. 106.

Chapter 6: Socializing Children: From Baby to Daddy

105 This isn't to say that there aren't: Interview with Carole Beal, 1998. See also Beal's *Boys and Girls: The Development of Gender Roles* (New York: McGraw-Hill, 1994), p. 43.

105 almost one hundred minutes: Carol Nagy Jacklin and Eleanor Maccoby, "Length

of Labor and Sex of Offspring," *Journal of Pediatric Psychology* 7, no. 4 (1982), 355–360.

105   Within hours of birth: Ann Moir and David Jessel, *Brain Sex: The Real Difference Between Men and Women* (New York: Lyle Stuart, 1991), pp. 17, 56.

105   Boys also take in less sensory data: Interview with Carole Beal. See also Moir and Jessel, *Brain Sex,* p. 18; Josef E. Garia and A. Scheinfeld, "Sex Differences in Mental and Behavioral Traits," *Genetic Psychology Monographs* 77 (May 1968), 169–195; and Barbara Lloyd and J. Archer, *Exploring Sex Differences* (London: Academic Press, 1976), p. 129.

106   When their babies are less than: M. Stern and K. H. Karraker, "Sex Stereotyping of Infants: A Review of Gender Labeling Studies," *Sex Roles* 20 (1989), 501–522. See also J. Rubin, F. J. Provenzano, and Z. Luria, "The Eye of the Beholder: Parents' Views on Sex of Newborns," *American Journal of Orthopsychiatry* 43 (1974), 720–731.

106   showed a group of more than two hundred adults a videotape: J. Condry and S. Condry, "Sex Differences: A Study of the Eye of the Beholder," *Child Development* 47 (1976), 812–819.

106   adults played in a more masculine way: M. Stern and K. H. Karraker, "Sex Stereotyping of Infants," pp. 501–522.

106   In point of fact, there are no differences: Beal, *Boys and Girls,* pp. 21–22.

106   Men are stereotyped: I. K. Broverman et al., "Sex-Role Stereotypes: A Current Appraisal," in Bill Puka, ed., *Caring Voices and Women's Moral Frames: Gilligan's View,* vol. 6: *Moral Development: A Compendium* (New York: Garland Publishing, 1994), pp. 191–210.

107   African-American children: M. F. Peters, "Parenting in Black Families with Young Children: A Historical Perspective," in H. McAdoo, ed., *Black Families* (Newbury Park, Cal.: Sage, 1988), pp. 211–244; J. T. Gibbs, "Black American Adolescents," in J. T. Gibbs and L. N. Huang, eds., *Children of Color* (San Francisco: Jossey Bass, 1989), pp. 179–223.

107   Similarly, girls are encouraged: D. Lewis, "The Black Family: Socialization and Sex Roles," *Phylon* 36 (1975), 221–237; L. R. Allen and S. Majidi-Abi, "Black American Children," in Gibbs and Huang, eds., *Children of Color,* pp. 148–178.

107   Men . . . even young educated ones: T. L. Ruble, "Sex-Stereotypes: Issues of Change in the 1970s," *Sex Roles* 9 (1983), 397–402.

107   single-earner fathers have more traditional: S. M. McHale et al., "Children's Housework and Psychosocial Functioning: The Mediating Effects of Parents' Sex-Role Behaviors and Attitudes," *Child Development* 61 (1990), 1413–1426.

107   In 1975, psychologists: H. L. Rheingold and K. V. Cook, "The Contents of Boys' and Girls' Rooms as an Index of Parents' Behavior," *Child Development* 46 (1975), 459–463.

108   In 1990 another group of researchers: A. Pomerleau et al., "Pink or Blue: Environmental Gender Stereotypes in the First Two Years of Life," *Sex Roles* 22 (1990), 359–367.

108   Girls . . . receive more dolls: M. R. Bradbard, "Sex Differences in Adults' Gifts and Children's Toy Requests at Christmas," *Psychological Reports* 56 (1985), 969–970. See also Pomerleau et al., "Pink or Blue."

108 "Sex-typed clothing serves very well": B. I. Fagot and M. D. Leinbach, "Socialization of Sex Roles Within the Family," in D. Bruce Carter, ed., *Current Conceptions of Sex Roles and Sex Typing: Theory and Research* (New York: Praeger, 1987), p. 93.

108 As a society that is supposedly struggling: Beal, *Boys and Girls*, p. 42.

109 "Several times that day": S. L. Bem, *The Lenses of Gender: Transforming the Debate on Sexual Inequality* (New Haven: Yale University Press, 1993), p. 149.

109 By age four or five: Phyllis Berman, "Young Children's Responses to Babies: Do They Foreshadow Differences Between Maternal and Paternal Styles?," in A. Fogel and G. F. Melson, eds., *Origins of Nurturance* (Hillsdale, N.J.: Erlbaum, 1987), pp. 25–51.

109 In one study, a group of three- to six-year-old: ibid.

110 "It may be that just as others": ibid., p. 49.

110 "It is likely that parenting or caregiving": P. W. Berman, "Children Caring for Babies: Age and Sex Differences in Response to Infant Signals and to the Social Context," in M. Woodhead, R. Carr, and P. Light, eds., *Becoming a Person: Child Development in Social Context*, vol. 1 (London: Routledge, 1991), pp. 300–327. See also Berman, "Young Children's Responses to Babies," p. 49.

110 In early childhood: Hilary Rose and Charles Halverson, "A Transactional Model of Differential Self-Socialization of Parenting," unpublished paper, University of Georgia, 1996. See also Carol L. Martin and Charles F. Halverson, "A Schematic Processing Model of Sex Typing and Stereotyping in Children," *Child Development* 52 (December 1981), 1119–1134.

111 Parents aren't the only ones: B. I. Fagot, "Consequences of Moderate Cross-Gender Behavior in Preschool Children," *Child Development* 48 (1977), 902–907.

111 Children themselves often operate: M. E. Lamb, M. A. Easterbrooks, and G. W. Holden, "Reinforcement and Punishment among Preschoolers: Characteristics, Effects and Correlates," *Child Development* 51 (1980), 1230–1236; M. E. Lamb and J. L. Roopnarine, "Peer Influences on Sex-Role Development in Preschoolers," *Child Development* 50 (1979), 1219–1222.

111 The result is that children from preschool age: E. E. Maccoby and C. N. Jacklin, "Gender Segregation in Childhood," in H. W. Reese, ed., *Advances in Child Development and Behavior* (Orlando, Fla.: Academic Press, 1987), pp. 239–287; E. E. Maccoby, "Gender and Relationships: A Developmental Account," *American Psychologist* 45 (April 1990), 513–520.

112 Teachers, for example, acknowledge: B. I. Fagot, "Beyond the Reinforcement Principle: Another Step Toward Understanding Sex-Role Development," *Developmental Psychology* 21 (1985), 1097–1104.

112 Boys view themselves: Carol Dweck and Teresa Goetz, "Attributions and Learned Helplessness," in J. Harvey, W. Ickes, and R. F. Kidd, eds., *New Directions in Attribution Research*, vol. 2 (Hillsdale, N.J.: Erlbaum, 1977). See also S. Ben Tsvi-Mayer, R. Hertz-Lazarowitz, and M. P. Safir, "Teacher Selection of Boys and Girls and Prominent Pupils," *Sex Roles* 21 (1989), 231–245.

112 As boys move through school: Moir and Jessel, *Brain Sex*, p. 17.

112 There is one area in which parents': B. I. Fagot, "Beyond the Reinforcement Principle: Another Step Toward Understanding Sex Role Development," *Developmental Psychology* 21 (November 1985), 1097–1104; B. I. Fagot, "Consequences

of Moderate Cross-Gender Behavior in Preschool Children," *Child Development* 48 (September 1977), 902–907.

112   Canadian fatherhood expert: Kerry Daly, "Reshaping Fatherhood: Finding the Models," *Journal of Family Issues* 14 (1993), 510–530.

114   In one study, two groups of children: R. S. Bigler and L. S. Liben, "The Role of Attitudes and Interventions in Gender-Schematic Processing," *Child Development* 61 (October 1990), 1440–1452.

114   Anthropologist Tom Weisner studied: T. S. Weisner and J. E. Wilson-Mitchell, "Nonconventional Family Lifestyles and Multischematic Sex Typing in Six-Year-Olds," *Child Development* 61 (1990), 1915–1933.

Chapter 7: Socializing Adults: From Husband to Father

116   The more satisfying men's marriages are: Shirley S. Feldman, S. C. Nash, and B. G. Aschenbrenner, "Antecedents of Fathering," *Child Development* 54 (1983), 1628–1636.

116   expectant fathers whose marriages were rated as "satisfying": ibid.

117   Martha Cox and her colleagues: Martha Cox et al., "Predictions of Infant-Father and Infant-Mother Attachment," *Developmental Psychology* 28 (1992), 474–483.

117   Eleven-month-olds . . . are less likely to look: Susan Dickstein and Ross D. Parke, "Social Referencing in Infancy: A Glance at Fathers and Marriage," *Child Development* 59 (1988), 506–511.

117   As John Gottman found: John Gottman, *Why Marriages Succeed or Fail* (New York: Simon & Schuster, 1994).

117   And kids who watch their parents fight: Mark Cummings, "Marital Conflict and Children's Functioning," *Social Development* 3 (March 1994), 16–36.

117   Not according to psychologist: Jay Belsky, B. Gilstrap, and M. Rovine, "The Pennsylvania Infant and Family Development Project, I: Stability and Change in Mother-Infant and Father-Infant Interaction in a Family Setting at One, Three, and Nine Months," *Child Development* 55 (1984), 692–705.

117   Adolescent fathers . . . have more positive: Michael E. Lamb and A. B. Elster, "Adolescent Mother-Infant-Father Relationships," *Developmental Psychology* 21 (1985), 768–773.

117   Overall . . . the quality of the marriage: Shirley S. Feldman, S. C. Nash, and B. G. Aschenbrenner, "Antecedents of Fathering," *Child Development* 54 (1983), 1628–1636.

117   Given the connection between marital satisfaction: Martha J. Cox et al., "Marriage, Adult Adjustment, and Early Parenting," *Child Development* 60 (1989), 1015–1024.

117   Studies in both the United States and Japan: Lamb and Elster, "Adolescent Mother-Infant-Father Relationships"; M. E. Durrett, M. Otaki, and P. Richards, "Attachment and the Mother's Perception of Support from the Father," *International Journal of Behavioral Development* 7 (1984), 167–176; Jane R. Dickie and P. Matheson, "Mother-Father-Infant: Who Needs Support?," paper presented at the annual meeting of the American Psychological Association (Toronto, August

1984); W. A. Goldberg and M. A. Easterbrook, "The Role of Marital Quality in Toddler Development," *Developmental Psychology* 20 (1984), 504–514.

118   "Can one parent bring up": 1994 National Opinion Survey cited in Lynn Smith, "Men Can't Be Good Dads If Moms Block the Way," *Los Angeles Times,* July 21, 1996, p. E3.

118   mothers play a "gatekeeping" role. . . . Fathers, they say: Michael E. Lamb, "The Changing Roles of Fathers," in Lamb, ed., *The Father's Role: Applied Perspectives* (New York: Wiley, 1986), pp. 3–27.

119   Others resent men's intrusion: Jane Dickie and Sharon Carnahan Gerber, "Training in Social Competence: The Effect on Mothers, Fathers, Infants," *Child Development* 51 (1980), 1248–1251.

119   Psychologist Ashley Beitel: Ashley Beitel and Ross D. Parke, "Paternal Involvement in Infancy: The Role of Maternal and Paternal Attitudes," *Journal of Family Psychology* 12 (June 1998), 268–288.

119   As it turns out, mothers' attitudes: ibid.

119   only about a third of divorced fathers saw their children: Graham Spanier and Linda Thompson, *Parting: The Aftermath of Separation and Divorce* (Beverly Hills, Cal.: Sage, 1984), p. 76.

119   37 percent of divorced fathers: Judith A. Seltzer and Suzanne M. Bianchi, "Children's Contact with Absent Parents," *Journal of Marriage and the Family* 50 (1988), 663–678.

119   Interestingly, studies of mothers who don't: Seltzer and Bianchi, "Children's Contact with Absent Parents."

120   "they no longer see themselves": Frank F. Furstenberg and Andrew J. Cherlin, *Divided Families: What Happens to Children When Parents Part* (Cambridge, Mass.: Harvard University Press, 1991), p. 34.

120   So it is no wonder that our legal system: Gordon H. Lester, *Child Support and Alimony: 1989,* U.S. Department of Commerce, Bureau of the Census, Current Population Reports, Consumer Income, Series P-60-173, September 1991, p. 7.

120   factors that contribute to fathers' "retreat from parenthood": Furstenberg and Cherlin, *Divided Families,* p. 34.

120   As many as half the mothers with custody: Julie A. Fulton, "Parental Reports of Children's Post-Divorce Adjustment," *Journal of Social Issues* 35 (1979), 126–139.

120   "bothersome, empty rituals": Judith S. Wallerstein and Joan B. Kelly, *Surviving the Breakup* (New York: Basic Books, 1980), p. 39.

120   To find out, researchers . . . studied: Jane Dickie and Sharon Carnahan Gerber, "Training in Social Competence: The Effect on Mothers, Fathers, and Infants," *Child Development* 51 (December 1980), 1248–1251.

121   "For almost an hour": Barbara Meltz, "Nurturing Nature: Stay-at-Home Dads Ease Stereotypes," *Boston Globe,* June 13, 1996, p. 85.

121   Kyle Pruett . . . has identified no negative effects: Kyle D. Pruett, *The Nurturing Father* (New York: Warner Books, 1987).

122   "They learn that love, discipline, just about everything": ibid.

122   Norma Radin, an expert on families in which the father: Norma Radin, "Primary Caregiver and Role-Sharing Fathers," in Michael E. Lamb, ed., *Nontraditional*

Families: Parenting and Child Development (Hillsdale, N.J.: Erlbaum, 1982), pp. 127–143.

122   reverse-role fathers spend more than twice as much: "Interesting News on Nurturing," *Working Mother,* July–August 1996, p. 74. Frank's work was also cited in Meltz, "Nurturing Nature."

122   Australian researcher Graeme Russell has found: Graeme Russell, *The Changing Role of Fathers* (St. Lucia, Queensland: University of Queensland Press, 1983), p. 128.

122   "Who does what around the house?": Norma Radin, "Primary Caregiving Fathers of Long Duration," in P. Bronstein and C. P. Cowan, eds., *Fatherhood Today: Men's Changing Role in the Family* (New York: Wiley, 1988), pp. 127–143.

123   Adolescents who grew up with dad: E. Williams, Norma Radin, and T. Allegro, "Sex-Role Attitudes of Adolescents Raised Primarily by Their Fathers," *Merrill-Palmer Quarterly* 38 (1992), 457–476.

123   "I enjoy the freedom from the routine pressures": Russell, *The Changing Role of Fathers,* p. 128.

123   "After going back to work": ibid., p. 131.

123   "They get teased by the men they know": Quoted in Meltz, "Nurturing Nature," p. 85.

123   "I had a lot of difficulty adjusting to the idea": Russell, *The Changing Role of Fathers,* p. 130.

123   "Even though a wife may be comfortable": Quoted in Meltz, "Nurturing Nature," p. 85.

123   Following up with his role-reversal families: Russell, *The Changing Role of Fathers,* p. 129.

Chapter 8: The Workplace

125   "I will not lose my family": Quoted in Sheryl Flatow, "I Will Not Lose My Family for the Job," *Parade,* July 14, 1996, p. 15.

125   "the best job I've ever had": Robert Reich, "My Family Leave Act," *New York Times,* November 8, 1996, p. A15.

126   "I told them I could not work nights": James A. Levine and Todd L. Pittinsky, *Working Fathers: New Strategies for Balancing Work and Family* (Reading, Mass.: Addison-Wesley, 1997), p. 21.

126   "the arena in which men struggle": Rosalind C. Barnett and Nancy L. Marshall, "Men's Job and Partner Roles: Spillover Effects and Psychological Distress," *Sex Roles* 27, no. 9–10 (1992), 455–472.

126   "what percentage of working mothers and fathers": Levine and Pittinsky, *Working Fathers,* pp. 14–15.

126   According to Levine, these views: Cited in Levine and Pittinsky, *Working Fathers,* p. 17.

126   They found that in dual-career families: Ellen Galinsky and James T. Bond, "Work and Family: The Experiences of Mothers and Fathers in the U.S. Labor Force," in Cynthia Costello and Barbara Kivimae Krimgold, eds., *The American*

Woman, 1996–97 (New York: W. W. Norton, 1996), p. 96. See also the special analysis conducted by James T. Bond of unpublished data from Ellen Galinsky, James T. Bond, and Dana Friedman, *National Study of the Changing Workforce* (New York: Families and Work Institute, 1993), cited in Levine and Pittinsky, *Working Fathers*, p. 234n.

126   "You work longer hours because of the fear": Galinsky and Bond, "Work and Family," p. 22.

127   In a 1995 poll of . . . DuPont employees: survey conducted by Boston-based consulting firm Work/Family Directions for DuPont, reported in *Working Mother*, December 1996, p. 18.

127   "This is a message we're hearing from employees": Catherine Popper, Rodgen and Associates, quoted in *Working Mother*, December 1996, p. 18.

127   "Today in corridors of business": Betsy Morris, "Is Your Family Wrecking Your Career?," *Fortune*, March 17, 1997, pp. 71–72.

127   Schneer and Reitman interviewed: Joy A. Schneer and Frieda Reitman, "The Importance of Gender in Mid-Career," *Journal of Organizational Behavior* 15 (May 1994), 199–207; Joy A. Schneer and Frieda Reitman, "The Impact of Gender as Managerial Careers Unfold," *Journal of Vocational Behavior* 47 (December 1995), 290–315.

128   "Ambitious beware": Morris, "Is Your Family Wrecking Your Career?," p. 72.

128   "Both opposing male attorneys": Susan Vogel, "Babies and Briefs: Rhetoric Yields to Reality," *New Jersey Law Journal* (January 30, 1995), 25. In Levine and Pittinsky, *Working Fathers*, p. 29.

128   "I find guys doing all kinds of strange things": Interview with James Levine, 1998.

129   "In all this talk": Cited in Arlie Hochschild, *The Time Bind: When Work Becomes Home and Home Becomes Work* (New York: Metropolitan Books, 1997), p. 146. Although we clearly disagree with Hochschild's earlier research on women's "second shift," we do think that her research on corporate America is accurate and up-to-date, but based only on a single company.

129   In addition, factory workers are putting in: Cited in "It's too Much of a Good Thing, GM Workers Say in Protesting Overtime," *New York Times*, November 22, 1994, p. A10.

129   Progressive employee policies: Robert Levering and Milton Moskowitz, *The 100 Best Companies to Work For in America*, rev. ed. (New York: Penguin, 1997).

129   only about 10 percent: Ellen Goodman, "Time to Expand the Family Leave Program," *Press Enterprise*, May 10, 1996, p. 11.

129   slightly fewer than half: Ellen Galinsky and James T. Bond, "Work and Family: The Experiences of Mothers and Fathers in the U.S. Labor Force," in Cynthia Costello and Barbara Kivimae Krimgold, eds., *The American Woman 1996–1997* (New York: W. W. Norton, 1996), p. 85. Cited in Levine and Pittinsky, *Working Fathers*, p. 136.

129   The Commission on Family and Medical Leave: *Commission on Family and Medical Leave, a Workable Balance: Report to Congress on Family and Medical Leave Policies 1996*, pp. 95–97, 272. The commission found that 58.2 percent of

women took family leave for any reason, compared with 41.8 percent of men; that 4.4 percent of men and 2.1 percent of women needed but didn't take family leave for childcare purposes; and that women take an average of 41 days for all Family and Medical Leave Act–related leaves, compared with 33 days for men.

129 Only 1 percent of fathers: John Cranford, "Pieces of the Package," *Congressional Quarterly Governing Magazine,* December 1993, cited in Levine and Pittinsky, *Working Fathers,* p. 137.

130 "The primary reason people were not taking advantage": Quoted in Melanie Busch, "Few Find Family Leave Affordable." *Press Enterprise,* July 21, 1996, p. H1. Neese is also the owner of Neese Personnel Services.

130 According to a survey of 1,206 worksites: Commission on Leave survey conducted by Westat, Inc., and the University of Michigan Survey Research Center. Reported in Donna Lenhoff, *The Women's Legal Defense Fund's Guide to the Family and Medical Leave Act: Questions and Answers* (Washington, D.C.: Women's Legal Defense Fund, 1995).

130 "New daddies need paternity leave": Malcolm Forbes, "Fact and Comment: With All Thy Getting, Get Understanding," *Forbes,* July 14, 1996, p. 17.

130 In 1986, when Catalyst: Joseph H. Pleck, "Fathers and Parental Leave: A Perspective," in *Parental Leave and Productivity* (New York: Families and Work Institute, 1992), pp. 17–18.

130 "There's been a lot more discussion": Interview with Marcia Brumit Kropf.

130 Houston Oilers football player David Williams: Sam Howe Verhovek, "At Issue: Hold a Baby or Hold That Line," *New York Times,* October 20, 1993, p. A1. See also "No Appeal of Pay Loss," *New York Times,* October 21, 1993, p. B8; and "Real Men in Sports Can Dunk a Ball and Diaper a Baby," *Salt Lake Tribune,* June 11, 1996, p. C1.

131 "I took him aside and said": Levine and Pittinsky, *Working Fathers,* p. 134.

131 A 1996 report from a bipartisan: Busch, "Few Find Family Leave Affordable."

131 "One worker found himself ": Cited in Hochschild, *The Time Bind,* p. 121.

131 "He actually asked me": Interview, 1998.

132 "To the women in the office": Cited in Hochschild, *The Time Bind,* p. 118.

132 Recently, Joseph Pleck: Joseph H. Pleck, "Are Family-Supportive Employer Policies Relevant to Men?," p. 229.

132 And in a study in four states: See James T. Bond et al., *Beyond the Parental Leave Debate: The Impact of Laws in Four States* (New York: Families and Work Institute, 1991).

132 In another study, Pleck interviewed: Pleck, "Are Family-Supportive Employer Policies Relevant to Men?," p. 229.

132 "An allotted span of time": Maureen Green, *Fathering* (New York: McGraw-Hill, 1976), p. 216.

133 "Although these associations do not": Pleck, "Are Family-Supportive Employer Policies Relevant to Men?," p. 229.

133 "Thanks to the Family and Medical Leave Act": Tom McMakin, "The Politics of Paternity Leave: Why Government Isn't Always the Problem," *Newsweek,* September 25, 1995, p. 26.

133   In 1991, for example, the Los Angeles: Personal communication, 1997.

133   Executives at IBM: ibid.

133   "It is what most people think of ": Levine and Pittinsky, *Working Fathers,* p. 61.

134   "My husband missed": Cited in Hochschild, *The Time Bind,* p. 67.

134   "I don't want to be like my dad": ibid.

134   Parents have to deal with a sick child: American Medical Association study cited in Josephine Marcotty, "Home with a Sick Child," *Minneapolis Star-Tribune,* February 25, 1996, p. 1B.

134   "Flexible use of time is the single most important": Levine and Pittinsky, *Working Fathers,* p. 69.

135   Another option: Correspondence with Suzanne Smith, co-director of New Ways to Work, San Francisco, California, 1998.

135   One study: Cited in Elizabeth Sheley, "Flexible Work Options," *HR Magazine* 41 (February 1996), 52.

135   In the same year, the American Management Association: Levine and Pittinsky, *Working Fathers,* p. 103.

135   And in its National Study of the Changing Workplace: Galinsky and Bond, "Work and Family," p. 84.

135   Recent as well as earlier evidence: See Marni Ezra and Melissa Deckman, "Balancing Work and Family Responsibilities: Flextime and Child Care in the Federal Government," *Public Administration Review* 56 (March–April 1996), 174–176; Fran Sussner Rogers and Charles Rogers, "Business and the Facts of Family Life," *Harvard Business Review* 89 (November–December 1989), 121–129; and Robert A. Lee, "Flextime and Conjugal Roles," *Journal of Occupational Behavior,* 4 (1983), 297–315.

135   Government workers in: Richard A. Winett and Michael S. Neale, "Results of Experimental Study of Flextime and Family Life," *Monthly Labor Review* 113 (1980), 29–32.

135   "Free time won't and can't be": James A. Levine, *Who Will Raise the Children?. New Options for Fathers (and Mothers)* (New York: Lippincott, 1976), p. 91.

136   Although the jury is still out: Hewitt Associates, 1995, cited in Rosalind Barnett and Caryl Rivers, *She Works/He Works* (San Francisco: Harper San Francisco, 1996), p. 66.

136   At Hewlett-Packard, 12 percent: Barnett and Rivers, *She Works/He Works,* p. 66.

136   Far too often: Jane Kiser, "Behind the Scenes at a 'Family-Friendly' Workplace," *Dollars & Sense,* January–February 1998, p. 19.

136   In a 1990 study of Fortune 500 companies: See U.S. Bureau of the Census, *Employed and Unemployed Workers, by Work Schedules: 1990–1993,* 1994.

136   Minorities, particularly Latinos: Kiser, "Behind the Scenes."

136   In one study, fewer than 20 percent: Hochschild, *The Time Bind.*

137   And in *Fortune* magazine's 1990 study: U.S. Bureau of the Census, *Employed and Unemployed Workers.*

137   "The only way to keep a part-time schedule": Hochschild, *The Time Bind,* p. 77.

137   In Norway: Erik Gronseth, "Work-Sharing: Adaptations of Pioneering Families

with Husband and Wife in Part-Time Employment," *Acta Sociologica* 18 (1975), 216–223.

137 "the children are the ones whose interests": ibid., p. 219.

138 The researcher David Maklan found: David Maklan, "The Four-Day Workweek: Blue-Collar Adjustment to a Nonconventional Arrangement of Work and Leisure Time" (Ph.D. diss., University of Michigan, 1976), cited in John P. Robinson, *How Americans Use Time: A Social-Psychological Analysis of Everyday Behavior* (New York: Praeger, 1977).

138 Ten years ago, fewer than 1 million: L. U. Callentine, "The Ecology of the Mobile Workplace: Influence on Household Composition and Home Workspace on Satisfaction, Stress, and Effectiveness." Unpublished thesis, Cornell University, 1995.

138 By the end of this century: Information provided by Charles Grantham, CEO of the Institute for the Study of Distributed Work, July 14, 1998.

138 Employees who telecommute: R. I. Hartman, R. C. Stoner, and R. Arora, "An Investigation of Selected Variables Affecting Telecommuting Productivity and Satisfaction," *Journal of Business and Psychology* 6 (1991), 207–225.

139 Although many work-family experts: Sharon L. Kagan and Bernice Weissbourd, eds., "Families and Work: The Importance of the Quality of the Work Environment," in *Putting Families First: America's Family Support Movement and the Challenge of Change,* (San Francisco: Jossey Bass, 1994), pp. 112–136.

139 "a cyberspace sweatshop": Jeffrey E. Hill, Alan J. Hawkins, and Brent C. Miller, "Work and Family in the Virtual Office: Perceived Influences of Mobile Telework," *Family Relations* 45 (July 1996), 294.

139 studied the perceptions of 246 IBM employees: ibid.

139 "is not surprising in view of the increasing number": ibid.

140 One Alabama construction company: "Corporate Centers Important to Working Dads," *Employee Benefit Plan Review* 49 (August 1994), 38.

140 daycare giant Kindercare: "Corporate Centers Important to Working Dads," *Employee Benefit Plan Review* 49 (August 1994), 38.

140 "Most of the workers go home": Laura Shapiro, "The Myth of Quality Time," *Newsweek,* 1997, pp. 62–69.

141 As Karen DeCrow, a former president: Correspondence with Armin Brott, 1995.

Chapter 9: The Men's Movement

142 "movements of all sorts tend": Ellen Frankel Paul, "Silly Men, Banal Men (The Influence of the Men's Movement)," *Society* 30 (September–October 1993), 38.

142 Or a man who is "a crybaby": Asa Baber, "Wake-up Call," *Playboy,* September 1993, p. 42.

143 "The women's movement drew": Bob Matthews, "Parts Are Parts — or Are They? The Men's Movement," in *Tracks in the Sand.* This article accompanies Gary S. Kalus's "Men's Groups — Gangs — Isolation?" Although this publication is undated, it can be found on the Internet at http://www.vix.com/men/orgs/write ups/tracks.html#movement.

143 "when the plight of woman": Myron Brenton, *The American Male* (1966), cited

in Cindy Tittle Moore, "Feminism/Terms" (July 1994), downloaded from the Internet: http://www.intac.com/man/faq/feminism/terms. This site contains a section on men's movements, contributed by Dave Gross.

143   "The men's movement . . . is largely": Ellen Frankel Paul, "Silly Men, Banal Men."

143   "The collapse of the breadwinner": Barbara Ehrenreich, *The Hearts of Men: American Dreams and the Flight from Commitment* (New York: Doubleday, 1984), p. 12.

144   "Men and women have cooperated": Richard Haddad, cited in Moore/Gross on the Internet.

144   It is perhaps because of this rejection: Susan Faludi, in *Backlash*, devotes five pages ("The Liberated Man Recants," pp. 300–304) to an ad hominem attack on Warren Farrell.

144   "We must not reverse the women's movement": Fred Hayward, keynote speech to the National Congress for Men, 1981. Cited in Moore/Gross on the Internet.

144   And in its pursuit of true gender equality: Men's Libbers, for example, are outspoken critics of circumcision. Certainly one can debate whether male circumcision is medically necessary, but we believe that to equate it with female circumcision (more accurately referred to as genital mutilation), as Men's Libbers do, is ridiculous.

145   Men who prefer egalitarian relationships: Armin Brott attended the orientation of a Sterling Institute men's weekend where founder Justin Sterling insisted that men who ask their wives or girlfriends for permission to do anything are "pussywhipped"; men who don't agree to plunk down $500 for a weekend workshop are pussywhipped; and men who give in to requests to "stop lying around on the couch, farting and smoking cigars" are pussywhipped.

145   These types of disturbing and ultimately damaging: Rich Zubaty, *Surviving the Feminization of America: How to Keep Women from Ruining Your Life* (Chicago: Panther Press, 1993).

145   They are very political, believing: Paul, "Silly Men, Banal Men."

145   "They may feel only a vague pricking": Anthony Astrachan, *How Men Feel: Their Response to Women's Demands for Equality and Power* (New York: Anchor, 1988), p. 303.

146   "For these men, the question": James Doyle and Michele Paludi. *Sex and Gender: The Human Experience* (Madison, Wis.: Brown and Benchmark, 1994), p. 341.

146   In short, this "stillborn offspring": A phrase coined by Ellen Frankel Paul in "Silly Men, Banal Men."

146   "Not seeing your father when you are small": Robert Bly, *Iron John: A Book about Men* (New York: Vintage Books, 1990), p. 31.

146   "I don't want to omit people": Woody Harper, interview with John Lee, *Men's Council Newsletter*, August 1990. Cited in Moore/Gross on the Internet.

147   "What I'm interested in": Tim Warren, interview with Robert Bly, *Baltimore Sun*, October 28, 1990. Cited in Moore/Gross on the Internet.

147   Bly and other mythopoetic leaders believe: Robert Bly, *The Naive Male* (St. Paul: Ally Press, 1988). Cited in Moore/Gross on the Internet.

147   "lovely, valuable people": Bly, *Iron John*, p. 2.

147   "They had learned to be receptive": ibid., pp. 3–4.

147   "Bly portrays men and women": Scott Coltrane, *Family Man* (New York: Oxford University Press, 1996), p. 194.

148   By 1963 the group . . . had changed its name: Richard F. Doyle, "Men's Movement History," in *A Men's Movement Organization Manual* (Men's Defense Association, 1976), which to our knowledge is available only on the Internet: http://www.vix.com/pub/men/history/rdoyle.html.

149   "Themselves seemingly afflicted": Doyle, "Men's Movement History."

149   "We organized it in just ten days": Interview, via e-mail, with David Usher, 1997.

150   The Good Fatherhood Movement: In the interest of full disclosure, Armin Brott attended a two-day working session in 1996 and helped to create the "Call to Action," a document of which he is a signatory.

151   the "New Father": David Blankenhorn, *Fatherless America: Confronting Our Most Urgent Social Problem* (New York: Harper Perennial, 1996), p. 102.

151   "I can hear you saying": In Al Janssen, ed., *Seven Promises of a Promise Keeper* (Focus on the Family, 1994), p. 6. See also "Promise Keepers Fact Sheet," October 1994.

152   Brown insists that men: In Janssen, ed., *Seven Promises,* cited in Russ Bellant, "Mania in the Stadia: The Origins and Goals of Promise Keepers," *Free Inquiry* 16 (Winter 1995), p. 28.

152   This message was seconded: Peter Steinfels, "Beliefs" column, *New York Times,* June 13, 1998, p. A9.

152   It has an annual budget: Information gathered from the Promise Keepers web site: http://www.promisekeepers.org/21ca.html. See also Steve Rabey, "Where Is the Christian Men's Movement Headed?," *Christianity Today* 40 (April 29, 1996), 46. See also Promise Keepers press release, February 18, 1998.

152   McCartney . . . has frequently — and publicly: Michael Romano, "Keeping the Promise of God," *Rocky Mountain News,* July 17, 1994.

152   which would have denied certain basic civil rights: Michael Mills, "Promise Keepers Send an Alarming Message," *Boulder Daily Camera,* July 28, 1994.

152   "Promise Keepers urges men": Bellant, "Mania in the Stadia," p. 28, quoting John Maxwell's speech at a Promise Keepers rally in Indianapolis, June 6, 1994.

153   At the October 1997 rally, 14 percent: *Washington Post* poll, *Washington Post,* October 11, 1997, p. C7.

153   "There is a growing number of men": James Dobson, *Straight Talk to Men and Their Wives* (Word Books, 1980), cited in Rabey, "Where Is the Christian Men's Movement Headed?"

153   "Here are men who": Joseph Sobran, "Smirking at Virtue . . . with Envy," *Washington Times,* October 11, 1997, p. C3.

153   "feel-good form of male supremacy": Quoted in Jonetta Rose Barras, op-ed piece, *Washington Times,* October 10, 1997, p. A23.

153   "the time has come": *Time*/CNN/Yankelovich Clancy Shulman poll, February 1992 (telephone poll of 1,250 adults).

154   "Men, it seems, are seeking": Betty Friedan, *The Second Stage,* rev. ed. (New York: Summit Books, 1986), p. 160.

154   "solidarity with women": Cathy Young, *Ceasefire: From Gender War to Real Equality* (New York: Free Press, in press).

154   "If one could imagine such a thing": ibid.

154   "I found myself in a tent": Cited in John Guarnaschelli, "Men's Support Groups and the Men's Movement: Their Role for Men and for Women," *Group* 18 (Winter 1994), 197–211.

154   "Men may best discover": John Guarnaschelli, "Men's Support Groups and the Men's Movement," p. 201.

155   "At their best, they serve two purposes": Ronald Levant, *Masculinity Reconstructed: Changing the Rules of Manhood — at Work, in Relationships, and in Family Life* (New York: Plume, 1996), p. 7.

156   "Could it be, then, that": Myriam Miedzian, " 'Father Hunger': Why 'Soup Kitchen' Fathers Are Not Good Enough," in Kay Leigh Hagan, ed., *Women Respond to the Men's Movement: A Feminist Collection* (San Francisco: Harper San Francisco, 1992).

156   "We believe that every child": "A Call to Fatherhood," National Fatherhood Initiative, 1997, Gaithersburg, Md., p. 1.

158   Ronald Levant has developed: Cited in Ross D. Parke, *Fatherhood* (Cambridge, Mass.: Harvard University Press, 1996), p. 245.

159   "powerful increase of 'ego strength' ": John Guarnaschelli, "Men's Support Groups and the Men's Movement," pp. 206–207.

159   "Adult men don't hide their feelings": ibid., p. 208.

160   "if the current focus on 'deadbeat dads' ": Wade F. Horn and Eric Brenner, *Seven Things States Can Do to Promote Responsible Fatherhood* (Washington, D.C.: Council of Governors' Policy Advisors, 1996), p. 12.

Chapter 10: The Women's Movement

161   "The care and welfare of children": Judith Hole and Ellen Levine, *Rebirth of Feminism* (New York: Quadrangle, 1971), p. 305. Also cited in Robert L. Griswold, *Fatherhood in America: A History* (New York: Basic Books, 1993), p. 245.

161   "marriage should be an equal": Cited in Griswold, *Fatherhood in America*, p. 246.

161   "It's clear that most American children": Gloria Steinem, "A New Egalitarian Life Style," *New York Times*, August 26, 1971, p. 37.

162   "the family, instead of being enemy territory": Betty Friedan, *The Second Stage*, rev. ed. (New York: Summit Books, 1986), p. 108.

162   Ellen Goodman . . . declared: Ellen Goodman, "Fatherhood Is Changing," *Boston Globe*, June 12, 1980, cited in Cathy Young, *Ceasefire: From Gender War to Real Equality* (New York: Free Press, in press).

162   "all over the country men": Letty Cottin Pogrebin, *Family Politics: Love and Power on an Intimate Frontier* (New York: McGraw-Hill, 1983), p. 206. Cited in Young, *Ceasefire*.

162   In 1990, Pogrebin made a complete U-turn: Letty Cottin Pogrebin, "Fathers Must Earn Their 'Rights,' " *New York Times*, June 17, 1990, p. E21. Cited in Young, *Ceasefire*.

162   "women have a capacity for understanding": Quoted in R. G. Ratcliffe, "Not a Tender Gender: Jordan Says Men Lack Care Package," *Houston Chronicle*, September 28, 1991, p. 1A.

162   "gender feminists": This term, which has been used by a number of commentators, was perhaps coined by Christina Hoff Sommers, in *Who Stole Feminism: How Women Have Betrayed Women* (New York: Simon & Schuster, 1994), p. 19.

163   "ideological feminists": Sam Keen, *Fire in the Belly: On Being a Man* (New York: Bantam Books, 1991), pp. 195–196.

163   "animated by a spirit of resentment": ibid.

163   "Men are rapists, batterers": Andrea Dworkin, *Pornography: Men Possessing Women* (New York: Perigee, 1981), p. 48.

163   "in a patriarchal society, all heterosexual intercourse is rape": Quoted in Daphne Patai and Noretta Koertge, *Professing Feminism: Cautionary Tales from the Strange World of Women's Studies* (New York: Basic Books, 1995), p. 129.

163   A 1994 *Time*/CNN poll: Cited in Richard Grenier, "The Myths and Lies of the 'Gender Feminists,' " *Washington Times*, June 22, 1994, p. A21.

163   a feminist is a woman who puts herself first: Deirdre English, "Fear of Feminism," *Washington Post*, September 4, 1994, (review of Sherrye Henry's *The Deep Divide: Why American Women Resist Equality* (New York: Macmillan, 1994).

164   "The evil that women do": Young, *Ceasefire*.

164   "No matter how much they themselves": David Popenoe, *Life Without Father* (New York: Free Press, 1996), p. 141.

164   three "slightly different" options: Warren Farrell, *The Myth of Male Power: Why Men Are the Disposable Sex* (New York: Simon & Schuster, 1993), p. 52. This point is also explored in some detail in Farrell's *Why Men Are the Way They Are* (New York: McGraw-Hill, 1987).

164   "I will do the dishes": "Where Have All the Cowboys Gone?," *This Fire*, Imago/Warner Bros., 1996.

164   Cole, who seems to be espousing: Cole was one of the headliners at the 1997 Lilith Fair near San Francisco, a concert-festival celebrating women and music.

165   In fact, two out of three women: Louis Genevie and Eva Margolies, *The Motherhood Report: How Women Feel about Being Mothers* (New York: Macmillan, 1987), pp. 358–361.

165   "a damper on men's involvement with their children": ibid.

165   "In these decisions": Susan Faludi, *Backlash: The Undeclared War Against American Women* (New York: Doubleday, 1991), p. 404.

167   "Ethics aside, is that a wise attitude": Cathy Young, "Phony War," *Reason*, (November 1991), p. 56.

167   "Given time and space, most women": Gloria Norris and Jo Ann Miller, *The Working Mother's Complete Handbook* (New York: New American Library, 1984), p. 299. Cited in David Blankenhorn, *Fatherless America* (New York: Basic Books, 1995), p. 79.

168   "Children are a joy; many men are not": Katha Pollitt, "Bothered and Bewildered," *New York Times*, July 22, 1993, p. A23. Cited in Young, *Ceasefire: From Gender War to Real Equality*.

168   "Men are like pinch hitters": Leslie Bennets, "Belle Michelle," *Vanity Fair*, September 1993, p. 164. Cited in Blankenhorn, *Fatherless America*, p. 76.

168   About 90 percent of the parents . . . but about 3,000: Blankenhorn, *Fatherless America*, p. 178.

168   And consider the recent case: Doreen Iudica Vigue, "Boston Clinic Sued over Use of Embryo," *Boston Globe*, August 20, 1998, p. A1.

168   "women can shape their reproductive experiences": Anne Donchin, "Procreation, Power, and Subjectivity: Feminist Approaches to the New Reproductive Technologies," Working Paper No. 260, Wellesley College Center for Research on Women, 1993, p. 13.

169   "It is no tragedy": Nancy D. Polikoff, "The Deliberate Construction of Families Without Fathers: Is It an Option for Lesbian and Heterosexual Mothers?," *Santa Clara Law Review* 36 (Midwinter 1996), 375–394.

169   "87 percent of single women": Faludi, *Backlash*, p. 404.

169   Fatherless children are twice as likely: U.S. Department of Health and Human Services, National Center for Health Statistics, Survey on Child Health, 1993.

169   children who exhibit violent behavior in school: Jonathan L. Sheline and Betty J. Skipper, "Risk Factors for Violent Behavior in Elementary School Boys: Have You Hugged Your Child Today?," *American Journal of Public Health* 84 (1994), 661–663.

169   at much greater risk of becoming teen parents: Department of Health and Human Services, Survey on Child Health.

169   Seventy-two percent of adolescent murderers: Dewey Cornell, et al., "Characteristics of Adolescents Charged with Homicide," *Behavioral Sciences and the Law* 5 (1987), 11–23.

169   "is it socially reprehensible": Penelope Leach, *Children First: What Society Must Do — and Is Not Doing — for Children Today* (New York: Random House, 1994), p. 39.

169   "It makes sense to ask women": Cathy Young, *Ceasefire: From Gender War to Real Equality.*

169   "a sad corollary of modern feminism": Suzanne Fields, "Feminism's U-Turn Leads Down Path of Motherhood," *Insight on the News*, February 12, 1996, p. 1.

170   But the majority of the commissioners: John Guidubaldi, *Minority Report and Policy Recommendations of the United States Commission on Child and Family Welfare*, July 1996.

171   "women are simply better equipped": Judith Regan, "In Defense of Gordon Clark: An Open Letter to Marcia Clark," *Newsweek*, March 13, 1995, p. 54.

172   women "give up something": Ann Snitow, "Motherhood: Reclaiming the Demon Texts," *Ms.*, May–June 1991, pp. 34–37.

172   "forced joint custody, like forced sterilization": Quoted in "History and Evolution of 'Young Child' Guidelines," unpublished document, Children's Rights Coalition, Washington, D.C., October 1992.

173   "The maternal custody preference . . . can coerce": Anne Mitchell, "The Maternal Bond," *American Journal of Family Law* 9 (Fall 1995), 125–133.

173   "because it disrupts the relationship": Richard A. Warshak, *The Custody Revolution:*

The Father Factor and the Motherhood Mystique (New York: Poseidon Press, 1992), pp. 192–196.

173   "At its best joint custody": Ross Thompson, "Fatherhood and Divorce," in L. S. Quinn, ed., *The Future of Children: Children and Divorce* 4 (Spring 1994), 17.

174   The officials examined nearly two dozen studies: Guidubaldi, *Minority Report.*

174   "did not appear to worsen": Jessica Pearson and Nancy Thoennes, "Custody after Divorce: Demographic and Attitudinal Patterns," *American Journal of Orthopsychiatry* 60 (1990), 238.

174   adolescents who often feared "being caught": Christy Buchanan, Eleanor Maccoby, and Sanford Dornbusch, "Caught Between Parents: Adolescents' Experience in Divorced Homes," *Child Development* 62 (October 1991), 1008–1029.

174   "Court-ordered joint physical custody": J. R. Johnston, "High-Conflict Divorce," in R. E. Behrman, *The Future of Children* 4 (1994), 165–182. Cited in Guidubaldi, *Minority Report.*

175   "in some cases, especially where parents": Johnston, "High-Conflict Divorce," p. 176.

175   But only 10 percent of these: C. R. Albistoma, E. E. Maccoby, and R. R. Mnookin, "Does Joint Legal Custody Matter?," *Stanford Law and Policy Review* 2 (1990), 167–179.

175   "should not serve as the basis": Guidubaldi, *Minority Report.*

175   Hugh McIsaac . . . reported that mediation: Los Angeles public hearing transcript, pp. 138–140, cited in *Achieving Equal Justice for Women and Men in the California Courts,* final report of the Judicial Council of California, Advisory Committee on Gender Bias in the Courts, July 1996, pp. 170–171.

175   90 percent of all clients said: *California Statewide Snapshot Study of Family Court Services,* Office of Family Court Services, 1992, p. i. Cited in *Achieving Equal Justice for Women and Men in the California Courts,* p. 171.

176   In one of the few experimental studies of mediation: See Robert Emery, *Renegotiating Family Relationships: Divorce, Child Custody and Mediation* (New York: Guilford Press, 1994).

176   a majority of mediation clients were satisfied: Jessica Pearson and Nancy Thoennes, "Mediating and Litigating Custody Disputes: A Longitudinal Evaluation," *Family Law Quarterly* 17 (1984), 497–517.

176   mediated agreements tended to include: Emery, *Renegotiating Family Relationships.*

177   "motherhood mystique": Warshak, *The Custody Revolution,* p. 14.

177   They've "come to believe in the tradition": Anne Mitchell, "The Maternal Bond."

177   roughly a third asked for less: See Eleanor Maccoby et al., *Dividing the Child: Social and Legal Dilemmas of Custody* (Cambridge, Mass.: Harvard University Press, 1992).

178   "Why are Mothers Losing?": Nancy Polikoff, "Why Are Mothers Losing? A Brief Analysis of Criteria Used in Child Custody Determinations." *Women's Rights Law Reporter* 5 (Spring–Fall 1992), 175–184.

178   In the Stanford child-custody study: Cited in Mitchell, "The Maternal Bond."

178   the mother got custody 46 percent of the time: Cited in Anne Mitchell, "The Na-

tional Organization for Women Declares War on Fathers: Do They Really Represent the Views of the Majority of Women?," *The Women's Freedom Network Newsletter* 4 (Spring 1997), p. 7.

179   Early in the trial: Richard Price and Jonathan Lovitt, "Prosecutor Pays Price: O.J. Scrutiny Adds to Stress of Her Divorce," *USA Today,* March 3, 1995, p. 1A.

179   "Because of the notoriety": ibid.

180   Boys in father custody were less anxious: K. Alison Clarke-Stewart and Craig Hayward, "Advantages of Father Custody and Contact for the Psychological Well-Being of School-Age Children," *Journal of Applied Developmental Psychology* 17 (April–June 1996), 239–270.

180   National studies confirm: James L. Peterson and Nicholas Zill, "Marital Disruption, Parent-Child Relationships, and Behavior Problems in Children," *Journal of Marriage and the Family* 48 (May 1986), 295–307.

180   Others, such as Herb Zimiles: Herbert Zimiles and Valerie E. Lee, "Adolescent Family Structure and Educational Progress," *Developmental Psychology* 27 (March 1991), 314–320. See also Valerie E. Lee et al., "Family Structure and Its Effect on Behavioral and Emotional Problems in Young Adolescents," *Journal of Research on Adolescence* 4 (1994), 405–437.

180   In one California study: C. M. Buchanan, E. E. Maccoby, and S. M. Dornbusch, *Adolescents after Divorce* (Cambridge, Mass.: Harvard University Press, 1996), p. 92.

181   Joint custody aside: Laura Meckler, "Government Wants Fathers Involved with Their Children's Lives," Associated Press news wire, July 4, 1998.

181   In a 1978 custody ruling in West Virginia: *J.B. v. A.B.,* 242 S.E. 2d 248 (W. Va. 1978). Cited in Ron Henry, " 'Primary Caretaker': Is It a Ruse?," *Family Advocate,* Summer 1994, 53–56.

181   "Behavioral science is so inexact": Henry, " 'Primary Caretaker.' "

182   "Every definition that has been put forward": ibid.

182   "for vacuuming the floors": ibid.

182   The primary-caretaker theory: Young, *Ceasefire: From Gender War to Real Equality.*

182   "for every mother who reduces her hours": Henry, " 'Primary Caretaker.' "

182   Even the most extreme studies: As we've discussed in detail earlier, we sharply reject the notion that men do only one-third of the childcare.

183   "WHEREAS organizations advocating": "NOW Action Alert on 'Fathers' Rights,' " *National NOW Times,* October 1996.

184   "It seems clear that NOW believes": Anne Mitchell, "NOW Declares War on Fathers."

184   five hundred fathers' rights groups: Interview with Stuart Miller, 1998.

185   "The collective message presented by 'fathers' rights' ": Phyllis Chesler, "The Men's Auxiliary: Protecting the Rule of the Fathers," in Kay Leigh Hagan, ed., *Women Respond to the Men's Movement* (New York: Harper Collins, 1992), pp. 133–140.

185   "Make no mistake about it": Gloria Steinem, in the foreword to *Women Respond to the Men's Movement,* pp. v–ix.

185   "The men's separatist movement is frightening": Carol Bly, "The Danger in Men's Groups," *Utne Reader,* November–December 1989, p. 59.

185   "Don't tell me 'it can't happen here' ": Laura S. Brown, "Essential Lies: A Dysto-
      pian Vision of the Mythopoetic Men's Movement," in Hagan, ed., *Women Re-
      spond to the Men's Movement*, pp. 93–100.
186   "not being possessed of a sense of irony": Ellen Frankel Paul, "Silly Men, Banal
      Men," *Society* 30 (September–October 1993), 38.
186   men "return to their relationships": John Guarnaschelli, "Men's Support Groups
      and the Men's Movement: Their Role for Men and For Women," *Group* 18 (Win-
      ter 1994), 195–210.
187   "The system encourages divorcing women": Quoted in Jack Kammer, *Good Will
      Toward Men* (New York: St. Martin's Press, 1995), p. 66.
187   "that almost all men are jerks": ibid., p. 68.
187   "[Radical] feminists may be": Interview with Karen Lehrman. This point is
      elaborated on somewhat in her book *The Lipstick Proviso* (New York: Anchor,
      1997).

Chapter 11: Where Do We Go from Here?

192   In one study, dads watched a videotape: Ross D. Parke et al., "Fathers and Risk: A
      Hospital-Based Model of Intervention," in D. Sawin, ed., *Psychosocial Risks in In-
      fant-Environmental Transactions* (New York: Bruner/Mazel, 1980).
193   Children with physically active dads: Kevin Macdonald and Ross D. Parke,
      "Bridging the Gap: Parent-Child Interaction and Peer Interactive Competence,"
      Child Development 55 (1984), 1265–1277.
193   "Men must allow themselves": John Gottman, *The Heart of Parenting* (New
      York: Simon & Schuster, 1997), p. 173.
193   Be a partner, not a helper: See S. Coltrane, *Family Man* (New York: Oxford Uni-
      versity Press, 1996), for a discussion of mothers as managers of the household
      routines and decisions.
193   "A push for old family values": Rosalind C. Barnett and Caryl Rivers, *She
      Works/He Works* (San Francisco: Harper San Francisco, 1996), p. 85.
194   Without taking part in the everyday: See Coltrane, *Family Man.*
195   "When fathers do spend time": John Gottman, *Why Marriages Succeed or Fail*
      (New York: Simon & Schuster, 1994), p. 183.
196   "Those who don't pay don't visit": See Frank Furstenberg and Andrew Cherlin,
      Divided Families (Cambridge, Mass.: Harvard University Press, 1991).
196   "Women usually measure": Interview with Jay Belsky, 1996. See also Jay Belsky,
      The Transition to Parenthood (New York: DTP, 1995).
196   "Every woman who asks her husband": Interview with Rikki Jones, 1996. See
      also Rikki Robbins Jones, *Negotiating Love: How Women and Men Can Resolve
      Their Differences* (New York: Random House, 1995).
199   In open preschools: B. D. Bianchi and R. Bakeman, "Patterns of Sex Typing in an
      Open School," in B. Liss, ed., *Social and Cognitive Skills: Sex Roles and Children's
      Play* (New York: Academic Press, 1983).
199   "Almost nothing in the prefatherhood learning": J. S. Chafetz, *Masculine, Femi-
      nine, or Human* (Itasca, Ill.: F. E. Peacock, 1978), p. 197.

199   By about age six: This idea is explored by Myriam Miedzian in *Boys Will Be Boys: Breaking the Link Between Masculinity and Violence* (New York: Anchor, 1992), p. 116.

200   a host of programs in operation: See James Levine and Edward Pitt, *New Expectations: Community Strategies for Responsible Fatherhood* (New York: Families and Work Institute, 1996).

201   Pediatricians can play a more active role: See Michael Yogman and Daniel Kindleon, "Pediatric Opportunities with Father and Children," *Pediatric Annals* 27 (1998), 1–6, for guidelines aimed at increasing fathers' involvement in doctors' visits.

201   People need to know about the connection: See Sara McLanahan and Gary Sandefur, *Growing Up with a Single Parent* (Cambridge, Mass.: Harvard University Press, 1994).

201   "welfare rules continue": Wade F. Horn and Eric Brenner, *Seven Things States Can Do to Promote Responsible Fatherhood* (Washington, D.C.: Council of Governors' Policy Advisors, 1996), p. 12.

Index